Kissing the World

The Universal Ti of the Great Perfection

With Tibetan Manuscript

Translated by

Christopher Wilkinson

The painting on the cover of a dancer is the work of Lobsang Jamyang, a master painter who is currently residing in Dharamsala, India.

No Artificial Intelligence tools were used in this translation.

Independently Published

ISBN: 9798870728285

DEDICATION

To all teachers and students of the Great Perfection.

Also Translated by Christopher Wilkinson

The Mahayana

Vajra Sky:
The Sutra that Brings Together the Contemplations of All the Buddhas
Volumes One, Two, and Three

The Mind Section

The All-Creating King: A Root Tantra of the Great Perfection

Atiyoga: The Eighteen Tantras

Astounding: Five Tantras of the Mind Section

Royal Ambrosia: Three Great Perfection Tantras for the King

The Bodhicitta Sutra: Ten Scriptures of the Great Perfection

The Tantra of Great Bliss:
The Guhyagarbha Transmission of Vajrasattva's Magnificent Sky

Secret Sky: The Ancient Tantras on Vajrasattva's Magnificent Sky

The Space Section

Natural Bliss: Five Tantras of the Space Section

Star Light: Eight Early Tantras of the Space Section

Sky Space: The Royal Tantra on the Great Perfection of the Bodhicitta

The Royal Tantra on the Brilliant Diffusion of Majestic Space

The Great Tantra of Vajrasattva: Equal to the End of the Sky

Perfect Wisdom: Four Early Tantras of the Great Perfection

The Secret Tantras of the Fish Wheel and the Nine Spaces:
Two Ancient Scriptures of the Great Perfection

Secret Wisdom: Three Root Tantras of the Great Perfection

The Upadeśa Instruction Section

The Jewel Maker: The Great Tantra on the Consequence of Sound

The Lion Stops Hunting: An Upadesha Tantra of the Great Perfection

CONTENTS

ACKNOWLEDGMENTS

First and foremost, I wish to thank my root teacher Dezhung Rinpoche for constantly bringing out the best in me and encouraging me to pursue a comprehension of every branch of Buddhist learning. It was he who introduced me to Dilgo Khyentse Rinpoche, and through his recommendations enabled me to receive full empowerments, transmissions, and permissions in the areas of Mahā, Anu, and Ati yogas. With the highest regard I wish to thank Dilgo Khyentse Rinpoche, Khetsun Zangpo Rinpoche, Nyoshul Khen Rinpoche, and Khenpo Palden Sherab for their kind instruction and encouragement in my effort to translate the literature of the rDzogs chen. There are many individuals, too many to name here, who have helped me in many ways over the years to become a qualified translator. At this time I want to acknowledge the kindness of Ngawang Kunga Trinlay Sakyapa, Jigdral Dagchen Sakya Rinpoche, Dhongthog Rinpoche, Karmapa Rangjung Rigpay Dorje, Kalu Rinpoche, Chogyam Trungpa Rinpoche, Geshe Ngawang Nornang, Carl Potter, David Ruegg, Turrell Wylie, Gene Smith, Karen Lang, Richard Salomon, Jack Hawley, David Jackson, Herbert Guenther, Eva Neumeier-Dargyay, Leslie Kawamura, Frits Staal, Robert Thurman, Paul Nietupski, Lou Lancaster, David Snellgrove, Jean-Luc Achard, Sarah Harding, Steve Landsberg, Tsultrim Allione, Carolyn Klein, Rob Mayer, Jonathan Silk, and Mark Tatz. I want to thank Nora Staffanell for proofreading the manuscript. I also want to thank Henry Frieder, Diana McPhee, Giovanni Santuz, Irv Beiman, Joel Shefflin, Rosanne Shaw, Michael Gregory, John Hoag and the Dakini Land Foundation, whose support has helped to make this translation possible. I owe special thanks to Lopsang Jamyang for painting the cover art. The many people who have contributed to my understanding and ability to do this work cannot be counted. I wish to thank everyone who has taken a kind interest in these translations, however slight, for their part in making this work a reality.

INTRODUCTION

It is said that the pinnacle of the Nine Vehicles of the Buddha's Dharma is the Great Perfection: The Atiyoga or Dzogchen. The innermost essence of the Atiyoga is said to be the Yang Ti. The quintessence of the Yang Ti is said to be the *sPyi Ti*: The Universal Ti. Kissing the World is a core Tantra of the Universal Ti. It was Translated into Tibetan in the Eighth Century of our era by Padmasambhava of Orgyan working together with the Tibetan translator Kawa Peltsek. It is preserved in the *Nyingma Gyubum*, the Hundred Thousand Tantras of the Ancients. This Tantra is not like any other. Here we find a direct discussion of masculinity, femininity, and family relations as they characterize our path. There are prophesies and many upadeśa instructions. It touches on things that other Tantras do not mention, such as what to do when you are in a war, how to evaluate gurus, relationships between couples and children, how to use a phurba, and many other interesting topics. This is the first time a Root Tantra of the yoga of the Universal Ti has been translated into any Western language.

For your convenience, and to help in the preservation of this ancient tradition, I have included images of the Tibetan manuscript.

KISSING THE WORLD

In the Indian language:

Bhaba Samapuṭa | Amṛita Rasa Khahila | Saṃpara Adi Anata Tseda Tantra Nāma

In the Tibetan language:

sNang srid Kha sbyor bdud rtsi bcud 'thigs 'khor ba thog mtha' gcod pa'i rgyud ces bya ba

In the English language:

The Tantra on Kissing the Apparent World
While Dripping an Elixir of Ambrosia
To Cut through Samsara from Start to End
.

THE BASIC SCENE THAT THOROUGHLY DISPLAYS OUR PERFECT STORE

I bow to the Blessed One,
The true sentience that has no sign and is beyond discussion,
The unborn All Good.

On one occasion I proclaimed these words:

In the abode of Akaniṣṭha
There is an infinite palace
That has no end or middle.
It is a hollow space for reality,
A mandala for the great and pervasive fullness
Of the basis of all things.

The lights of great price gathered there.
The three bodies that are our hearts' purpose
Dwelt in this abode where light rays glowed.
Through growth and through darkness
There was the body of the Dharma
Which is beyond thought,
Beyond the intellect,
And is not to be discussed.

There was the body of pleasure
Which does not stop.
It is beyond thought,
And is unborn.

There was the manifest body,
Which is an all-encompassing compassion
That has no agenda.

This is the perfect store of our teacher.

His entourage was also like this:

There was the intended audience,
The audience that had been present from the beginning,
And the audience of the three times.

The intended audience was as follows:

Our true sentience has no birth
So there is the audience that is
An awareness that does not stop.
Reality does not change,
So there is the audience that is
The variety of changes in our attitudes.

Our true sentience is non-dual,
So there is the audience of those
Who crave to define their dualistic visions
Of what they take in and what they hold onto.

The audience that has been present from the beginning
Was as follows:

The earth,
The water,
The fire,
The wind,
And the sky.

The audience of the three times was as follows:

There were the Buddhas of the past,
The Buddhas of the future,
And the Buddhas of the present.

Moreover,

The hosts in the audience were as follows:

The Anuyoga,
The Atiyoga,
And the Mahāyoga.

The audience of my own true nature
Was as follows:

There were the audience of natural views
And the audience of natural understanding.

As for these,
They are the perfect store of an audience.

The meaning of the teachings was as follows:

There are teachings that have never been exemplified.
There are the Buddhas of the Dharmas that exemplify these things,
There are teachings from those who are not Buddhas.

The thing to be exemplified
And the act of exemplification
Are non-dual.
So there is a teaching that does not reject
Words and letters.
This is a perfect store of teachings.

As for the teaching on the time,
It is like this:

Do not cut off the trails of the past!
Do not greet a premonition of the future!
Do not let present conditions be lost in your mouth!

There is a time in which
The three times are inseparable.
There is a time for the puppet lineages
Of those who enter the trails of what happened before.
This is a perfect store of time.

Then from out of the hosts in the audience
Vajrasattva made inquiry with these words:

Kye Kye!
Teacher!
Our own sentience is All Good!
As the meaning of a perfect store is like that,
Our teacher must speak on these things
In their profundity!

The way of being of the primary base,
The borderline between Buddhas and sentient beings,
The difference between our higher delusions and our lower delusions:
What is the answer and what is the benefit of our validations?

What are the methods by which we are to work toward
An understanding of thusness,
The way in which we acquire a reward
After we have understood,
The way that we are seized by an unchanging resolve,
The way it is with the Yang Ti and the Universal Ti,
And the methods by which those who follow our trails may understand?

From the Tantra on Kissing the Apparent World while Dripping an Elixir of Ambrosia to Cut through Samsara from Start to End, this is Chapter One: The Basic Scene that Thoroughly Displays Our Perfect Store.

A WAY OF EXPLANATION THAT TAKES UP THE TOPIC

Then from out of the audience
Vajrasattva rose up from his seat.
He planted his knees,
And joined his palms.
Then he made an address with these words:

What is the way in which we are to discuss the great word?
O True Sentience of the All Good,
I beg you to speak!

Thus was he addressed.

Our teacher,
The True Sentience of the All Good,
In his effort to teach the hosts who had gathered
Entered into the equanimity of the samadhi
In which all the Dharmas that are within
The empty reality of this great dominion,
This infinite palace of the blazing light of jewels,
Do not move.

Then he saw that the hosts who had gathered
Were organized in their totality.
Then he got up from that samadhi
And he gave instruction to those audiences
With these words:

This is my yoga of the Universal Ti.
I will teach it to the audience that has gathered.
My audiences must listen respectfully
And not be distracted.

This is the way to explain the Yang Ti and the Universal Ti.
It will not arise from out of any other vehicle.
It has not arisen.
It is not arising.
It will not arise.

We explain the great word
With the three ways of explanation:
The explanation of the unborn that is not exemplified,
The explanation that uses words that are nouns,
And the explanation that uses a symbolic exemplification
To liberate us.

The ways that we explain what is universal
Are also of three kinds:

The explanation that uses blessings,
The explanation that uses our own essence,
And the explanation that uses poetic words.

As for the way we explain the Yang Ti and the Universal Ti,
There is the way of explanation
Of the unborn body of the Dharma,
The way of explanation
Of the unstopping body of pleasure,
And the way of explanation
Of the compassionate body that is manifest.

When we divide them three by three
There are nine.
You must understand that we have three common purposes.

As for the way of explanation of the unborn that is not exemplified,
By the Dharmas that we exemplify we will not become Buddhas.

We need the one Dharma that is beyond exemplification.
By the Dharmas of explanation we will not become Buddhas.

We need the one Dharma that is not explained.
By having nothing to teach we will not become Buddhas.
We need the one Dharma that is not taught and has nothing to teach.

By the Dharma of permanence we will not become Buddhas.
We need the one Dharma that is beyond the intellect.

By Dharmas of creation we will not become Buddhas.
We need the one Dharma that was not created and is self-originating.

By the Dharmas of our practices we will not become Buddhas.
We need the one Dharma where there is nothing to do
And is not complicated.

This is the way of explanation for the unborn
That is not exemplified.

As for the way of explanation that uses words that are nouns,
There are the ways of explanation of the three characteristic sections,
The way of explanation of the three sections of the Kriya yoga,
And the ways of explanation
Of the three kinds of generation and perfection.

As for the way of explanation of the nine stages,
We do not discuss it here.
We are at peace with ourselves.

As for the way of explanation that uses symbolic exemplifications
For liberation,

A He He He!
A La La La Ho!

No one else has this kind of Universal Ti and Yang Ti!
This is a word of extremely great amazement:

A La La!

My own true nature is like this:
My existence is nothing at all.
My appearance is that I may appear to be anything.
I have no substance at all.
I create the roots for all my attributions.

There is no success in the objectives that we talk about.
We create the roots for all our words and names.
We are not stained by any conventionalities.
We create the roots for all conventionalities.
We are beyond all birth and death.
We create the roots of our birth, age, sickness, and death.

We are beyond everything that is generated.
We create the Base that gives birth to all things.
No basis for what happens has been established.
The birth and shaking of the apparent world
Are the basis for what happens.

We are beyond all extremes and middles,
All directions and all borders.
We work to support all positions,
Be they extreme or middle.
If we divide the rest of them
We leave behind our thoughts.
We create the roots for an unknown thought.

As for the true nature of the blazing jewel light,
There is no time whatever in which to exemplify it.

As for teachers,
We teach that there are two kinds.

As for happenings,
There happen to be eighty-four thousand.

As for summaries,
We summarize this into the nine stages of our vehicles.

As for La,
It is the utterance of the Universal Ti and the Yang Ti.

As for being,
It is actually the Bodhicitta.

Those who are living
Live in the dominion of the unborn.

As for clarity,
It shines out from within the light.

As for appearance,
It totally encompasses the apparent world.
There is no substance that is marked for us to see.
There is no essence that we visualize in our discussions.

Upon thought,
This is beyond being an object for our intellects.
We cut through to the roots
Of the feeling that we are aware of our awareness.
We do not find any basis for our sentience
In our memories.
This being so,
We are beyond all signs and exemplifications.
This is the way of explanation that uses symbolic exemplification
For liberation.

As for the way of explanation
For the unborn body of the Dharma,
We explain that Dharmas are dominions of the unborn.
We explain the essence of the unchanging body of the Dharma.
We melt into a space where there is no speech.
Then we settle.

As for the way of explanation of the body of perfect pleasure,
We teach that Dharmas have no cessation.
The body of pleasure is an unceasing pervasive fullness.

As for the way of explanation of the compassionate body that is manifest,
The non-duality of the apparent world
Is the body that is manifest.
A variety of things may appear,
But we do not recognize them.

An appearance has no attachment or craving
For any object.
This is the way of explanation for the manifest body
That is not a memory.

As for the way of explanation that uses blessings,

The teacher who is indistinguishable
From the primordial beginning,
The primordial abode,
And the primordial dominion,
Is me.

I am explaining this.
I,
The All Good One am explaining this
From out of the space of my heart.
Vajrasattva listens
From out of the abode of clear light.

The little child of self-clarity
Is explained to come from
A ball of clear light.
A great self-clarity
Abides throughout all things
And it listens.

Magnificent self-clarity
Is explained as being from
The abode of total clarity.

Prahe Vajra listens from the peak of Mt. Meru.
Prahe Vajra explains things from the peak of Mt. Meru.
Mañjuśrī Mitra listens from the side of Mt. Meru.
Mañjuśrī Mitra explains things from the side of Mt. Meru.
Takshaka the King of the Nagas listens from the bottom of the ocean.
When he teaches
There is no understanding.
This is the way of explanation that uses blessings.

As for the explanation that uses our own essence,
It is the wisdom of the Bodhicitta.
Our teacher arises into a body of earth.
He does not teach through words or letters.
We do not conceptualize a self.
We do not conceptualize an other.
We teach a contemplation of non-conceptual equanimity.
When all the sentient beings of the three realms understand this
They will be the equals of all the Buddhas.

Our dominion is not moved
By thoughts of strife.
In the light rays of the Bodhicitta
Our teacher arises in a body of water.
He does not teach using words or letters.
He does not discriminate any self.
He does not discriminate any other.
He teaches the necessity of indiscriminate equanimity.

When all the sentient beings of the three realms
Understand this,
They will be the equals of all the Buddhas.

Our dominion is not moved by our thoughts of strife.
This is the wisdom of the Bodhicitta.
Our teacher arises in a body of fire.
He does not cling to any self.
He does not cling to any other.
He teaches the necessity of non-dual interaction.
When all the sentient beings of the three realms
Understand this
They will be the equals of all the Buddhas.

Our dominion is not moved by thoughts of strife.
This is the true nature of the Bodhicitta.
Our teacher arises in a body of wind.
He does not work toward any self.
He does not reject any other.
He teaches a contemplation
In which cessation and propitiation are non-dual.
When all the sentient beings of the three realms
Understand this,
They will be the equals of all the Buddhas.

Our dominion is not moved by thoughts of strife.
This is the wisdom of the Bodhicitta.
Our teacher presents himself in the body of the sky.
He does not work toward any goodness.
He does not reject any evil.
He teaches a contemplation in which there are no clear distinctions.
When all the sentient beings of the three realms
Understand this,

They will be the equals of all the Buddhas.

Our dominion is not moved by thoughts of strife.
In this way,
We do not use the totality of the apparent world
To teach in any words or letters.
We teach a Dharma
In which each of us is inseparable.
This is the way of explanation for our own essence.

We use the way of explanation of poetic words
To teach a lineage that is from ear to ear.
This is the way of explanation of the Universal Ti and the Yang Ti.

That is what he said.

This is Chapter Two: A Way of Explanation that Takes up the Topic.

TEACHING THE WAY OF BEING OF THE BASE

Then Vajrasattva questioned his own sentience,
The All Good:

How is it that each and every Buddha and sentient being
Lives within a sphere that has not yet arisen?
Please speak to the hosts that have gathered!

So did he address him.

The true sentience that is the All Good One,
From out of the infinite palace
That Guards the Light of Jewels,
Entered into the equanimity of the samadhi of indivisibility.

He looked upon the hosts who had gathered.
He got up and gave instructions to his audience:

Long before there were Buddhas and sentient beings
No substance of any kind had been realized.
There is no reversal by exemplifying things.
We are liberated from extremes.

In the basis of our beginning
We are inseparable.
Buddhas and sentient beings
Do not even have a name.

There are no craftsmen
Who bind symbols to conventionalities.
There are no craftsmen who teach
That there are analogies and meanings.
There are no craftsmen who bind words to letters.
There are no craftsmen who bind happiness and sorrow into a pair.
There are no craftsmen who move into a duality of cause and result.
There are no craftsmen who divide self and other into a duality.
A duality of Buddhas and sentient beings
Has not been established.

This is nothing at all.
We live in our essence.
The Buddha that we would exemplify
Is beyond any words.
He is beyond being an object
That we might think or talk about.

The way that we discuss things
Is beyond any exemplification.
For this reason,
We are inseparable at base.
This is why we are free from all attributions and cravings.
We are beyond the limitations
That are in exemplifications.

Vajrasattva addressed him with these words:

O Teacher,
True Sentience of the All Good,
What is the way of being of the base of all things?

That is what he asked.

Our teacher gave instruction to the audience:

You must understand that the analogies for the base are three:

A bank of treasure,
A field of earth,
And an icicle.

The vastness of the Base
For Buddhas and sentient beings
Is not limited,
Even in samsara.

In nirvana,
Our vastness is not limited.
Our vastness is also not limited
In non-duality.
Our vastness is also not limited
By conventionalities.
We do not experience any existence.
We do not experience any non-existence.
We do not experience emptiness.
We do not experience clarity.
In this same way,
We do not experience any clear happiness or sorrow.

Being,
Non-being,
Being empty,
Desire,
Strife,
Craving,
Attachment,
Proving that good and evil exist,
Entering meditation,
Delusions and obstructions we take in and hold onto,
Understanding,
Misunderstanding:
We experience none of them.

We are not split into two,
Nor into one.
The duality of causes and conditions
Has no birth or ending.
Our essence does not change.
We do not visualize any true nature.
We also do not limit the vastness
Of any birth or ending.

We are not exemplified.
We have no words.

We have no support.
We have no Dharma.
We have no teacher.
We have no audience.
We have no middle.
We have no end.
We have no Buddhas or Bodhisattvas.
We have no awareness.
We have no minds.
We also have no sentience.
We have no attachments to places.
We have no cravings.
We have nothing to take in or hold onto.
We are liberated from collective understandings.
We also do not divide our form into anything.

That is what he said.

This is Chapter Three: Teaching the Way of Being of the Base.

TEACHING THE GREATER VIRTUE OF THE BUDDHA

Then Vajrasattva again questioned our teacher,
The All Good:

What is the borderline between Buddhas and sentient beings?
Please give us instructions
That are extremely profound
On the difference between upward growth
And downward delusion!

That is what he asked.

The King of Teachers,
The True Sentience of the All Good One
Entered the equanimity of the samadhi
That reveals the union of precious light.

Then he got up,
And he spoke these words:

As for the borderline between
Buddhas and sentient beings,
It is exemplified by the marks
Of awareness and ignorance.
It is the borderline between
Understanding and non-understanding.

To look upward while being deluded downward
Is as follows:

In the past,
In our true beginning,
We have been living since the primordial
Without birth and without any separation.

One child is born.
He uses a great and indivisible stupidity
To teach his father:
The King of Methods.
He is beyond all birth and ending.
This is the way of the mother.

One child is born who does not make judgments.
He has no beginning.
This is the way of the father.
He has no ending.
This is the way of the mother.

This child is not to be divided or cleared away.
He makes a determination about both beginnings and endings.
His true nature is primordially present.
This is the way of the father.
His magnificent space encompasses all things.
This is the way of the mother.

As a reality of clear light
One child is born.
The Dharmas melt into the dominion of equality.
His habitual patterns are moving.
This is the way of the father.
He is totally in motion.
This is the way of the mother.
They give birth to a flickering.
This is the way of the child.

Happenings are present
In the way of the father.
The five lights spin
In the way of the mother.
The five winds are born

In the way of children.

He finds resolve in the force.
Understanding dawns.
The child melts into the core of the mother.
The child melts into the mother
And does not distinguish any separation.

The father and mother melt into an unchanging dominion.
The children that are the unceasing force of awareness
Swell forth from out of the sky-space
That is the heart-essence of the father and mother.

We do not find any earth for their swelling.
The rays and the knowledge of the space of our hearts
Melt into the unmoving.

The triad of father, mother, and child
Are inseparable,
So from the beginning we are primordial Buddhas.
When our reality meets with the base
Our wisdom takes its own place.

We cut through our ideas at the root.
Our delusions are liberated into their own places.
We dissolve into unchanging space.
Our hearts are liberated into the body of the Dharma.
We smash the dark house of ignorance.
We do not limit the vastness of our wisdom.
We open the door to the arising of wisdom.
We lock the door of ignorant delusions.

The heart that awakens the vastness of samsara
Grows within the body of the Dharma.
When we awaken from our works and quests
There grows an uncomplicated lack of anything to do.

Growing upward,
The All Good One knows things in this way.

We ask for a validation
Of what benefit there may be.
There is no benefit in any work or quest.

We are melting into our own places.
We are actually inherently liberated.
We actually understand this by ourselves.

This is not any rejection or acceptance,
Any termination or production.
Once we awaken our ideas
Our wisdom grows.

No one whosoever is not included in this growth.
We actually grow by ourselves.
In this way,
When we simply understand
Unchanging Buddhahood,
We have no ignorance.
There is a majestic experiential radiance.

Our wisdom is primordially present.
There is a majestic experiential radiance.
We have no ideas.
There is a majestic experiential radiance.
Reality has been a majestic experiential radiance
From the beginning.

There are no three times.
There is a majestic experiential radiance.
The three bodies are primordial.
There is a majestic experiential radiance.
The five great poisons
Are a majestic experiential radiance.

There is no stopping.
This is a majestic experiential radiance.
There is no pain.
This is a majestic experiential radiance.
Age and death do not exist.
This is a majestic experiential radiance.

There is no emptiness.
There is a majestic experiential radiance.
There are no dualities.
There is a majestic experiential radiance.
Objects and minds are not a duality.

There is a majestic experiential radiance.

What we take in and what we hold onto
Are not a duality.
There is a majestic experiential radiance.
The dualities of termination and projection,
Of rejection and acceptance,
Do not exist.
There is a majestic experiential radiance.

The dualities of work and quest,
Of positions and preferences,
Do not exist.
There is a majestic experiential radiance.

The dualities of division and clearance,
Of accounting and judging,
Do not exist.
There is a majestic experiential radiance.

There is no experience of awareness.
There is a majestic experiential radiance.
There are no flashes of sentience.
There is a majestic experiential radiance.
There are no visualizations for our minds.
There is a majestic experiential radiance.

We do not crave to attribute names, words, and discussions.
There is a majestic experiential radiance.
We do not study or travel over
Any stages or pathways.
There is a majestic experiential radiance.
Our collective ideas have no names.
There is a majestic experiential radiance.
Every basis for discussion
Is a majestic experiential radiance.

The greater virtue of the Buddhas
Is like that.

That is what he said.

This is Chapter Four: Teaching the Greater Virtue of the Buddha.

PUTTING OUR LOWER DELUSIONS INTO ORDER

Then Vajrasattva questioned our teacher,
The All Good:

What is the problem with the three realms of samsara?

That is what he asked.

He gave instruction to the audience that had gathered:

Abidara Radna Saṃpara Alemema Kye Ma Ho!

Those who have deviated from their proper purpose
Are the ones who take their ideas to be their selves.
When the sky takes in the sky
There are clouds.

We use our own feet
To hold down our heads.
We chain our own necks and limbs.
We throw away our own wealth.
We put out our own lanterns.
We sink our own suns and moons.

Kye Ma!
Sentient beings who cling to a self
Have big problems with their emotions.
For the sake of equality

They give rise to positions and preferences.

The basis for both Buddhas and sentient beings
Is a universal essence,
A wind that moves the earth.
Our awareness of being born
Is present to us equally.

As an analogy,
This is like the icicles on a lake.
Our flickering is the equal of our wind.
Our reply uses the three ways
That we do not hold onto our own place.

We do not understand the purpose of Buddhahood.
Our motion, flickering, and non-flickering
Rays, light, and knowledge,
Luster, fluttering, and lack of support:
Our aware memory uses a flickering
Through areas and their boundaries.

A drop of sweat brings the awakening of fortune.
The awareness that thinks that it exists
Gives birth to lust and hatred.
We do not know the purpose of our presence.
We are not aware of any meaning.
This is described as being the darkness of ignorance.

Our flickering creates a cause for the wind.
A darkness that covers our obstructions
Arises as a condition.
We do not open the door
To the arising of wisdom.
So the door to the cycle of darkness
Arises as our condition.
We are wandering through the doors
Of our ignorant delusions.

When we hunt with our awareness
We create wrath.
Our sentience is accompanied by an actual flickering.

As for the mind,
It is described to have five clarities:

It is clear.
It does not move.
Its vastness is not limited.
The unchanging moves and changes.

The ways that the mind appears
Are described as being five.
The form of light and the form of awareness
Arise in a form of flesh.
In the form of our awareness
The form of light is a delusion.

There is a mother.
There is a father.
When they work together
We wander through the door of the womb.
The form of flesh
Is wrapped within a form of radiance.

By cause of the father's hatred
We become attached to the way of flesh and bones.
By the condition of the mother's lust
We become attached to the way of blood and urine.

By cause of the three times
There are bodies, speech, and minds.
This is the reward
For the ripening of our delusions.

In our vision of the conditions of substances
We are delusional in these ways.

Fathers, mothers, children, relatives, nations,
And all the rest:
We appear to be them.
We hold onto them.
We define them,
We crave for them.

These three:
Delusion, apparent definition, and craving:
At first awareness is born.
It flickers in our sentience.
There is a clarity in our minds.
We define this in a name.

As for names,
They have no meanings.
This is our sentience.

As for the mind,
It is a noun that we discuss and conceptualize.
We hunt everywhere,
And we put things into systems,
We are deluded into the three wheels of forced certitude.

In the reality of our majestic equality
We use a variety of false ideas and knowledges
To hold onto the essence of inequality.
Because of this,
Our delusions develop into our rewards.

Delusion and non-delusion are not a duality.
It is because our craving ideas develop into names
That we hold Dharmas that do not exist to exist.
Because of this,
They ripen into delusional rewards.

There is no one to blame,
But blame has arisen.
Rejection and acceptance have arisen.
From out of the lack of anything to terminate or to work on,
Strife and practice have arisen
From out of the lack of any work or quest.
Because of this,
We ripen into a delusional reward.

There is no self or other,
But we hold to a self.
Then even though things are not this way
We hold them to exist.

We experience sorrow
In the way of a dream.
The movement to be born among the six classes
Arises from this.

We hold untruths to be true.
There is nothing to the base of our collective ideas.
We are holding onto ideas.

Due to our clinging,
We crave.
Then we are attached.
We are deluded.

Do not be deluded like this!
Put yourself into order!

If you ask how we are to answer,
We answer by ourselves.
We are hurt by the three ways
In which we do not hold our own ground.

We do not meet up with reality.
Our self-awareness is very dark for us.
Our wisdom does not take its own ground.
We are actually very ashamed of ourselves.
Our ideas do not awaken into their own place.
We vomit on ourselves in our reversion.
Our hearts do not rise up from within us.
We cover ourselves in darkness by ourselves.
We do not liberate our delusions into their own place.
We torture ourselves by ourselves.

No one swims to cause harm.
We reply that our minds and the body of the Dharma
Are not confused.
We reply that we do not cut the roots
Of the three poisons.
We reply that our cravings do not come from reverting ourselves.
We reply that the five poisons
Are not separate from this.
We reply that the darkness of our stupidity
Has not been removed.

We reply that the sun of wisdom has not arisen.

We have put ourselves in samsara
By ourselves.
We have put ourselves into delusion
By ourselves.

That is what he said.

This is Chapter Five: Putting Our Lower Delusions into Order.

TEACHING THAT THERE IS NO LIBERATION BY DHARMAS THAT ARE DUALISTIC VISIONS

Then Vajrasattva questioned our teacher,
The All Good,
With these words:

Please teach us the method
By which we are to understand the body of the Dharma.

That is what he asked.

Our teacher,
The All Good One,
Entered the samadhi of peace
In the blazing light of precious jewels.

Then he got up from it,
And he spoke these words:

Aya Kari Maha Ati Tala!

The Yang Ti of the Universal Ti
Is the king of the vehicles!
It is described as being the universal ancestor
Of the three vehicles.
It is unborn, wordless, and beyond exemplification.

E Ma!
Sentient beings do not understand things this way.

There is no substance,
But they want to show something.
This is also a big emotional problem
For sentient beings.

They want to say something
About something that is unborn.
This is also a big emotional problem
For sentient beings.

For something that is insubstantial
They want there to be a substance.
This is also a big emotional problem
For sentient beings.

My true nature is not universally realized.
It has been forced into the oral traditions
Of the eight vehicles.
This is also a big emotional problem
For sentient beings.

The eight vehicles do not see me.
This is also a big emotional problem
For sentient beings.

Their pride is turned backward by looking at others.
This is also a big emotional problem
For sentient beings.

Where there is no duality
They divide things into two.
This is also a big emotional problem
For sentient beings.

The five poisons do not exist,
But they want to give them up.
This is also a big emotional problem
For sentient beings.

The five bodies do not exist,
But they want to work toward realizing them.
This is also a big emotional problem
For sentient beings.

Sentient beings do not exist,
But they want to reject them.
This is also a big emotional problem
For sentient beings.

Buddhahood does not exist,
But they want to work toward realizing it.
This is also a big emotional problem
For sentient beings.

Ignorance does not exist,
But they want to reject it.
This is also a big emotional problem
For sentient beings.

Wisdom does not exist,
But they want to work toward realizing it.
This is also a big emotional problem
For sentient beings.

Objects and minds do not exist,
But they want to reject them.
This is also a big emotional problem
For sentient beings.

They believe that there is nothing
To take in or hold onto.
This is also a big emotional problem
For sentient beings.

Are you not aware
That these and all the rest
Of our dualistic visions
Are Dharmas made by our intellects?
Are you not aware that they are fantasy visions?
Are you not aware that they are nouns?
Are you not aware that they are
A conventional basis for discussion?

Are you not aware that they are
What the mean minded teach as Dharma?
Are you not aware that everything is an intellectual game?
Are you not aware that the Dharmas of the intellect
Are of interpretable intent?

The triad of fantasy, vision, and craving
Does not gather any Dharma that is for the Dharma.

That is what he said.

This is Chapter Six: Teaching that There Is No Liberation by Dharmas that Are Dualistic Visions.

REALITY BEYOND EXEMPLIFICATION

Then Vajrasattva questioned our teacher,
The All Good,
With these words:

Please teach us the meaning
Of the reality that is not to be exemplified.

That is what he asked.

The true mind of our teacher,
The All Good,
Entered the equanimity of the samadhi
On the meaning of the blazing light of precious jewels,
Which is not to be exemplified.

Then he got up from that samadhi,
And gave instruction to the audience that had gathered:

Ataba Turi Abama!

I am explaining something that is beyond all exemplification.
Vajrasattva,
Take this into your understanding!

Nothing came before the unborn.
It is beyond being exemplified.

Those who exemplify it
Will not become Buddhas.

We need a single Dharma
That is not to be exemplified.
By working toward the realization of the three bodies
We will not become Buddhas.
We need a single Dharma
That is free from that.

The trinity of appearance, emptiness, and the unborn:
By working toward realizing these three
We will not become Buddhas.
We need a single Dharma
That is free from that.

The trinity of mind, awareness, and thought:
By working toward realizing these three
We will not become Buddhas.
We need a single Dharma
That is free from that.

The trinity of mind, wisdom, and habitual patterns:
By believing in these three
We will not become Buddhas.
We need a single Dharma
That is free from that.

The trinity of awareness, emptiness, and non-duality:
By working toward realizing these three
We will not become Buddhas.
We need a single Dharma
That is free from that.

The trinity of collection, exemplification, and definition:
By working toward the realization of these three
We will not become Buddhas.
We need a single Dharma
That is free from that,

The trinity of what we must accept, what we must reject,
And having nothing to grasp:
By working toward the realization of these three

We will not become Buddhas.
We need a single Dharma
That is free from that.

The trinity of the unchanging, our hearts, and reality:
By working toward the realization of these three
We will not become Buddhas.
We need a single Dharma
That is free from that.

The trinity of total vision, clarity, and non-grasping:
By working toward the realization of these three
We will not become Buddhas.
We need a single Dharma
That is free from that.

The trinity of strife, practice, and work:
By believing in these three
We will not become Buddhas.
We need a single Dharma
That is free from that.

The trinity of what we must view, what we must meditate,
And what we must practice:
By working toward the realization of these three
We will not become Buddhas.
We need a single Dharma
That is free from that.

The trinity of vision, fantasy, and craving:
By working toward the realization of these three
We will not become Buddhas.
We need a single Dharma
That is free from that.

The trinity of intellectual objects, thought without a prayer,
And forms:
By meditating on these three
We will not become Buddhas.
We need a single Dharma
That is free from that.

The trinity of the wish to succeed, getting what we need,
And our cause:
By believing in these three
We will not become Buddhas.
We need a single Dharma
That is free from that.

The trinity of collective ideas, reception, an attachment:
By working toward the realization of these three
We will not become Buddhas.
We need a single Dharma
That is free from that.

The trinity of stopping letters, processing them, and nouns:
By working toward the realization of these three
We will not become Buddhas.
We need a single Dharma
That is free from that.

The trinity of visions, prejudices, and colors:
By working toward the realization of these three
We will not become Buddhas.
We need a single Dharma
That is free from that.

Dualistic, vision, non-duality, and all the rest:
They transcend our thoughts.
So we divide them in a mere summary.
Real success happens because
We are disappointed.

Regarding the true sign for what we call
A single Dharma,
It is an instruction that is definitive.

Moreover,
You must understand that it is like this:

The name of what we call a single Dharma
Is also actually alone.
We leave behind the one.

As for the meaning of leaving it behind,
We have nothing to say.
As for the meaning of leaving it behind,
We have nothing to show.
As for the meaning of leaving it behind,
We have nothing to receive.

As for a purpose that is beyond thought,
We have no reason for our beliefs.
We have no work or quest.
This is the meaning of leaving it behind.

As for the meaning of leaving it behind,
We have nothing to accept or reject.
As for the meaning of leaving it behind,
We have nothing to throw out or compile.
As for the meaning of leaving it behind,
We have no view or meditation.
As for the meaning of leaving it behind
We have no practice or rewards.
As for the meaning of leaving it behind,
We have no causes to protect.
As for the meaning of leaving it behind
We have nowhere to travel.

The reason we get the meaning
Of leaving it behind
Is that we have left our own existence behind.

In this there is nothing to be contrived by our intellects.
In this there is nothing that is complicated or uncomplicated.
In this there is nothing that is finished or unfinished.
In this there is nothing that happens or does not happen.
In this there is no clear division between good and evil.
In this we have no reason to work on forecasting calculations.
In this there is nothing that is clear or unclear.

As for the reality of the secret that is supreme,
It will not happen that our ears do not hear others.
About this there is nothing we can say with our tongues.
By speaking we will not get any higher.
Everything we say is a noun.

In words that are nouns there are no Buddhas.
From the beginning this has been beyond
Speech, thought, and discussion.
We have no reason to settle on an attitude
That is not mindful.

There is nothing to think about.
This is beyond being an object for our intellects.
The Buddha is primordially absent.
We have nothing to do
To work toward realizing anything.

The unchanging and unborn body of the Dharma
Has been present from the primordial.
We do not need to work toward its realization.
The body of the Dharma
Has been unborn from the beginning.
The unborn is not affected by any imputations of blame.

There are some fools
Who say this sky does not exist.
They are throwing out their critical thinking.

Since long ago,
The wise have not held to any existence.
We have lacked any duality
From the beginning.
Refute this clinging to two truths!

The All Good cannot refute
The supreme intent of non-duality.
This being so,
You must understand things this way.

That is what he said.

This is Chapter Seven: Reality Beyond Exemplification.

TEACHING THAT WE WILL NOT BE LIBERATED BY STOPPING, STARTING, REJECTING, OR ACCEPTING

Then Vajrasattva addressed our teacher,
The All Good One,
With these words:

Regarding this intent that is not to be exemplified,
Will there not be a contradiction
If we engage in strife and projection?

That is what he asked.

Our teacher,
The All Good One,
Entered the equanimity of the samadhi of unchanging jewel light.

Then he got up,
And he spoke these words:

For me,
This is the yoga of the Universal Ti.

If stopping and starting
Or rejection and acceptance
Are happening,
There is a contradiction.

If you reject the five poisons,
You reject me.
If you work to realize the five bodies,
You are rejecting me.
If you abandon ignorance,
You abandon me.

If you work to realize wisdom,
You abandon me.
If you reject ideas,
You are rejecting me.
If you work to realize reality,
You abandon me.

If you reject samsara,
You are rejecting me.
If you work to realize nirvana,
You are rejecting me.
If you reject sentient beings,
You are rejecting me.

If you work toward Buddhahood,
You are rejecting me.
If you reject yourself and others,
You are rejecting me.
If you are working toward selflessness,
You are rejecting me.

If you work preferentially,
You abandon me.
If you give up friends and enemies,
You give up me.
If you reject dualistic clinging,
You reject me.

If you work toward non-duality,
You abandon me.
If you discontinue your clear visualizations,
You abandon me.
If you work toward clarity,
You abandon me.

If you use a view to see,
You abandon reality.
If a meditator is meditating,
He is abandoning reality.
If you are protecting samaya,
You are abandoning reality.

If you hunt for good works,
You are abandoning reality.
If you travel on levels and paths,
You abandon reality.
If you are working toward a reward,
You are abandoning reality.

Moreover,
You may ask why this is so.

All of these things are either stopping or developing.
The views and the act of viewing
Have the disease of strife.
The meditators and the act of mediation
Have the disease of strife.
The practitioners and the act of practicing
Have the disease of strife.
The act of working toward a reward
Has the disease of strife.
The act of traveling over levels and paths
Has the disease of strife.

When we practice like that
We will not be liberated.
If we do not use our knowledge
To cut through dualistic vision,
Going to the other side will be very dear.

That is what he said.

This is Chapter Eight: Teaching that We Will Not Be Liberated by Stopping, Starting, Rejecting, or Accepting.

METHODS FOR EXPERIENTIAL ACCEPTANCE AND SETTLING

Then Vajrasattva questioned our teacher,
The All Good,
With these words:

Speak to this audience!
Teach the instructions
On the methods for attaining the body of the Dharma
That are not delusional!

Our teacher,
The true mind of the All Good
Entered the samadhi of the preciousness that has no fixed estimate.

Then he got up,
And he spoke these words:

Our method for attaining
The unchanging body of the Dharma
Is that we do not seek to perform any strife or development.
We experience the giving up of all our works.
Our own selves are settled into their own places,
And so we seek them.
We are free from the diseases of rejection and acceptance,
Attachment and craving.

As for the traditional teachings
On my own great word,
They have never been taught
To those of the other vehicles.

A La La Ho!
This is the heart-blood of my own ambrosia!

As for me,
I appear throughout all the apparent world.
Appearance is for appearance,
But you do not see me.
Come into the experience of not seeing!

As for me,
I encompass the totality of our vessel and its contents.
It is because I encompass everything
That no one recognizes me.
Come into the experience of having nothing to recognize!

As for me,
I am the real basis for everything.
As I am the real base,
Nothing encompasses me.
Come into the experience of having nothing to realize!

Everything is opened up by me.
There is not even one actor or thinker.
Come into the experience of not being open!

As for me,
I am apparent to everyone,
But everyone will not have a vision of me.
Come into the experience of being invisible!

Everything was created by me.
I was not created by anybody.
Come into the experience of being uncreated!

I control everyone.
I am not controlled by anyone.
Come into the experience of being uncontrolled!

I seek everyone,
But no one seeks me.
Come into the experience of being unsought!

I abandon everyone.
No one abandons me.
Come into the experience of not being abandoned!

I work toward the realization of everyone,
But no one works toward the realization of me.
Come into the experience of not working toward anything!

I define all things,
But nothing defines me.
Come into the experience of not being defined!

I exemplify all things,
But nothing exemplifies me.
Come into the experience of not being exemplified!

I know everything,
But there is no natural knowledge of me.
Come into the experience of the unknown!

I give birth to everyone,
But no one gives birth to me.
Come into the experience of ungenerated perfection!

I understand everyone,
But no one understands me.
Come into the experience of not being understood!

Use your unborn awareness!
Come into the experience of having no experience!

Use the absence of any flickering in your thought!
Come into the experience of there being no motion!

Use the absence of any designated name for the mind!
Come into the experience
Where we do not hold onto complex attributions!
Come into the experience of an unchanging way of being!
Come into the experience

Of the self-luminescence of the way things appear!
Come into the absence of any clear division between these two!
Come into the absence of any substance to the way things are!
Come into the absence of any stopping or starting of appearances!
Come into the absence of any accounting for these two!

Let the totality of our objects:
Outer, inner, white, and red
Come into the absence of any true nature to their appearance.
Let our every way of being,
The forceful visions of our minds,
Come into the invisible absence of any true nature!

Let all our taking in and holding onto dualistic visions
For the interim
Come into the experience where we cut the ropes of our complexities.
Come into the experience where there is no birth!
Come into the experience where there is no change!
Come into the experience
Where there is no speech, thought, or discussion!
Come into the space of the unceasing body of the Dharma!
Come into the experience in which our ideas are not dualistic!
Let even the words that we plant
Come into non-duality!

That is what he said.

This is Chapter Nine: Methods for Experiential Acceptance and Settling.

SETTLING INTO AN UNCONTRIVED NATURE

Then Vajrasattva addressed our teacher,
The All Good,
With these words:

What are the upadeśa instructions
On the method for settling
In which we settle into our own uncontrived nature?

So did he address him.

Then our teacher,
The true mind of the All Good One,
Entered the samadhi of the jewel light that does not beam.

Then he got up,
And he spoke these words:

This is the method for settling oneself
In uncontrived self-purity.
Vajrasattva,
You must understand this!

You who wish to look upon me,
Come into the personal joy
Of not working out views!

There is no object that we see by looking.
By settling down without looking

We meet with God.

You who wish to meditate on me,
Come into the experience of having no meditation!
To settle into the experience of the unchanging
Is to meet with me.

You who wish to practice with me,
Come into the experience of having no practice
And nothing to do!
In the experience of having nothing to do
We are actually settled.

You who desire to protect me,
Come into the experience that we do not protect
And we do not transgress.
To settle into the experience
Of having nothing to protect
Is our samaya.

You who desire to hunt for me,
Come into the experience where there is no strife
And we do not strive.
To settle into a resolve that is without strife
Is actually a good work.

You who desire to travel to me,
Come into the experience
Where we are indivisible without traveling!
Settling into the experience of indivisibility
Is the perfection of the levels and paths.

You who desire to propitiate me,
Come into the experience that we do not work toward
Where there is nothing to work on!
Settling into the experience of having nothing to propitiate
Is the realization of our objectives.

You who desire to acquire me,
There is nothing for you to acquire.
So come into your own places!

It is because there is nothing anywhere else
That our rewards are great.
With nothing to acquire,
You meet up with your original purpose.

Let all the Dharmas in their infinite variety,
Whatever may appear,
Come into the experience of leaving things alone.

As for the true nature of our hearts
As embodiments of the Dharma:
Whatever may appear,
Come into the absence of any true nature!

You with a vision for the collective ideas
That are objects for our intellects,
Come into the absence of any true nature to appearances!

You for whom this is a dualistic vision
Of taking things in and holding onto them,
Come into the absence of any clear divisions or accounting!

You who are aware of the memories
Of the mind that enjoys thinking,
Come into the experience of a great self-awakening!

Your collective ideas are the miracles of your minds.
Come into the experience of a magnificent self-luminescence!

You who would define flickering awareness,
Come into the experience of a majestic shining luminescence!

The totality of our settled experience
May be condensed into three things:
We achieve the three bodies,
Which we have no reason to achieve.
By overwhelming the three worlds
We mount our own level
Without oppressing the three levels.
By cutting through the three poisons at the root
We sweep the three realms of samsara with a broom.
This is a vision of essence, true nature, and compassion.

That is what he said.

This is chapter Ten: Settling into an Uncontrived Nature.

TEACHINGS ON THE TRINITY OF DEVIATIONS, OBSTRUCTIONS, AND DELUSIONS

Then Vajrasattva questioned our teacher,
The All Good,
With these words:

There is no name for the heart
Of an unchanging embodiment of the Dharma.
So how was it given a name?

So did he address him.

With the true mind of a teacher,
The All Good One
Entered the samadhi of blazing jewel light.

He got up from it,
And said these words:

Dharmas have no names
And no exemplification.
So it is said that we deviate
By using names that would exemplify.

I am explaining the characteristics of deviation and obstruction.
Vajrasattva,
Hold this in your mind!

There is no Buddha.
So there is also no name for any Buddha.
When he believes that he does not exist,
The Buddha is deviating.

There is no body of the Dharma.
So there is also no name for any body of the Dharma.
By believing that they do not exist
The bodies of the Dharma are deviating.

There is no body of pleasure.
So there is also no name for the body of form.
By believing that they do not exist,
Form bodies are deviating.

There is no samsara.
So there is also no name for samsara.
By believing that it does not exist,
Samsara is deviating.

There is no nirvana.
So there is also no name for nirvana.
By believing that it does not exist,
Nirvana is deviating.

Ignorance does not exist.
So there is also no name for ignorance.
By believing that it does not exist,
Ignorance is deviating.

There is no wisdom.
So there is also no name for wisdom.
By believing that it does not exist,
Wisdom is deviating.

There are no ideas.
So there is also no name for ideas.
By believing that they do not exist,
Ideas are delusional.

Reality does not exist.
So there is also no name for reality.
By believing that it does not exist,

Reality is delusional.

Preferred positions do not exist.
So there is also no name for preferred positions.
By believing that they do not exist,
Self-awareness is delusional.

All of these things are non-dual.
When it happens that we are dividing the things we take in
Dualistically,
That is an obstruction.

None of these things have a name.
There is nothing to discuss.
When it happens that we talk about giving things names
That is an obstruction.

We mistake the door
To the path that we would go on.
So we deviate.

By wandering through the five doors
We are delusional about what we take in.

The totality of the two thousand five hundred
Deviations and obstructions,
When divided are infinite.
When summarized they are subsumed into three.

That is what he said.

This is Chapter Eleven: Teachings on the Trinity of Deviations, Obstructions, and Delusions.

TEACHINGS ON A CORE THAT IS NOT STAINED BY DEVIATIONS AND OBSTRUCTIONS

Then Vajrasattva questioned our teacher,
The All Good,
With these words:

Is there any conclusion to deviation and obstruction?

So did he address him.

Our teacher,
The true mind of the All Good,
Entered the samadhi that brings together
The circle of the precious Sutras.

Then he got up,
And he spoke these words:

The deviations and obstructions of the vehicles
Are infinite,
But the Universal Ti of the Yang Ti
Is said to be conclusive.

Misunderstandings appear to be deviations and obstructions.
In the intent of the heart
There are no deviations or obstructions.
There are no names.
To give a name is to deviate.

When we leave discussion behind
We do not deviate.
We are obstructed by the bonds
Of what we take in and what we hold onto.
There are no clear differences.
So there are no obstructions.

The ideas of the demonstrators
Are intellectual delusions.
When we leave speech and thought behind,
There are no delusions.

Our deviations and obstructions
May be inconceivable,
But our deviances, obstructions, and delusions
When summarized are three.

Through the door of what arises we may be delusional,
But we understand the methods for turning things around
So we do not deviate.

Those who remain
May be obstructed by misunderstandings,
But in the dawning of the purpose of our hearts
There is nothing to obstruct.

We may be delusional about our wanderings
Through the five doors,
But once we have cut through the roots of our thoughts
We have nothing to be delusional about.

One who has the resolve to be decisive
Has no hope or fear.
Nothing obstructs our understanding
Of the purpose of our hearts.

A balance that has no preference
Is not delusional.

To understand the meaning of non-duality
Is to have no position or preference.
To understand the meaning of indivisibility

Is to have nothing to take in or hold onto.
To understand the meaning of wisdom
Is to have no ignorance.
To understand the meaning of the three bodies
Is to have none of the three poisons.
To understand the meaning of the five bodies
Is to have none of the five poisons.

To understand the meaning of Buddhahood
Is to have no sentient beings.
To understand the meaning of decision
Is to have no object or mind.

That is what he said.

This is Chapter Twelve: Teachings on a Core that Is Not Stained by Deviations and Obstructions.

OUR ABODE IS HOPELESS

Then Vajrasattva asked our teacher,
The All Good,
What this means:

We have had this within ourselves from the beginning.
So are we not seeking out works, quests, and strife?

So did he address him.

The true mind of the All Good One
Entered the samadhi in which the five jewel lights
Abide within ourselves.

He got up from it.
Then he gave instruction:

We have had this from the beginning
Within ourselves.
So we do not need to strive, practice, or work.

Vajrasattva,
Take this into your mind!
If you understand that experiential radiance
Is a viewpoint,
You must not look for a view!

If you understand that experiential radiance
Is a meditation,

You must not meditate on any meditation!

If you understand that experiential radiance
Is a practice,
You must not practice any practice!

If you understand that experiential radiance
Is a reward,
You must not work toward any rewards!

If you understand that experiential radiance
Is the three bodies,
You must not work toward realizing any three bodies!

If you understand that experiential radiance
Is Buddhahood.
You must not work toward realizing Buddhahood!

If you understand that your own mind
Is the body of the Dharma,
Do not seek the body of the Dharma
In anyone else!

It is not possible that you find it by searching,
Even in an eon.
You may seek through the three times,
But you will not find it.
What we do not find by seeking
Is Buddhahood.

What is successful
Without being worked on
Is the realization of the three bodies.

If you find anything
It is an idea.

That is what he said.

This is Chapter Thirteen: Our Abode Is Hopeless.

AMBROSIA MELTS ITSELF AND IS LUMINOUS BY ITSELF

Then Vajrasattva questioned our teacher,
The All Good,
With these words:

What is this magnificent self-radiance?

So did he question him.

Our teacher entered the equanimity of the samadhi
On the precious jewel light that does not boil.

Then he got up from it.
He gave instruction:

It is said that ambrosia melts itself
And is radiant by itself.
O Audience,
Listen respectfully!
Do not be distracted!

Asara Tsita Api!
The three bodies are a majestic self-radiance
That does not change.

Without abandoning the three poisons
We are already in a majestic self-radiance.

Without seeking any wisdom
We are already in a majestic self-radiance.
Without abandoning our ignorance
We are already in a majestic self-radiance.
Without searching for reality
We are already in a majestic self-radiance.
Without rejecting our ideas
We are already in a majestic self-radiance.

Without accepting Buddhahood
We are already in a majestic self-radiance.
Without abandoning sentient beings
We are already in a majestic self-radiance.
Without working to realize nirvana
We are already in a majestic self-radiance.
Without there being any samsara to reject
We are already in a majestic self-radiance.
Without having any preferred positions or planetary referents
We are already in a majestic self-radiance.

The unchanging body of the Dharma of our hearts
Is already in our majestic self-radiance.
Our true selves are unchanging.
For we are already in a majestic self-radiance.

We have no base.
We do not change.
We are already in a majestic self-radiance.

Everyone who appears to be in bondage
Is already in a majestic self-radiance.

That is what he said.

This is Chapter Fourteen: Ambrosia Melts Itself and Is Luminous by Itself.

THE SHINING LANTERN OF AMBROSIA

Then Vajrasattva addressed our teacher,
The All Good,
With these words:

Please teach us the meaning
Of the magnificent clear depths of reality!

That is what he asked.

Our teacher,
The All Good One,
Entered the equanimity of the samadhi of blazing jewel light.

Then he got up from it,
And he spoke these words:

Amuna Taripe Tayati!
I will explain the shining lantern
That is an elixir of ambrosia.
Audience,
Listen respectfully!
Do not be distracted!

From out of the space that is the body of the Dharma,
Our unchanging hearts
Are an unceasing knowing awareness
That transforms into all the many things.
We do not find any place to go anywhere.

Reality melts into the space of our hearts
Without stopping,
And melts into a vision of the force.

At the first we introduce the mother to the child
That is primordial Buddhahood.
Being indivisible,
We melt into ourselves.

Wisdom takes its own place.
Our delusions awaken themselves.
Our ideas are liberated into their own places.
We hold to the level of the unborn.

Our hearts are shining in space.
We do not create visions in our minds.
This is the great and shining deep.

We do not create emptiness in our minds.
This is the great and shining deep.

We do not create non-duality in our minds.
This is the great and shining deep.

We do not create the three bodies in our minds.
This is the great and shining deep.

We do not create the five poisons in our minds.
This is the great and shining deep.

We do not create any appearance or emptiness in our minds.
This is the great and shining deep.

We do not create happiness and sorrow in our minds.
This is the great and shining deep.

We do not create the unborn in our minds.
This is the great and shining deep.

These and all the rest
Are a great and shining deep.

That is what he said.

This is Chapter Fifteen: The Shining Lantern of Ambrosia.

TEACHINGS ON THE MANDALA THAT IS NOT DRAWN

Then Vajrasattva again questioned our teacher,
The All Good:

What is the undrawn mandala
For the yoga of the Universal Ti of the Great Perfection?

So did he address him.

Then our teacher,
The All Good One,
Entered the equanimity of the samadhi in which
Precious jewels do not move.

Then he got up from it,
And he gave instruction to the audience:

Bhona Hrita Hana Maṇḍala!
I will describe the mandala of perfection
That we do not draw.
Audience,
Listen respectfully!
Do not be distracted!

The true nature of our hearts does not change.
The mandala of the Bodhicitta dawns
On the pervasively encompassing sky space

That is the basis for all things.

With both scripture and reason
We make attributions about the earth foundation
That is a pervasively encompassing reality.
Then knowledge is taken up by our mother.
The reality that is the basis of all things
Is a spacious abode.

In the house of worship
Of the pure dominion of the Dharma
We are brought together
Into a magnificent encompassing pervasion
That fills the earth.

We use the water of enlightenment
To clear away the dust of our ideas.
We work to spread out into a true equality.

The unchanging circle exemplifies wisdom.
Our unchanging hearts are rolled together at center.
The eight collections of consciousness
Dawn by themselves.

A lotus has eight petals.
We possess five wisdoms.
We are in the center of the four directions.
The immeasurable square is the door of our validation.
There are four marked corners
For the four kinds of awareness.
They are clear, unmoving, and their vastness is not limited.
They are unchanging, stable, and possess the five.
So white, yellow, red, blue, and green are the five colors.
They are ornamented by goddesses of unceasing playfulness.

The Dharma and reality are blended.
So the nets, half-nets, and silk
Are melodious,
And are ornamented by a clear vision of reality.
They are beautified at their four doors
With four wheels that leave behind the four extremes
And cut through complications.

We plant the pillar of an unchanging heart.
We are ornamented by the sun and moon
Of a shining experiential radiance.

The Dharma cycle of the Universal Ti
Is for an umbrella.
It is the vajra horn
That overwhelms the nine stages.

When a view that is a serious bondage
Has taken your mind,
Meditate!

In order to burn up
Our logic, creation, practice, hopes, fears, and rewards
We are surrounded by a wall of fire.

If we are to raise a mandala,
We raise it in our minds.
This is the mandala that is the reality of our original purity.
It will not come up in the other vehicles.

That is what he said.

This is Chapter Sixteen: Teachings on the Mandala that Is Not Drawn.

TEACHING THE DEFINITION OF A MANDALA

Then again Vajrasattva asked:

If the mandala that we do not draw is like that,
What is the definition of this mandala?

That is what he asked.

The All Good One gave instruction:

I will explain the definition.
Listen,
O Audience!

This is the mandala of the very pure dominion of the sky.
Reality abides in the Bodhicitta.
Our center is the unchanging body of the Dharma.
Our circumference is that the force of our awareness
Does not stop.

This being so,
Our mandala is perfected in our mind.
We are an unmistaken center
With an uncontrived circumference.
Our mandala is not mistaken and is not contrived.

Reality is perfected in the Bodhicitta.
Our hearts are at center.
The way things appear is the circumference.

Our hearts and the way things appear
Are perfected in our minds.

The unchanging is at center.
The uncontrived is the circumference.
The unchanging and the uncontrived
Are perfected in our minds.

The unborn is at center.
The unceasing is the circumference.
The non-duality of birth and ending
Is a mandala.

The indivisible is at center.
The apparent world is the circumference.
And indivisible variety is a mandala.

The non-dual is at center.
The uncounted is the circumference.
Non-dual accounting is a mandala.

That is what he said.

This is Chapter Seventeen: Teaching the Definition of a Mandala.

TEACHINGS ON THE HOSTS OF GODS WHO ARE COMPLETELY PERFECT WITHOUT BEING GENERATED

Then Vajrasattva questioned our teacher,
The All Good,
With these words:

If the definition of a mandala is like that,
Then who is its god and where does he dwell?

That is what he asked.

The All Good One entered the equanimity of the samadhi
Of the light that encompasses us all.

He got up from it,
And he gave instruction:

In the mandala
That is the dominion of the sky for us all
The dominion of the Dharma does not transfer or change.
It is very pure.
It is inconceivable.

In the mandala of blazing jewel light
Our own minds are unchanging
And are supreme leaders.
They are accompanied by an entourage

Of the unceasing force of awareness.

Our god is completely perfect,
Without being generated.

In the central position,
Upon a throne that is the sky,
Our very pure stupidity
Transcends our intellects
Without thought,
Without birth.
There sits the body of the Dharma.

In the Eastern position,
Upon a throne of the sun and moon,
Our very pure hatred
Has no birth or ending.
There sits the self-arising body of perfect pleasure.

In the Southern position,
Upon a throne that is a garuda,
Our very pure pride
Is without any mindfulness.
There sits the manifest body
That we do not create in our minds.

In the Western position,
Upon a throne that is an ocean,
A very pure lust,
In its three embodiments,
Sits in a body of indivisible true essence.

In the Northern position
Upon a throne of wind
Our very pure jealousy
Perfects our four bodies.
There sits the magnificent body
Of genuine enlightenment.

It does not sit there
Due to being generated.
It is beyond strife and projection.
It sits in its own place.

Our five families accord in their parts,
Which is especially noble.

Upon the four borders
There sit goddesses who are not generated.

In the South-East,
Upon a lotus throne
We are aware that our deluded writings
Are the Bodhicitta.
We settle into our cravings
For definition to our smell.

Great goddesses live as the wives of awareness.
On the North-West border there is a lotus.
Our memories have nothing to do with our minds.
The true nature of sound is very pure.
The great goddesses live as happy wives.

On the North-East border there is a lotus.
Upon it there is a self-radiance
That makes flickerings in our minds.
Our feelings of taste are all awoken.
The goddesses of non-duality
Live as empty wives.

The agreeable aspect of being a goddess
Is its special nobility.

As for the way in which
The ungenerated sentinels sit:

At the Eastern door
Upon a throne of clouds,
He who cuts the miracle of birth
At the roots
Sits in the great experiential radiance
Of a door protector.
He subjugates the demons
Of our five poisonous emotional problems.

At the Western door,
Upon the throne of a mirage,

He who cuts through the sorrows of old age
At the roots
Sits in a magnificent self-awakening
As a door protector.
He subjugates the demons
Who are the children of the gods.

At the Northern door
Upon a throne of fog,
He who cuts through the sorrow of death
At the roots
Sits in the shining deeps of reality
As a door protector.
He totally subjugates the demons
Of the Lord of the Dead.
Then he dwells in the experience
Of there being no birth or death.

From the beginning,
These four kinds of door protectors
Have subjugated the four kinds of demons
And have left behind the eight kinds of limitations.

They have emerged from out of a lake
Of attachment, clinging, and craving.

They have broken free from the chains
Of both taking things in and holding onto them.

They have escaped from the swamp
Of terminating, developing, rejecting, and accepting.

The hosts of gods that are the visible force of our awareness
Are also not generated
By any strife, propitiation, or invitation.

From the very start
They have lived like that.
The hosts of gods that cooperate in their factions
Are especially noble.

It will not happen that any other vehicles arise
From out of this yoga of the Universal Ti.

That is what he said.

This is Chapter Eighteen: Teachings on the Hosts of Gods Who Are Completely Perfect Without Being Generated.

THE NON-CONCEPTUAL IS OUR BOUNDARY

Then Vajrasattva questioned the All Good One:

If the way that the hosts of gods dwell is like that,
What is the great cutting off of borders?

So did he address him.

The All Good One gave instruction:

As for a border,
We cut through our own minds for ourselves.
We use the victorious borders
Of non-conceptual wisdom
To remove the king of obstacles,
Who is our own ideas.

We use this victorious karma
Where we have nothing to do
To expel the obstacles
Of taking things in and holding onto them,
Of I and self.

The king of wrath uses an unchanging experiential radiance
To expel the demons
Of delusion, ideation, fantasy, and craving.
The wrathful ones of self-arising wisdom
Clear away our obstacles and ideas.
They live within their own arising.

They use an indivisible and primordially present wisdom
To clear away the obstacles that are our preferred positions.
This is a space of equality.

They use a wisdom of uncorrupt and total perfection
To clear away the obstacles there are in accounting.
They live without counting things.
They use a wisdom of self-luminous success as their purpose
To clear way the obstacles there are
In believing in names and signs.

They abide in a contemplation of reaching the end
Without changing.

That is what he said.

This is Chapter Nineteen: The Non-Conceptual is Our Boundary.

SUMMONING, DWELLING, AND WORSHIP

Then Vajrasattva questioned the All Good himself
With these words:

How are we to summon, dwell with, and worship
The hosts of gods who have unchanging hearts?

So did he address him.

The All Good One gave instruction:

According to the way it is
In the meaning of reality,
There are no invitations, dwelling with, or worship,
But I will explain how
The apparent force of reality
Is playful.

Even though your heart is the ultimate truth
Of the body of the Dharma,
Please come here
From out of a dominion that we do not visualize!

Even though the body of pleasure,
That has no birth or ending,
Comes from a spacious and very pure
Space of clear light,
Please come here

From your abode in Akaniṣṭha!

Even though your manifest body
Encompasses everything without trying
From out of the pervasive sky-space
If the apparent world,
Please come here for the sake of living beings!

We attach all our ideas
About taking things in and holding onto them
To the hosts of gods who have originally pure hearts,
Then we seek for some unchanging ultimate truth.
We are accepted into a space
That is non-dual and empty of extremes.

In the infinite palace
Of the spacious space of the sky,
Upon the actual throne chairs of equality
There dwell the hosts of gods who have unceasing hearts.
They have no names,
But are stable in their own places.

When we do not hinder or develop
Any of the particulars in the objects that appear
We offer them in worship.

When there is no substance
To the memories and ideas
That our minds cling to,
We offer them in worship.

When there is no clear distinction
In any of the appearances
Of any external or internal duality,
We offer them in worship.

When the white and the red
That appear to be objects
Are in a majestic individual settlement,
We offer them in worship.

When there is no accounting for

The private force of the things
That come out of our minds,
We offer them in worship.

When our binding
By both what we take in and what we hold onto
Is not a complicated rope,
We offer it in worship.

When none of the many appearances of external objects
Has any private radiance,
We offer them in worship.

When there is no visible appearance
To this sentience that shines inside us,
We offer it in worship.

When we have no attachment or clinging
To any of the Dharmas that appear
And that are possible,
We offer them in worship.

Please come down from your seat
And take them!

Those who remember
With minds that hold to ancient ways,
In their magnificent experiential radiance
Offer them in worship.

In a dominion that we do not visualize
We offer them in worship.

When we offer our own views to ourselves
We will get great and wondrous siddhis.
When we offer in worship
We make offerings to our own minds.

As for the worship
That is the heart of our own sentience,
The other vehicles never speak of it.
A worship that all factions agree on
Is especially noble.

That is what he said.

This is Chapter Twenty: Summoning, Dwelling, and Worship.

PRAISE FOR THE PURPOSE OF OUR HEARTS

Then Vajrasattva questioned the All Good himself
With these words:

How are we to use praise
To make these hosts of gods in the mandala happy?

That is what he asked.

The All Good One gave instruction:

It is certainly true
That we have nothing to divide in our intent,
But I am teaching about praises in signs and symbols.

In the infinite palace
That is the dominion of the originally pure Dharma
There is a god who lives alone in a circle.
He is the supreme leader of all the gods.

I bow to the Bodhicitta!

Unchanging and all encompassing,
Your body is like the sky!
Clearing the darkness of ignorance,
Your eyes are the sun and moon.
You are beyond all desire.
You have a wish-fulfilling heart.
I praise your body of perfect pleasure!

You are insubstantial,
While you encompass all things.
You work to cut through all kinds of complications.
I bow to the compassionate and all-pervasive
Guardian of living things,
The manifest body!

The indivisibility of the three bodies
Liberates us from extremes.
I praise the one who works to gather
All the infinite Dharmas,
That leave our thought behind,
Into an experiential reality,
The body of our true essence.

All the karmas of strife, production, work, and hunting
Which are fantasies used by the childish
Are not to be worked on.
Our freedom from complications is spontaneously realized.
We praise the body of genuine enlightenment!

Once we have cut through all the complications
Of our attachments and clinging,
A great friendship will encompass us all.
I praise and bow to the body of aware wives
Who work to remove all our collections of smells.

Once you are free from all stopping and projecting,
All rejection and acceptance,
Use your great compassion
To guide living beings!

In objects that are tangible
There are no clear distinctions.
I praise and bow to the body
Of the wife who is clear.

The non-duality of the outside and the inside
Is an experience of reality.
The karmas of our joy are totally perfect.
The true nature of sound is free from complications.
We bow to the body of the wife of bliss.

We are beyond all the eight extremes of dualistic clinging.
Our cravings and bondage to taste are very pure.
You make our equanimity totally perfect.
We bow to the body of the wife of emptiness.

We are beyond the totality of causes and conditions,
Of birth and endings.
Those who are playful about their ideas that cling to extremes
Bow to the door guard in the East,
Who shines by himself in the sky of our reality.

Everyone is perfected in the experience of equality.
All the flickerings of our feeling awareness,
None excepted,
Are actually radiant in the experience of self-origination.
We bow to the door guard in the South.

All of our delusional visions
Arise from out of themselves
And are pure in themselves.
The unclear actually awakens into its own place.
We bow to the door guard of the West.

The signs of our fantasies and cravings
Are self-liberated.
Our liberation is pure in its own place.
Our clarity is actually the essence of our radiance.
We bow to the door guard of the North.

The praise in which our factions agree
Is especially noble.

That is what he said.

This is Chapter Twenty-One: Praise for the Purpose of Our Hearts.

WE OFFER EVERYTHING IN THE APPARENT WORLD AS A VERY PURE AMBROSIA

Then Vajrasattva addressed the true mind of our teacher,
The All Good:

How are we to make the ambrosia and medicinal offerings
For the gods of the mandala of reality?

So did he address him.

The All Good One gave instruction:

O Audience,
Listen with respect!
Do not be distracted!
I will explain the ambrosia
That is a medicine of worship.

The self-originating has been very pure
From the primordial.
The medicines that are concocted into eight thousand roots,
The hundred thousand roots,
Are elixirs that are spacious.

The ambrosia of immortality is the *Rasayana.*
This is the heart that brings everyone together.
It liberates all the sentient beings of the six classes.

It is the supreme ambrosia that clears away the five poisons.

We offer medicine to the gods of the unchanging heart.
We offer it into a dominion that is not a visualization.
Grant us the siddhi of unborn great bliss!

The true nature of our hearts
May be unchanging,
But we teach that all the Dharmas of the apparent world,
None excluded,
Are contemplations on the categorization of ambrosias.

The self-originating has no cause or condition,
No birth or ending.
From out of the primordial clear light of the Base
Delusional vision and ignorance are very pure.
Our root is actually the Bodhicitta.

As for eight,
There are the eight collections of consciousness.

As for the thousand,
There are eighty thousand vehicles.

As for concoctions,
They are concocted in a space of balance.

As for medicine,
It is medicine for our eighty thousand emotional problems.

Our root is a single solitary circle.
The hundred thousand are visions of the force of our circle.
Our spaciousness is that we are spacious
Due to the playfulness of reality.

As for elixir,
Our hearts do not transfer or change.

As for demons,
They are our five poisonous emotional problems.

As for juice,
It is the five kinds of wisdom.

As for Ra,
It is both me and myself.

As for Sa,
It is the reality that overcomes the self.

Yana is the vehicles in their eight stages.

Everything is condensed into the Great Perfection.
Our heart is the yoga of the Universal Ti.
We use instructions that are for
Both beginnings and endings,
And so we cut through the abyss
Of the six classes of living things.

We use the transmission of the word
On cutting a rope by slicing it
To liberate all sentient beings,
None excepted,
Into this dominion.

We settle the unborn
Into the space of our reality.
The five poisons,
The five kinds of hatred, lust, and holding on,
Clear out our knowledge,
Understanding, views, meditations,
Practices, and rewards.

As for demons,
They are the positions of our ideas.
Clear jewel light is the best knowledge.
The demons do not crave.
They are overcome in their experience.

As for juice,
There are two diseases and three dangerous passages.

As for methods,
The apparent world is a space of great bliss.

As for worship,
We worship without visualizing anything.

Delight
Is to delight in a great equality.

As for being real,
Our own minds are unborn.

Our success is the wisdom in our ideas.

E Saṃkora A Siddhi A!

That is what he said.

This is Chapter Twenty-Two: We Offer Everything in the Apparent World as a Very Pure Ambrosia.

WE PRESENT OUR MINDS AS TORMAS

Then Vajrasattva questioned our teacher,
The All Good:

How are we to send off a torma of reality
That is not thrown together or glamorous
To these gods of the mandala?

So did he address him.

Then our teacher,
The All Good One,
Entered the equanimity of the samadhi in which
The precious jewel light has no clear distinction
Between growing and shrinking.

Then he got up from it,
And he said these words:

I will explain how reality is a torma of the mind!

O Audience,
Listen respectfully!
Do not be distracted!

In the unchanging true nature of our hearts
We send out ceaseless visions of the force
As torma.
We send out a torma that is stamped

With the seal of the apparent world,
And is not made out of stuff that has been thrown together.

The world that is a vessel
Is a vessel of gold and silver.
The inner elixir of the world
Is the stuff of a torma.

Birth, living, bodies and such things
Are ornaments for our torma.

The five ambrosias that emerge from themselves,
The five poisons,
The five originally pure wisdoms,
And the three poisons
Are our originally pure bodies, speech, and minds.

Our five kinds of consciousness
Are ornaments for our tormas.
The objects of our five senses
Are supports for our tormas.
Personal purity is the elixir
Of the contemplations of the Victorious Ones.

We use the blessings from these three:
Oṃ Ā: Hūṃ
So that the six classes of living things
In the three realms of the three worlds
Who are brought together by the outer and inner
Vessel and its contents
Will turn into an ocean
Of the ambrosia of equality.

Bless us so that we have no births or endings!

We offer in worship
All the Dharmas that have been gathered
By the apparent world
Into the dominion of the unborn.

Bless us so that we may cut through the roots of the tree of birth!

The Sugatas of the three times
Are beyond our thoughts.
We stamp the apparent world with a seal
And we offer it in worship.

Please enjoy it in the absence of any birth!
Bless us so that we do not change!
In worship we offer the fantasy visions of our minds
To the unsurpassed Three Jewels.
Please enjoy them without thought or speech!
Bless us so that we may be liberated
From signs and visions!

We offer our eighty thousand emotional problems
As tormas
To our gurus and yidams,
And to the dakinis.
Please enjoy them in a radiance that is on our own level!
Bless us so that our sorrows may be originally pure!

We offer the memories and ideas in our minds
In worship.
Please enjoy them throughout unchanging space!
Bless us so that we have no birth!

We offer all our feelings as they arise
As tormas
To the gods who are our heart's purpose.
Please enjoy them as you cut the ropes of complications!
Bless us so that we have nothing to account for!

We offer our dualistic apprehension of outside and inside
As a torma
To the five families, the five bodies, and our fathers and mothers.
Please enjoy them where there are no clear distinctions!
Bless us so that we have nothing to boil!

We offer our awareness, thought, memory, and minds
As Torma
To the goddesses who include Bliss Wife.
Please enjoy them without any divisiveness!
Bless us in the great liberation of the East!

We offer both our objectives and our minds
As tormas
To the door guard of the South,
Who awaken themselves.
Please enjoy them without stopping!
Bless us so that we are without any duality!

We offer our ignorance and our grasping at dualities
As tormas
To the door guard of the West,
Who is self-radiant.
Please enjoy them in a space of clarity!
Bless us so that our wisdom is in its own place!

We offer our view, meditation, practice, and rewards
As tormas
To the door guard of the North,
Who shines in the deeps.
Please enjoy them without any disposition of desire.
Bless us into our majestic original purity!

We offer all the names that we give things
As tormas.
Bless us so that we have no fantasy visions!

We offer all our works and quests
As tormas.
Bless us into a magnificent lack of anything to do!

We offer everything good and evil
As tormas.
Bless us into a magnificent lack of any rejection or acceptance!

We offer our visions of the base and of the force
As tormas.
Bless us so that mothers and children are inseparable!

The torma of the mind
Which lacks anything to send or any act of sending
Is especially noble.

That is what he said.

This is Chapter Twenty-Three: We Present Our Minds as Tormas.

THE DEFINITION OF A TORMA

Then Vajrasattva asked our teacher,
The All Good,
Who is a hero:

What is the definition of a torma?

So did he address him.

Our teacher gave instruction to the audience:

A torma is called a "torma."
We send off the six classes of living things,
So we say: "Tor."
Ma is because we cut through the abysses of these six.

We must say: "Tor" or "Send"
Because we offer up our dualistic visions.
We say: "Ma" because we are without any duality.

We say "Tor"
Because things happen without stopping.
We say "Ma"
Because we have nothing to account for.

We call a vision of the force of our awareness "Tor."
We call our melting into the force of the Base "Ma."

A variety of things appears,
So we say "Tor."
We are gathered into one.
So we say "Ma."

Our discussions are infinite,
So we say "Tor."
We have nothing to discuss,
So we say "Ma."

"Ma" is because we understand that the Dharmas are one.
The liberation of everyone by a single knowledge
Is the best torma.

That is what he said.

This is Chapter Twenty-Four: The Definition of a Torma.

IMPARTING EMPOWERMENT INTO THE MEANING OF THE UNIVERSAL TI

Then Vajrasattva questioned the All Good himself
With these words:

What is the method of imparting empowerment
For the yoga of the Universal Ti of the Great Perfection?

So did he address him.

Then our teacher,
The All Good One,
Entered the equanimity of the samadhi
In which the blessings of light blaze within us.

Then he got up from it,
And he gave instruction to the audience
On the methods for imparting empowerment:

In the way things are,
Which is the purpose of our hearts,
There are neither anything to impart
Nor any act of imparting anything,
But when we are starting out
We impart the empowerment of the force
Of the mind that is aware
Upon those with intellects that do not understand.

The basis for all things
Is the infinite palace of spacious space.
In the dominion of the sky,
Which is not a compounded thing,
Those who wish to understand
The original purity of reality
Will use the way where there is no strife
To engage.

First there is the empowerment of the vase.
Second there is the empowerment that is secret.
Third is the empowerment of knowledge and wisdom.
Fourth is the empowerment of the most precious word.

We conclude with the anointing vase
For the investiture of a king.

First we impart the empowerment of the vase.
Students who have the karma and the fortune
Who have instructions for their hearts
Will offer their request to the guru.
The guru will give it to them.

They work to acquire the implements and requisites.
Then in a place on earth where our reception and retention are pure,
A place on earth where we abandon our prejudices,
In a house of worship
That is the spacious space of the sky,
In a mandala that is an unchanging dominion,
There is an infinite palace of shining ignorance.
There live the gods who are totally perfect
Without being generated.
Their students receive empowerment from them.
These students are from fortunate families.

In the mandala that is
The supreme abode of Akaniṣṭha
We set out a feast and our tormas of worship
According to the proper way.
We must gather the implements of propitiation,
And the implements for the mandala,
Without limiting their vastness.

Then students who have purpose
Will go for a refuge that is supreme
And will generate an enlightened attitude.
They will use a river of the waters of great enlightenment
To wash the filth from their minds
Into purity.
They will work with their intellects
To hold onto positions.
They will confess their sins.
They will offer things
Without cravings, attachments,
Or clinging to anything as being real.

The Master sits on a throne.
His three doors are pure.
So he questions with these words:

E Ma Ho!
From the beginning
We have been at the heart of the Sugata,
But by the power of our emotional problems,
Ignorance, and karma
We do not recognize our own thusness.

We have been accompanied by it for eons,
But we have not found it.
We live together with it,
But we do not see its face.
The true identity of our emotional problems
That are the five poisons
Wanders through the three realms of samsara.

We are introduced to the Buddhas
Who are of the beginning.

In our effort to introduce a mother and her child
To reality
We show them the mandala of unchanging reality.

Please pull us out from
The inside of samsara!
May our Master bless us!

Into the supreme city of Originally Pure Light
We seek to enter.
We are spirits without refuge!

So did he act to present his request.

To this our Master spoke out:

Kye Ma!
Fortunate Child of Good Family,
If you want to get into unchanging ease
Shake off the chains
Of both what you take in and what you hold onto!
You must purify the filth from your minds!
Do not create a disposition of desire in your intellects!
You must be free from attachments and cravings
To enter!

He said this.
So we did it like this.

Then our Vajra Master
Covered the eyes of his students
With silk.
He led them from the outside of the curtain
To the inside.
He expelled the obstacles
That were our heaps of collective ideas.
He placed the gods of our hearts
Into their own clarity.
He cleansed away our cravings
For the total fantasies of the nine stages.
He cut through our deviations, obstructions, and delusions
At the root.

Then the students who had faith
Also used their hands
To sweep out their ideas.
Then they offered the body of a vase
Of five precious things
Into the dominion of the insubstantial.

Then they questioned the Master:

We must see this mandala of the unchanging mind,
So open our eyes of ignorance
And show us the gods that are the purpose of our hearts!

They offered up this request.

Then the Master spoke:

Child,
You are fortunate!
A Child of Good Family!
Through time that has no beginning
We have not known the meaning of our lives.
We do not see any purpose.
Due to the darkness of our ignorance
Our eyes are blind.

Use the clear light
That is a knowledge of this
To open your eyes
From the blindness of ignorance!
We must look at the unchanging gods!

This shows you the clear light of your own jewels!
This is the introduction to the first Buddha!

By saying this
He opened our eyes
And showed us the face of God.

Then the students scattered flowers.
They were given secret names
For their families and for what they were.

Then the Vajra Master
And the students who were fortunate
Worked to attend on
The god of original purity.

Once we came to understand

That we were living by ourselves without hope
He imparted the four empowerments
To perfection.

He placed a vase on the crowns of the students' heads.

Hūṃ!
I place this vase
Of the very pure dominion of the Dharma
On the crown of my child.
I impart the empowerment of the wisdom vase.
So may you attain an empowerment
Without partiality into the body of the Dharma,
For the apparent world will never stop.

Then we wore our head ornaments
And the five families of Victorious Ones
Imparted empowerments.

May the five kinds of wisdom shine
And may we become embodiments of the five unsurpassed families
Who live by themselves,
And do not seek anything from others.

Then he enacted his vajra eye.
By sending out this wisdom vajra
May we use a vajra that is unchanging and stable,
Which is unmistaken and not contrived
For which there is nothing to be done
To attain growth in the Dharmas
Of samsara and nirvana.

Then he enacted his bell eye.
By giving you this bell of reality
May you use your own unceasing voice
That comes out of the true nature of insubstantial emptiness
So that the Dharmas may radiate
Into their own places!

Then he gave us tormas of ambrosia
And a symbolic empowerment
To teach us his secret purpose.

As for the second one,
The imparting of the empowerment of secrets,
Bonds and attachments
Are methods for publicizing visions
In which our insubstantial true nature
And the mother of knowledge
Are brilliantly united in their non-duality.
May you attain them
Without any clear distinctions.

As for the third,
The knowledge and wisdom,
The dominion of the Dharma is not divided into nations.
The body of the Dharma is not thought of by the mind.
The body of the Dharma and dominion of the Dharma
Are an unspeakable space.

You have attained the imparting of the empowerment
Of knowledge and wisdom.

That is what he said.

As for the fourth,
The empowerment of the precious word,
Our own minds are self-radiant jewels.
We come from the collection of our demarcated ideas.
You have attained the self-empowerment
Into a reality that shines by itself.

The crown vase of royal investiture
Is the final empowerment.
It presents an introduction
Into analogies, meanings, and signs.

The Universal Ti plants a secret samaya.
We send out our gathered tormas,
Which are an unceasing force.

That is what he said.

This is Chapter Twenty-Five: Imparting Empowerment into the

Meaning of the Universal Ti.

THE WAY OF PERFECTION THROUGH THE FOUR EMPOWERMENTS

Then Vajrasattva questioned our teacher,
The All Good One:

What is the tradition that has attained
A way to impart the empowerment?

Our teacher gave instruction:

Our hearts are originally pure.
We have no names.
Attaining and non-attaining are non-dual.
When we do not understand things this way
They arise in dualities.

As for the perfect tradition
On the way of attaining empowerment,
We live in an uncontrived reality.
So we have attained the imparted empowerment
For living anywhere else.

We have transformed into the unchanging body of the Dharma.
So we have attained the great empowerment of the body.

We live in an experience
For which there is nothing to speak or say.
We have attained the great empowerment of speech.

We melt into a dominion
Where there is no motion.
We attain the great empowerment of the mind.

Through our perfection in an experience that is not imparted
We attain the empowerment of our bodies, speech, and minds.

As for the teaching on the tradition
Of the perfection of our empowerment,
The empowerment of the vase is perfected in our minds.

As for the vase,
It is a vase of heart light.

As for Pa,
Reality is unceasing.

Empowerment
Is empowerment into the meaning of the unborn.

Imparting
Is imparting onto non-duality.

Attainment
Is the attainment of the Dharma body of the heart.

For these reasons,
The vase empowerment is perfected in our minds.

As for the perfect tradition
For the empowerment that is secret,
A secret does not turn out to be
An object for our intellects.
It is beyond speech, thought, and discussion.

As for empowerment,
We are empowered into the meaning of the unspeakable.

Imparting
Is imparting onto the absence of anything to signify.

As for attainment,
We attain an essence that is beyond speech.

For these reasons,
The secret empowerment is perfected in our minds.

As for the perfect tradition on knowledge and wisdom:

As for knowledge,
Our knowledge comes from the light of the Base.

As for excellent,
A mother and her child both recognize each other.

As for primordial,
It has no beginning.

As for wisdom,
We know the self-liberation of the origin of all things.

As for empowerment,
We are empowered into the body of the Dharma.

As for imparting,
We impart without any agenda.

As for attaining,
We attain an unchanging reality.

As for perfection,
Our own minds are perfect in our selves.

As for the perfect way
Of the empowerment of the precious word:

As for the price,
Our own minds are very precious.

As for great,
We are transformed by our five greatnesses.

As for the word,
It is a word that is not to be spoken.

As for empowerment,
We are empowered into the reality of clear light.

As for imparting,
It is imparted onto an unchanging dominion.
We attain the five original Buddhas.

For these reasons,
The empowerment of the word is perfected in our minds.

That is what he said.

This is Chapter Twenty-Six: The Way of Perfection through the Four Empowerments.

THE KING OF IMPARTED EMPOWERMENTS

Vajrasattva again asked:

What is the empowerment into the force of our awareness
That overwhelms the four empowerments?

So did he address him.

Our teacher gave instruction to the audience:

As for the imparting of the empowerment
Of the universal vase of our awareness:

Pata Ata Sangkari!
That is what this is called.

We use a method for imparting
The empowerment of the universal vase,
For we are being taught by the naked body of the Dharma.

All those who are gathered
In the apparent and possible world
Are imparted an empowerment
That does not stop or start.
We attain the pure clarity of a reality of radiant experience.

Those of the two truths
Who have the dualistic vision
Of taking things in and holding onto them

Are imparted an empowerment
That cuts through the roots
Of their delusional vision,
And that cuts the ropes
Of our indivisible complications.
We attain self-empowerment
Into a great self-awakening.

The apparent world is very pure.
Whatever we do within the space of the sky
Is an ornament of the playfulness of reality.

The reality of keeping to the Dharma
Is to meet with our mother.
We attain the self-empowerment
In which the mother and child are inseparable.

An overwhelming awareness
Is the empowerment of the universal vase.
To be stamped with the seals
Of the four empowerments
Is the king of empowerments.

To change the apparent world
Into an empowerment,
There is the seal of the unborn.

We do not change.
The upper and the lower are indivisible.
We give up all our work.
We do not stop or start anything.

Buddhahood is an empowerment in our own minds.
We stamp the apparent world with a seal.
We cut through the roots of our delusions.
We attain self-empowerment by ourselves.
This is a space where there is nothing to say.

To live by ourselves without changing
Is the king of empowerments.

This imparts the empowerment of the Bodhicitta.
It does not come up in any of the other vehicles,

For they are striving.
How would it be possible for it to come up from them?

The imparted empowerment of the Universal Ti
Is better than the others.

This is Chapter Twenty-Seven: The King of Imparted Empowerments.

PRESENTING OUR OWN MINDS AS TSATSAS

Then Vajrasattva questioned the true mind of our teacher,
The All Good:

How should we mold the tsatsa of our own minds?

That is what he asked.

Then our teacher,
The All Good One,
Entered the equanimity of the samadhi of self-originating reality.

He got up from it,
And he gave instruction:

The reality of primordial space is indivisible.
Still,
From out of the unmoving true nature of our hearts
We mold the tsatsas that are our branch forces.

O Audience,
Listen respectfully!
Do not be distracted!

Regarding the molding of tsatsas,
It is a reality
That we do not need to work, hunt, strive, or practice for.

On the unchanging earth foundation of reality
We use a sharp joining that is not a burden or a hassle
To mold eighty-four thousand earths.
We pound our memories, ideas, fantasies, and cravings
Into a paste.
The heart of the circle is wrapped into one.

In a true equality we make the individual pieces.
We bless them so that they do not change.
We use hands that are methods and knowledge
To make each lump into a single circle.
The Dharmas are wrapped into
The one body of the Dharma.

We pour the force of our awareness
Unceasingly into the mold
Which is the spacious dominion of the Dharma.
Our outer and inner apparent worlds
Are united in non-duality.
They are cast from what is common
In the three realms of samsara.

From out of the mandala of the very pure dominion of the sky
There appear stupas
Which are aware visions of the force.
We use a mixture of hearts and branches
As stupas of the indivisible force of the base.

The basis for all things
Sits in an abode of emptiness.
We request that you stay without changing
On a throne that is the spacious space of the sky.

Regarding the characteristics of this kind of stupa,
It has no periphery or center.
So its shape is round.
It is due to the specific characters of people's senses
That they live on the nine tiers
That are degrees of status.

They are equal to the end of
The sky that we would measure.

As for their forms,
They are invisible.
They are the substance of all things.
They live without transfer or change
Through the three times.
There are absolutely no characteristics
To be apprehended.
They live in their inclusion of all true natures.
Their essence is beyond being an object that may be visualized.

They are a lineage that is beyond
Speech, thoughts, and signs.
The stupas that we characterize
Are not beyond destruction.
When we cast tsatsas,
We attain them in our minds.
We do not need to strive or practice!
It is a great wonder!
The tsatsas that do not accord
Are especially noble.

That is what he said.

This is Chapter Twenty-Eight: Presenting Our Own Minds as Tsatsas.

TEACHING THE DEFINITION OF A STUPA

Then Vajrasattva questioned the All Good
With these words:

How do we build an unborn stupa
To be an abode for the tsatsa of our minds to dwell in?

That is what he asked.

Then our teacher,
The All Good One,
Entered the equanimity of the samadhi
Of the unchanging and indestructible
Light of great price.

Then he got up from it,
And gave instruction:

Our hearts are unborn and do not change.
A stupa is an unceasing vision of the force.
On an earth foundation
Of a great and encompassing pervasion
We draw a line
For the dominion of our original purity.
We spread out a stone cupola
For our unchanging stability.
We build a stupa that brings
That apparent world together.

We stamp everything,
With no exceptions,
With a seal.

We erect a reliquary.
Those who have friendship and compassion
Are pounded by the mud of eighty thousand emotional problems.
The I and the self make friends internally.
They are stuck on the thrones
Of samsara's three realms.

The final stage has three characteristics.
It is made out of the triad
Of the interim and what comes after.
The third is the Mahāyoga.

The Anuyoga has four stages.
The Great Perfection is a support for the vase.
The heart that is the vase
Of the Universal Ti
Is put into the unchanging tree of life.

In the wheel of thirteen wisdoms
Where the dakinis conceal the rain-spout of their spaciousness
Our hearts and limbs are stuck into a project.
Our methods and knowledge are ornamented
By the sun and moon.
We place our own minds
At the summit of a jewel.

We harmonize with the silk
Of uncorrupt complete perfection.
We attach the cymbals
Of the signless that is beyond speech.

The little bird
That is the unceasing force of our awareness
Flies.
It is ornamented by the ornaments
Of its nineteen ways of appearance.

As for its dominion,
It is present like the sky.

Its measurement encompasses
The totality of the apparent world.

As for its size,
It does not turn out to be an object
For our eight collections of consciousness.
There is no object that appears.
This is beyond any visualization.
Substances are fields of practice for those who name things.
How could those with the intellect of a child,
The rude,
Or the skeptical
Ever see this?

This is beyond the entire infinity of characteristics.
There is nothing whatever to be taken in.
The lights from a variety of colored jewels
May shine
But their recognition goes beyond any names.

We work to count and count
With indivisible accounting.
Our taking things in and holding onto them
Are filthless.
We smear them with white juices.
In our equality we abide
Where there are no clear differences.

That is what he said.

Then Vajrasattva questioned the All Good again:

What is the definition of a stupa?

That is what he asked.

The All Good One gave instruction:

The true nature of our hearts does not move.
So the stupa of our branch forces arises.
This is what we call a stupa,
A support for our worship.

As for worship,
We worship the indivisible three bodies.
As for support,
There is nothing to join or leave.

As for worship,
We worship because we have nothing to think about.
As for support,
This is beyond being an object for our intellects.

As for worship,
We worship in that we have no births.
As for support,
Our support has no stopping.

As for worship,
We worship without any memories.
Our support
Supports the absence of anything to do in our minds.

As for worship,
It is visible and is possible.
As for support,
Our accounting makes no clear difference.

As for worship,
It is our knowledge of the five doors.
As for support,
We do not practice and we do not engage.

As for worship,
It is the outer and inner white and red.
As for support,
It is without attachment and has no craving.

As for worship,
It is the spacious space of our hearts.
As for support,
The body of the Dharma does not change.

As for worship,
Sky-space is the basis of all things.
As for support,

It is a vision of the force of our awareness.

As for worship,
We melt into a vision of unceasing force.
As for support,
We abide in the experience of non-duality.

As for worship,
It is a great circle.
As for support,
It is beyond every kind of complication.

As for worship,
The many things are perfect.
As for support,
We will give up anything.

As for worship,
It is a great bliss.
As for support,
It is beyond all sorrow.

As for worship,
We give up a variety of names.
As for support,
Our non-conceptual wisdom grows.

As for worship,
It is a Dharma of unborn significance.
As for support,
It is an unchanging body.

As for worship,
All our dualistic visions are cleansed.
As for support,
We are fulfilled in our great non-duality.

For these reasons,
The great enlightenment of the world,
This stupa from an unchanging dominion,
Will not arise from out of
Any of the other vehicles.

The stupa on which the factions agree
Is especially noble.

That is what he said.

This is Chapter Twenty-Nine: Teaching the Definition of a Stupa.

BURNT OFFERINGS

Then Vajrasattva again questioned our teacher,
The All Good One:

What is a magnificent burnt offering?

That is what he asked.

Then our teacher,
The All Good,
Entered the equanimity of the samadhi
That is called: "Using jewel light to burn up all complications."

Then he got up from it,
And gave instruction:

The true nature of our hearts does not change,
But children with a vision of the force
Must make burnt offerings.
I have contemplated the four kinds of disciples
Using the four kinds of unborn good works.
So I speak:

Peace, production, power, and growth:
These are burnt offerings
For the yoga of the Universal Ti.
Vajrasattva,
You must understand this!

Of these,
Regarding burnt offerings for peace,
The spaciousness of space
In a round stove-pit:
Sentient beings who have been ensnared
By taking things in and holding onto them
Must all be made peaceful.

To do this,
We hook all the markings of our ideas
And put them into the stove-pit.
The fire of our knowledge burns the owners of the earth.
Our differences are burned up.
We are burned into an experience of peace.

Implements for burning, offering, and praises
Are not necessary.
We use the implements for burning, offering, and praise
Of the mind
To pacify all our ideas about the five poisons.

As for the teaching on the burnt offerings of wrath,
In a fire-pit that is the potential of the dominion of the Dharma
Sentient beings who crave for two truths
Are wrathfully finished off.

To do this,
We light the fire of great wisdom.
Those who hold onto dualities
Are burned up in the experience of non-duality.
Those who cling to substances
Are burned into an absence of any accounting.

We give up worshiping,
Implements for burning,
And our praises.

As for our power,
In the crescent moon of the dominion of the Dharma
Everyone is brought together under our power.
Sentient beings who are born, age, and die
Are drawn in.

They are liberated into an experience
Where there is no birth or death.
Stopping and starting are non-dual.
They are empowered into our purpose.

As for the teachings on burnt offerings for growth,
The self-luminescence of our wisdom must grow.
To do that,
All the sentient beings who crave and are attached to
Views, meditations, practices, and rewards
And all of their views that are intellectual fantasies
Are burned by the fire
Of a blazing and self-radiant jewel light.

Everyone who meditates by taking things into their thoughts
Is burned.

Everyone who practices with intentional activities
Is burned.

All of the rewards that we pray for in our thoughts
Are burned.

We do not look.
There is nothing to see.
We grow in our greatness.

We do not meditate.
There is nothing to think about.
We grow in our greatness.

We do not practice.
There is nothing to contrive.
We grow in having nothing to do.

We do not propitiate.
There is nothing to work toward.
We grow without impediment.

Worship, praise, and implements of burning
Are unnecessary.
The burnt offerings of the mind
Are especially noble.

This is Chapter Thirty: Burnt Offerings.

THE THREE POISONS OPPRESS THE I AND THE SELF

Then Vajrasattva again addressed out teacher,
The All Good:

How must we press the ashes
From burning up the five poisons
And the three poisons?

So did he address him.

Then our teacher gave instruction:

Our hearts for our mothers do not change,
But those who have the Dharma
Are pressed by an awareness of the force.

Vajrasattva,
Take this into your understanding!

In the rugged lands of the Great Perfection
A person who cuts through delusion at the root
With methods and knowledge in his hands
Takes hold of the bequeathed bowl
Of self-originating awareness.

The very pure dominion of the Dharma
Fills the pit for the effigy.

We put our emotional problems
Into the skull of the dominion of the Dharma.

We are very pure,
Self-liberated,
And fierce with our hopes.
We use the colored threads of the five wisdoms
To make the knot of the unchanging cross.

The I and the self are drawn into the dominion
Of enemies and obstacles.
The Dharma of our originally pure resolve
Is covered by ashes.
We are pushed beneath
The unchanging king of the mountains.

The place where the three bodies grow
Is thrown down.
Even our vow to never be reborn
Had been beaten.

E Ma Ho!
All sentient beings have been ensnared
By the I and the self.
I do not now liberate
Those who were not liberated in the past.
The great damage that harms them
Is the demon root of I and myself.
The three poisons support their backs.
On their trunks there are the eighty-four thousand,
Which press them into an experience of the unborn.

May there not arise
Any awareness of being born!
They are ensnared!
They are ensnared in the dominion of reality.
May their memories and ideas
Not be changed by their attitudes!

The unchanging owner is stamped with a seal.
May the habitual patterns of karma
Not rise up!

We cut through!
We cut through the roots of the three poisons.
May our sentience and our five poisons
Not rise up!

We are pressed!
We are pressed beneath the three bodies.
May we not rise up,
Even in a hundred eons!

We cut through views!
We cut through and we see!
We are stamped with a seal
That has no position,
And is beyond limitations.

May meditators be joyful and quiet!
Our attainment is by a seal
Of having no deceit or fraud.

Our practice is to cut through
The complete totality of it all.

Our attainment is by the seal
Of being beyond obstacles and complications.

Little by little,
We carry on relishing our experience.
Our attainment is by the seal
Of having no birth or ending.

We are given our rewards haphazardly.
The three bodies do not join or part.
Our attainment is by the seal
Of living by ourselves without hope.

That is what he said.

This is Chapter Thirty-One: The Three Poisons Oppress the I and the Self.

TEACHING THAT OUR OWN MINDS ARE PHURBAS

Then Vajrasattva again questioned our teacher,
The All Good:

How do we plant the phurba dagger of self-liberation
Into the enemies and obstacles
That are both the I and the self?

That is what he asked.

Then our teacher,
The All Good One,
Entered the equanimity of the samadhi
In which our hearts are self-originating jewel lights.

He got up.
Then he gave instruction to the audience:

In the experience of primordial space
We are indivisible,
But children with a vision of the force
Have enemies and obstacles.
So I will explain the method for planting the phurba
That cuts through to the roots.

We use the phurba of an unchanging mind
And plant it into the dominion of the Dharma

Where we have nothing to work toward.
We cut through the enemies and obstacles
Of samsara and nirvana
At the root.

We use the phurba of our unborn original purity
And plant it into the insubstantial dominion of the Dharma.
We cut through the enemies and obstacles that are substances
At the root.

We use a genuine phurba that is insubstantial
And plant it into the dominion of self-originating self-radiance.
We cut through the enemies and obstacles that are our ideas
At the root.

We use the phurba of living by ourselves without hope.
We plant it into the experience of an unsought dominion.
We cut through the enemies and obstacles of hope and fear
At the root.

A phurba is a symbol for the Bodhicitta.
We use the phurba of the Bodhicitta
To cut through the symbolic flesh
Of the living beings in the three worlds.

It seems that we do not plant it.
It is perfected spontaneously.
It seems that we do not work on it.
We have succeeded from the beginning.

The king of equality
Lives within our awareness.
A phurba is a planting of the dominion of the Dharma.
There is no other place to plant it.
Our self-awareness is planted in the Bodhicitta.
A phurba is something to hold onto:
It is nirvana.

We plant it into our actual ideas
About taking things in and holding onto them.
A phurba is beyond all substantial things.
We use the phurba of an insubstantial sentience.
We plant it into reverted substances.

We are beyond the limited visualizations
That we plant or do not plant.

Phurba is the meaning of the unborn.
We use the phurba of our unborn sentience.
We plant it in our minds
And our awareness dawns.
We plant it into our dominion.
We are spontaneously realized.
Non-duality is an experience that is pervasive.

We use the phurba of a great and encompassing pervasion.
Our lives encompass the whole of the apparent world.
When we understand things this way
We are planting.
When this turns out to be real
It is our understanding.

When we go beyond words,
That is Buddhahood.
When we leave behind counting
We will have nothing to discuss.
We are not separated into ones or twos.

That is what he said.

This is Chapter Thirty-Two: Teaching that Our Own Minds Are Phurbas.

PRESENTING OUR TRUE MIND TO BE GRACEFUL

Then Vajrasattva again questioned our teacher,
The All Good:

If we are not to kill our enemies,
What is a method to kill them gracefully?

Then the true mind of the All Good
Entered the equanimity of the samadhi
That is called: "Killing the enemies of jewel light rays
In a heap."

He got up from it,
And he gave instruction:

Our reality is indivisible from our mother,
But children with a vision of the force
Take it to be an enemy.

The root enchanter is I and my self.
The lords of our emotional problems
Are the five poisons.
Supporting their backs there are the eighty-four thousand.

War lords that are reverted spirits
And are makers of roads,
Those who hold the untrue to be true,
And those who do not get into working on roads
That are not made:

These three keep the doors
To the wheels of darkness.
They are not clear.
They are not free.
They are not at ease.

Those who abide in the nations of samsara
Wear what they take in and hold onto
In a reverted sleep of ignorance.
They are stuck in the chains of both attachment and hatred.
They are whipped by the irons of hope and fear.
They wander through the three realms.
There is no time in which they will be free.

They wail and scream.
There is no time in which they will be Buddhists.
They live in black darkness.
There is no time in which they will understand.
They hold that being sentient
There is an I or a self,
But they rise up as their own enemies.

The method for killing enemies of this sort
Is that a Master whose embodiment of the Dharma
Is his heart
Will seek out students
Who by knowing one thing liberate everyone.
He will acquire a phurba for this unchanging dominion.
He will recite the wrathful mantras
Of self-origination and self-awakening.
His flickering will be self-evident.

He casts his spell,
And strikes the heart of the I and self of the sorcerer,
And the selfless is liberated into the dominion of self-liberation.
He will use the phurba of the unchanging dominion of the Dharma
To cut through the life-roots of the lord of the three poisons,
And liberate him into the space
Of the king who has three bodies.

He will strike up a session
For a great self-origination,
And decimate all our emotional problems

At one time.

He will awaken us from all attachment, craving,
And clinging to permanence.
He will liberate us into space,
Where non-awareness is not present.

By cutting through the one root
That is our enemy,
We kill all our enemies
At one time.
This is called: "Magnificent grace."

As for our grace,
It is the totality of the apparent world.
To be magnificent
Is not to give up,
And not to remain.

As for grace,
It is a child who makes Dharma.
To be magnificent,
Is that we are great because reality is our mother.
Magnificent grace does not stop and is not to be visualized.

The Great Perfection is the magnificent grace of our minds.

That is what he said.

This is Chapter Thirty-Three: Presenting Our True Mind to Be Graceful.

CASTING OUR OWN MINDS INTO HAIL

Then Vajrasattva again questioned our teacher,
The All Good:

How are we to cast down the hail of the mind?

That is what he asked.

Then our teacher,
The All Good,
Entered the equanimity of the samadhi
In which our hearts beam out a jewel light
To everyone,
And we are gathered into the space of reality.

He got up from it.
Then he gave instruction:

The experience of reality does not change us,
But the children who are our branches
Cast down a great hail
On the earth foundation of samsara's three realms.

A harvest of the five poisonous emotional problems
Grows.
It ripens into a fruit
That is a grasping at an object and mind duality.
We eat the fields of our ignorance,
And our sorrows are pure.

For sentient beings who do not understand,
A self-radiant Vajra Master
Will put the taking in and holding onto
An object and a mind
Into a skull that has both
An outside and an inside,
But his heart will use a self-originating mantra
To count out the rosary
Of cravings and personal reversions.
His strength will emerge
And he will chant the wrathful mantra of self-liberation.

A man of the unchanging three bodies
Is stuck in a dangerous place:
The Universal Ti of the Mahayana.

In the very pure skull of sky-space
The things we view,
The things we meditate,
Our practice and rewards,
Are made into blood,
And boiled.

Then our method will be
To have no god,
To have no meditation,
And to have nothing to do.

A self-originating experiential radiance
Overwhelms our wrathful methods.
The spacious space that is the sky of our reality
Is covered by the black clouds
Of our perfect pleasure.

We send down a hail
Of unceasing manifest bodies.
The harvest of the five poisons
Overcomes our grasping at dualities.
The extreme darkness of our ignorance
Is pounded into ashes.

We grind the stopping and starting
Of objects and minds
Into gruel.
We find this in the harvest
Of our eighty thousand emotional problems.

We cast down a great hail
That is a door to the Dharma.
When the I and the self cling to two truths
The body of the Dharma sends down the great hail
Of our own minds.

On the harvest of our dense ignorance
There falls a great hail of shining wisdom.

That is what he said.

This is Chapter Thirty-Four: Casting Our Own Minds into Hail.

A SYMBOLIC TEACHING THAT WE TAKE INTO OUR EXPERIENCE

Then our teacher,
The All Good One,
Entered the equanimity of the samadhi of symbolic precious jewels.

Then Vajrasattva again questioned the All Good One:

Teach us how we are to take
The Universal Ti into our experience!

That is what he asked.

He got up from his samadhi
And gave instruction to the gathered audience:

Basa A 'Ga' Yaya | Mahā Suka Ho!

The upadeśa instructions for the Universal Ti
Are taught symbolically.

Vajrasattva,
Take this into your thought!

We pound an oath into the sky.
We acquire sustenance on the mountain face.
We stick a spear into white snow.
We use objects that are in the sky

To build a house on the sea.

We hoist silk at the face of a pass.
We build a castle on a central mountain.
We wear the atmosphere on our bodies.
We wear the fog on our heads.

We tie shooting stars on our waists.
We carry the sun on our right.
We carry the moon on our left.
We wear boots made of clouds.
We use a cooking of the five elements.

We eat visions for our food.
We put the world into our stomachs.
We hoist a victory banner of rainbow colors.

We kill the one.
We reject the two.
We support the three.

One brings forth an object.
Three bring forth their hearts.
Two cut their necks.

Alone we are thrown
To the keepers of the earth.

The three will conquer enemy armies.
The two will be carried as friends.
The sun covers the eyes of the blind woman.
When fire burns we kill it with water.

We stick our earth foundation into irons.
We shoot our arrows into the wind.
We recognize the ones who pile things.
The pass is gained by being calm.

We use a knife to cut through extreme beginnings.
We overcome the armies of our enemies.
We enter into fortresses.
We protect the castles that are crucial.
We lock the passage at the bridges.

That is what he said.

This is Chapter Thirty-Five: A Symbolic Teaching that We Take into Our Experience.

TEACHING THE INSTRUCTIONS FOR TURNING BACK THE BATTALIONS OF THE ARMIES IN SAMSARA'S WARS

Then Vajrasattva again questioned our teacher
The All Good:

What is the stopping of our core
By which we turn back the battalions of samsara
That does not come up in any of the other vehicles?

That is what he asked.

Then the true mind of the All Good One
Entered the equanimity of the samadhi
In which the jewel light never boils.

He got up from it,
And he gave instruction:

Crush the mountain!
Kill the fire!
Dry the lake!
Untie the knot!

Get it with a broom!
Kill old men and women,
And remove the orphans!
Ride the river!

Guide the lions!

Wear the sky!
Spread out the foundation of the earth!
Put the apparent world into your stomach!
Drink the ocean!

With eyes looking at the sky
Stick your finger into a cloud!
Sleep at the bottom of the great sea!
Stick the sun and moon into your eyes!

Give yourself to the wind,
For you must be subdued.
Send your optical illusions
Into the dominion of the sky!

Kill the monkey!
Rest in your dominion!

The little boy who would go to the sky
Does not find any place to go,
But lives on the edge.

In the dominion of the sky
He is nourished for one month.
He dedicates his legacy
At the border of the sun and moon.
Then he enters onto the pathway
Of the five rainbow colors.

In going we find no place to go.
We kill ourselves.
We open up a clear understanding
That darkness and vision are a duality.
On the borderline between two enemies
We seek the pathway
Where we may be born without fear.

We wear hard armor.
We carry sharp weapons.
We rely on friends who do not deceive us.
We ride the horse that runs

At the hidden entry
To the inside of the three dangerous passages.

We recognize our enemy,
And we kill him till he is finished.
We put him into the walls
That are within our three cores.

The king is held in prison,
And we have killed the children of our enemies.
Our kingdom will go into prosperity.

The two enemies will have finished with fighting.
Then our core fortresses will protect our ruler.
We are supported within three castles.
So we sleep.

We guard the borders of our nations.
We seal the three dangerous passages.
If our enemy is a great army of warriors,
And if they do not turn back,
They will cut through our lives,
And the war lords will be in command.
Be serious in your generation of armor and weapons!

Wear the magnificent mail of meditation
On your body!
Buckle on the belt of the core upadeśa instructions!
Put the blood of your able and gracious blessings
On your hands!
Wear the pants of non-duality!

Tie the three connections and three cycles
To your body!
The best methods and knowledge
Are in the blowing of a fresh breeze.

Our handle is the solitary eye of the sky.
It has nothing inside it.
It has the spirit of a mountain.

There is no pain in a shaft.
So it is illuminated with the feathers

Of the four immeasurables.
We are stricken by the bullets
Of those whose sharpness is intense.

We hunt in our quivers
For a pure atmosphere.
We have shields for our views
And helmets for our meditation.

We wear them,
And then we go to war.
We go.

There are four kinds of great war lords:

The unborn,
The unchanging,
The unceasing,
And the non-dual.

They hunt for four great heroes.
Path makers who cut through bonds
Have supernatural knowledge.
In this way the eight,
And all the rest of the great heroes who are most mighty,
Are inconceivable.
They smash our big dispute about dualities.

In a precious jewel that is empty
The seven clarities and the two types
Do not agree.
So we shoot an arrow into our enemies'
Armies of war.

One woman pounds on a fresh wind bow.
There are a thousand arrows
That are free from eight faults.

Keepers of dualities are rolled into one.
We join with the groove of the arrow.
The great sky is filled with watchers.
The enchanter strikes our unity with an iron hook
Without holding onto any damage

We spontaneously die.

We use an arrow
That is the majestic individual placement of the ocean
To strike at the heart of the wheel of black darkness.
In a space where the sun and moon are pure
We die.

We use the arrow of the atmosphere's insubstantial wind
To strike at the heart of dualistic clinging,
Acceptance and rejection.
When there is no medicine or poison
We die in our own places.

We use the arrow of a great and flawless crystal egg
To strike at the heart that separates positions.
When there are no differences,
We spontaneously die.

We shoot the arrows of the sun and moon
Into the bottom of a lake,
And we strike the hearts of five hundred enemies.
We decimate the five and are free from the eight.
We die in space.

We use a foreword bail
To decide on some advice
And all the enemy warriors
Turn their faces from the battle.

Their roots overcome,
Both old men and old women,
All the armies of war,
None excluded,
Are swept with a broom.

We win our disputes.
So we plant them with buttons.

This being so,
We savor the excellent tastes of all foods.
We drink the elixir
That is the ambrosia of immortality.

We cut through the roots
Of our old associations with our five enemies.

That is what he said.

This is Chapter Thirty-Six: Teaching the Instructions for Turning Back the Battalions of the Armies in Samsara's Wars.

PUTTING INTO ORDER THE SYMBOLIC TEACHINGS ON THE DHARMAS OF SAMSARA AND NIRVANA

Then Vajrasattva again questioned our teacher,
The All Good:

How are we to practice the symbolic Dharma
Of the Universal Ti,
Which puts the Dharmas into order?

That is what he asked.

The All Good One gave instruction:

In one realm of a nation
There is one Master.
He has a jewel that is dear to him.

What is the vessel that brings forth treasure?
What is the method for acquiring it?
When we recognize the demon of not acquiring it,
Should we kill it?

The jewel is hidden.
Will we recognize it?

This jewel has no positions.
There is one nation.

Will we recognize what that nation is?

There are two lords of wealth.
Will we know their faces?

There are two doors that bring forth this wealth.
Will we know them?

There are three methods to work toward acquiring this.
As signs of our attainment,
There are four things.
Will we know the faces of what they are?

In the great and universal nation
Where everything is light,
There are two great empowerments
And one universal wealth.
Of these two we kill one and engage in one.

We must acquire this wealth by ourselves.
We clear away the pitch-black darkness
That has no eyes.
In the Dharma of living on the border
Of the sun and moon,
We look into a mirror of magnificent visions.

Our clothes are of earth.
Our seat is the sky.
We wear the fog casually.
We sleep in the atmosphere.
We care for the waters of the little monkeys,
And take them with our hands.

We press the wind down under our feet.
With rainbow colors stuck in our heads
We sit on the peaks of mountains.
We drink a river into our mouths.
We are wrapped in silk.

On the border of vision and great darkness
Whatever we plant in the garden of our birth
Will all grow to be attractive flowers.
Our reward is a self-radiant precious jewel.

We have all given birth to a desire for it.
Not acquiring and not agreeing are non-dual.
Both of them create big disruptions.

The boy shines in a vision of experiential radiance.
Total Awareness has a mirror of delusion.
Your borders turn out to be a universal place.
Three, two, and six men will enter there,
And in two large copper pots
They will boil their medicines and poisons.

Then the old men and old women,
The triad of the heap makers,
The little children,
And the siblings
Who are patronized by three war lords
Will come to a war that is only the twilight.

We make poisonous water
To smash the armies of our enemies.
If it does not kill them
Their stomachs will reject it.

We go to the peaks of snow
And we ride the lions.
We spin our spears
Through the realm of the sky.

At the summit of a glacier mountain
We burn a great fire.
At the bottom of the ocean
We carry a butter lamp.

On the inside of the darkness
We carry the sun and moon.
On the inside of the wind
We spin our own knives.

We drink the elixir of the ambrosia of immortality.
We take a golden phurba to a meadow.
When the sun rises
We stick it in the snow.

By doing this,
The armies of our enemies
Will be cut off at the root.

From among our relatives and our worlds
We do not have a single enemy.
So when the worldly groups are gathered
We give them medicinal ambrosia for food.
We liberate them from all their sorrows.
Then they attain Buddhahood,
Which is that they embody the Dharma of great bliss.
All clear divisions and accounting
Are killed.

The method for collecting wealth that removes poverty:

The little boy of experiential radiance
Goes to do business.
He mounts the horse of reality.
He carries four items.
He opens up his provisions for giving.

He eats samadhi.
He wears hard armor.
He carries sharp weapons.
He is surely able to frighten us.

In a lake of conflict
On the wide plains of our divided realities,
We travel over four great and dangerous passageways.
We climb four passes.
We practice four fields.
We cross four passes.

We seal up three dangerous passageways.
We open three roads.
We enter four castles.
We sleep on four beds.
We rise up in the four kinds of rising places,
And we go.

We travel over three destinations.
On the other side

In a garden on the border of darkness and vision
In the experiential radiance of a self-radiant jewel
There is the precious jewel of our own minds.

Within the darkness
There are the sun and moon that dispel it.
We have a razor that will cut through delusion.
We have an ambrosia
That will heal us all
From the death of our lives.
We have a great treasure of inexhaustible rarity.

The little boy of experiential radiance will go there.
On one side there is darkness.
On one side there is vision.
At the border between darkness and vision
No one finds anything.

We do not see.
No one knows anyone.
We are insubstantial.
No one understands anyone.
We do not change.
No one hears anything.
We do not speak.
The origin of all things is an unchanging jewel.

The little boy buys the clear light of experiential radiance
He gives the blind old woman who owns the wealth
Three kinds of occasional knowledges.
He uses both scripture and reason
To make business friends.
He weighs the horse of his intellectual fantasies
For a price.
He weighs the meditations that he likes into his thoughts
For a price.
He weighs the practices that he does intentionally
For a price.
He weighs the rewards that he prays for in his thoughts
For a price.
He weighs desires that have no price
For satisfaction.
He weighs the phurba for holding on

For a price.
He weighs the lake of craving
For a price.
He weighs the door to the wheel of darkness
For a price.

By weighing eight prices,
He gets one jewel.

After we have finished with accumulating things
In our non-duality,
We return to our own places.
We go to a house
That is a dominion of reality.

We drink a fountain of beer
That is the ambrosia of immortality.
We savor the excellent taste of samadhi for our food.
We are clothed in great bliss.
Our seat is unchanging.
In a space where we have no position
We sleep soundly.

Do not do work that is stressful!
It is not to be done!
We give up all our work.
We settle into our own way of living.
In the dominion of reality
We wake up from our sleep.

The upadeśa instructions for symbols
Are the core of our purpose.

Vajrasattva,
Come into my heart!

That is what he said.

This is Chapter Thirty-Seven: Putting into Order the Symbolic Teachings on the Dharmas of Samsara and Nirvana.

TEACHING ALL THE DHARMAS WITH EXEMPLIFYING ANALOGIES

Then Vajrasattva again questioned our teacher,
The All Good:

How are we to use analogies to exemplify the Dharmas?

That is what he asked.

Then our teacher,
The All Good One,
Entered the equanimity of the samadhi of shining jewel light.

He got up from it,
And gave instruction:

O Audience,
Listen respectfully!
Do not be distracted!

The way of being that is our heart purpose
Does not turn out to be an object that may be exemplified,
But we start out by exemplifying things
Through the door of analogies.

A lake,
A treasury of silk,
And the foundation of the earth:

You must understand that these three are analogies
That exemplify the base of all things.

Water,
A block of ice,
And a sesame seed:
These three are explained to be
Analogies that exemplify our way of being.

A cairn,
A rope,
And a mirage:
These three are explained to be
Analogies that exemplify delusion.

A sun beam,
A razor,
And a crystal rosary:
These three are explained to be
Analogies that exemplify that
A vision of the force is connected.

A pigeon,
A crystal egg,
And camphor:
These three are explained to be analogies
That exemplify the way things appear.

Sandalwood,
Musk,
And garlic:
These three are explained to be analogies
For the unceasing arising of the force.

A sword,
A razor,
And a tooth:
These three are explained to be analogies
That exemplify knowledge.

Children,
Index fingers,
And milk:

These three are explained to be analogies
That exemplify sacred instructions.

The dawn,
An eye,
And the sun:
These three are explained to be analogies
That exemplify understanding.

Clouds,
Cataracts,
And darkness:
These three are explained to be analogies
That exemplify obstruction and concealment.

Mistaken roads,
Birds' eyes,
And stomach cramps:
These three are explained to be analogies
That exemplify grounds for deviation.

Thorns,
Spear tips,
And arrow tips:
These three are explained to be analogies
That exemplify awareness.

A vulture,
The sky,
And a garuda:
These three are explained to be analogies
That exemplify a view.

A mirror,
Rainbow colors,
And a lantern:
These three are explained to be analogies
That exemplify meditation.

A bee,
An elephant,
And a madman:
These three are explained to be analogies

That exemplify practice.

Big hail,
Lightning,
And avalanches:
These three are explained to be analogies
That exemplify good works.

Fog,
Water bubbles,
And revelations of the heart:
These three must be explained
To be analogies for experience.

The gods that are in the temples,
The butter lamps that are in vases,
And the reflections that are in mirrors:
These three are taught to be analogies
For the inner clarity of our own minds.

A tiger skin,
A leopard skin,
And the eye-feathers of a peacock:
These teach by analogy
The outer clarity of our own minds.

A crystal egg,
A *zi* stone,
And shimmering water:
These three are explained to be analogies
For the non-duality of the outer and inner.

Black charcoal,
Black silk,
And black wool:
These three are explained to be analogies
For the unchanging.

The wind,
The clouds,
And the fog:
These three are explained to be analogies
For exemplifying what we have taken into our experience.

A harvest,
A flower,
And the splendor of a pasture:
These are explained to be analogies
That exemplify impermanence.

The water and the mud are mixed.
The waves melt into the water.
The colors of a rainbow fade into the sky.
You must understand that these three
Are analogies for inseparability.

The striking at poison with a mantra,
The water from the canal going to the sea,
And the salt melting into water:
These three are explained to be analogies
For not turning back.

A lotus,
A peacock,
And a conch:
You must understand that these three
Are analogies that exemplify samaya.

The moon,
The light,
And the great stars:
You must understand that these three
Are analogies for wisdom.

A human lineage,
A stream of water,
And a bow's string:
These three are explained to be analogies
For the absence of any break in our continuum.

Lightning,
Shooting stars,
And shooting arrows:
These three are said to be analogies
To measure our understanding of the bardo.

Gold,
A mountain,
And a jewel:
You must understand that these are
Analogies for rewards.

In the way of being
That is the purpose of reality
There are basic similarities,
And these are exemplified in analogies.
There is no real basis for them.
There is nothing to visualize.

This is unborn,
Inconceivable,
And unchanging.

There is nothing to exemplify.
This is beyond analogies.
Once we start out exemplifying things
We teach for the sake of understanding.
The essence of our purpose is beyond any speech.

That is what he said.

This is Chapter Thirty-Eight: Teaching All the Dharmas with Exemplifying Analogies.

THE PURPOSE OF INTRODUCTION

Then Vajrasattva again questioned
The All Good:

What is the symbolic introduction
To the body of the Dharma?

That is what he asked.

Then our teacher,
The All Good,
Entered the equanimity of the samadhi in which
Our hearts hold the resolve
Of an indivisible mother and child.

He got up from it.
Then he gave instruction:

Our hearts have the true natures of our mothers.
When they move,
The children who are our limbs do not understand.
They become engaged in objects.
In this there is the teaching
On the symbolic introduction to the body of the Dharma.

Vajrasattva,
Take this into your thought respectfully!

The unchanging introduction has three parts:

The introduction into an unchanging way of living,
The introduction to the indefinite way that things appear,
And the introduction to non-duality.

First there is the teaching on our way of living.
We are beyond causes and conditions,
Birth and destruction.
Our essence is unchanging.
Our true nature is not to be visualized.

In the infinite palace of blazing jewel light
There lives one body that has no form.
It encompasses all things.
His name is unborn
And is beyond being spoken.
He is called:
"The total vision of our own blazing mind."

We introduce thusness to ourselves.
We melt into the space of the body of the Dharma.
Then without changing
We use a seal for our attainment.

I will teach you what it means
That the way things appear is indefinite.
At the very moment
When things appear nakedly
In the mirror of our clear vision
Of the dominion of the Dharma
We are individually settled in an experiential radiance
That is indivisible.

There lives one body that is self-originating
And self-destroying.
His name is Blazing Non-Dual Self-Liberation.
He introduces thusness to himself.
There is no outer or inner
Object or mind to hold onto.

Self-awakening and personal radiance
Are non-dual.

We use a seal that does not count clear distinctions
For our attainment.

The way things are and the way they appear
Are not a duality.
A precious jewel that does not expand or contract
Is a house of magnificent clear light.
One body that does not grow or shrink
Lives there.
His name is Beyond Holding.
He is beyond cutting through complications.
He introduces thusness to himself.

Neither objects nor minds exist.
There is no vision or emptiness.
The outer and inner are non-dual.
There is nothing to negate or prove.
There are no objects for our five doors.
There is no attachment or craving.
Neither self nor other exist.

We have no position or preference.
Appearances and minds are not a duality.
We have nothing to take in or hold onto.
There is no thought, awareness, or sentience.
There is no flashing.

This is not something that does not exist.
It is empty and visible.
It is not something that exists.
It is visible and empty.
It is not both.
There are no clear distinctions.

It is not unique.
It is beyond exemplification and discussion.
It is self-originating and self-destroying.
It is liberated from grasping and craving.

We use the seal of experiential radiance.
We are awakened from our attachment.
This is our attainment.
When these three are wrapped up,

They are condensed into one.

As for the introduction to the solitary embodiment of the Dharma,
We have a mandala of heart-light.
In the infinite palace of never-ending light
We do not visualize our hearts,
For they are beyond discussion.
There sits the stainless and very pure
Body of the Dharma.

This is a method for introducing thusness to ourselves.
There are the analogies,
The meanings,
And the validations.

As for the analogies,
You must understand that they are like this:
We do not divide oceans and streams into separate things.
We do not divide a mixture of milk and water into separate things.
We do not divide the salt that melts into water into separate things.

The particularities of the forms
That arise when pressed
Inside water, a crystal egg, or a mirror
Are not boiled into anything
Other than themselves.
Outer and inner objects and minds
Have nothing to take in or hold onto.

In the mandala of three indivisible analogies
Any two people who purely liberate
The one and the many
Are one.
This is the experience of the sky.
We live in a dominion
Where our clear depths are spontaneously realized.

As for meaning,
You must understand that it is like this:

The apparent world melts into the space
That is the basis for all things.
Our vision of the force melts into the space

That is our base.
Our subjectivity melts into the space
Of our hearts.
Characteristics melt into the space
Of reality.

Into the center of the space
Where reality is the Bodhicitta
Melt the complications of our intellects,
However many they may be.

There is no accounting that will recognize
The moment of the melting.
In the awareness that lets us be born
We melt into the unborn.
Indivisibility and unity are mixed.
They are not separate.

Non-duality is one.
This is the experience of the sky.
We are liberated from both unity and separateness.
Our hearts and the body of the Dharma
Are one circle.
We melt into an unspeakable space.
We are stamped with seals.

Moreover,
Regarding the instructions on introduction,
The thing we are introducing and the act of introduction
Are non-dual,
But in our effort to exemplify this
For intellects that do not understand,
Everything that we must discuss
Is an introduction to a dominion that we do not discuss.

Everything that we are to exemplify
Is introduced to the experience
Of having nothing to exemplify.

All the names that we would give
Are introduced to the experience of having no name.
All of our desires are introduced
To an absence of attachments and cravings.

Everything that we would take in or hold onto
Is introduced to the experience of having nothing to hold onto.
The stopping and starting of objects and minds
Are introduced to the experience of non-duality.

Our ideas and our clinging at a self
Are introduced to the experience of self-destruction.
The sorrows of our delusions
Are introduced to the experience of experiential awakening.
Our knowledge, memory, fantasy, and logic
Are introduced to a dominion where there is nothing to discuss.

The insubstantiality of anything that appears
Is introduced to the space of our hearts.
The mind of knowledge and awareness
Melts into a space of emptiness.
We plant the spike of indivisibility.
We live within the unchanging body of the Dharma.

The introduction to validations
Is as follows:

Clarity and emptiness are non-dual.
We do not divide them separately.
Our hearts and limbs do not melt or separate.

We melt as rays into the body of the Dharma.
We do not divide them separately.
The force melts into the base.
We do not divide them separately.

There is no mixing or dividing of Dharmas and reality.
Appearance and sentience are mixed.
So we do not divide them separately.
Intellects and substances are mixed.
So we do not divide them separately.
Our ignorance is clear and empty.
We do not divide them separately.

The three poisons and the three bodies:
We do not divide them separately.
The five poisons and the five bodies:
We do not divide them separately.

Pervasive encompassing and complete fulfillment:
We do not divide them separately.

Dualistic thinking and self-destruction:
We do not divide them separately.
The five doors and a lack of understanding:
We do not divide them separately.
Awareness and emptiness are not a duality:
We do not divide them separately.

All of us are inseparable.
We meet our mothers.
We do not change.
We are not destroyed.
We take our own places.

Our delusional ideas
Are radiant in their own place.
We do not change.
We strike the core.
We arise from out of space.

The body of the Dharma
Sits in an unborn space.
The indestructible vajra
Is harder than a rock.

In the reality of the empty heart
That is the basis for all things,
Those who are born into awareness
Encompass and pervade
All appearance, sentience, fantasy, and craving
Are introduced to a great and total fulfillment
In a space that is the basis for all things.

Accounting and clear differentiation are non-dual.
We are stricken by a spike.

That is what he said.

This is Chapter Thirty-Nine: The Purpose of Introduction.

TEACHING THAT OUR OWN MINDS ARE OUR GURUS

Then Vajrasattva again questioned
The All Good One:

We have adjusted our own minds
To be gurus.
So what is the way in which
The instructions are to be explained?

That is what he asked.

The All Good One gave instruction:

The true nature of our hearts is unchanging,
But I will explain how our limbs
Are gurus of awareness.

Vajrasattva,
Take this into your thinking!

There are nine ways
In which our own mind is our guru:

There are gurus of the base of our original beginning.
There are gurus of all-pervasive primordial space.
There are three kinds of gurus
For whom origins and pervasions are non-dual.

There are gurus of the original base.
There are gurus of the unceasing force.
There are gurus for whom the base and the force are non-dual.
There are gurus of the complete pervasion of the basis of all things.
There are gurus of the unceasing family of rays.
There are three kinds of gurus for whom total awareness is non-dual.

Gurus of the base of our primordial origin
Teach Dharmas that are not objects for
Our eight collections of consciousness,
Which are beyond being visualized.

Gurus of all-encompassing primordial space
Teach Dharmas that are indivisible.

Gurus of non-dual origins and encompassment
Teach Dharmas that are not open and are not utilized.

Gurus of the original base
Teach the Dharmas of our unchanging hearts.

Gurus of the unceasing force
Teach Dharmas that have no birth or death.

Gurus of the non-duality of the base and the force
Teach Dharmas for which there is no accounting.

Gurus of the universal pervasion
Of the base of all things
Teach the place of origin
For the base of all things
To their wives.

Gurus of the unceasing rays of awareness
Teach Dharmas that have no positions
Of limitations to their vastness.

Gurus of the non-duality of total awareness
Teach an indivisibility in which the force melts into the base.

These are the nine kinds of gurus of unborn sentience.

Our hearts and our vision of the force
Are not two things.
So we teach our branches in nine stages.
The guru of the base is our own mind.

We tell gurus who talk about the way things appear
About the six Mahāgurus:

Gurus for whom the awareness in their thought does not flicker,
Gurus of uncontrived sentience,
Gurus of unborn purpose,
Gurus of a magnificent encompassing pervasion,
Gurus who are reward minded,
And gurus who introduce us to the meanings of symbols.

Gurus for whom the awareness of their thoughts creates flickering
Teach the essence of the unborn body of the Dharma.

Gurus of uncontrived sentience
Teach the essence of the body of perfect pleasure.

Gurus of unborn purpose
Teach an embodiment of manifest non-duality
In which the many things
Are beyond speech, thought, and discussion.

Gurus of majestic encompassing pervasion
Teach a body of true essence
That is inseparable from
The lack of any clear distinctions
In the apparent world.

Gurus whose reward is just their sentience
Gather all the rewards
From that majestic space that has no end or center
Into one.
Their hearts melt into an unchanging space.

With a seal that is the absence of birth and death
We are attained.
We do not transfer or change.
We suppress our praises.

The basis for our bodies
Is an indivisible reward,
But we do not work.
This is beyond all deeds and quests.
We have nothing to say.
We melt into the true dominion of great bliss.

As for gurus who introduce us
To the meanings of the symbols,
In their study, contemplation, and meditation
They use a lantern that clears away the darkness of ignorance
To cleanse their intellects.

They use words to exemplify correct meanings.
Then they live by themselves without hope,
And work to teach the rewards of Buddhahood.

The six classes of Mahāgurus
Are even more strict than the Buddhas.

Moreover,
You may ask why this is so.

Even the Buddhas of a thousand eons
Grew by depending on their gurus.
For this reason,
The Mahāgurus must be respected
As if they were our hearts or eyes.

Gurus of the future will use the teachings,
And their inner gurus will become clear.

That is what he said.

From the Tantra on Kissing the Apparent World while Dripping an Elixir of Ambrosia to Cut through Samsara from Start to End, this is Chapter Forty: Teaching that Our Own Minds Are Our Gurus.

It is finished.

Pasa Anvari | Buddhakāya | Dharmakāya Bāka Siddhi A!

THE LATTER TANTRA ON KISSING THE APPARENT WORLD WHILE DRIPPING AN ELIXIR OF AMBROSIA TO CUT THROUGH SAMSARA FROM START TO END

PUTTING THE START AND END OF SAMSARA INTO CONTEXT

Then Vajrasattva questioned the All Good himself
With these words:

The Tantra on Kissing the Apparent World while Dripping Elixir
Brings the words of the Sugatas
That stamp the totality of the apparent world with a seal
Into one.
What is the way in which it is to be explained?

That is what he asked.

Then our teacher,
The All Good One,
Entered the samadhi of the precious jewel light
For which there is no accounting.

Then he got up from it,
And he spoke these words:

Vajrasattva,
Take this into your thought!

When we say: "Kissing the apparent world,"
Appearance is called an external object.
A world is called an inner sentience.
In kissing there are no dualities.

Appearance is an object or an idea about
Our five doors.

The world is the five kinds of consciousness.
Kissing is unchanging and is without any accounting.
Appearance is an external object,
Be it white or red.

The world is an aware memory in our minds.
In kissing there are no clear differences.
Appearance is this vessel of a world.

The world is all sentient beings.
In kissing there is no good or evil,
Nothing to stop or work toward.
This is what we call: "Dripping an elixir of demon juice ambrosia."

As for demons,
They are collections of ideas from our minds.
As for juice,
It is the non-conceptual body of the Dharma.

As for demons,
They are the flickerings of aware memories in our minds.
As for juice,
It is the absence of three things.

As for demons,
They are the darkness of our ignorance.
As for juice,
It is a great wisdom.

As for demons,
They are doorways to the wheels of darkness.
As for juice,
It is a doorway for the arising of awareness.

As for demons,
They are the three ways we are delusional.
As for juice,
It is the three ways that we turn around.

As for demons,
They are the delusions of the three realms.
As for juice,
We cut off the basis for our delusions at the root.

As for demons,
They are the three poisons that are our emotional problems.
As for juice,
It is our bodies, speech, and minds.

As for demons,
They are the five poisons
That are our emotional problems
As for juice,
It is the five bodies and the five wisdoms.

As for demons,
They are our eighty thousand emotional problems.
As for juice,
It is the eighty thousand doors to the Dharma.

As for demons,
They are the sentience of samsara's three realms.
As for juice,
It is the heart of the Victorious Ones of the three times.

As for demons,
They are the sentient beings of samsara.
As for juice,
It is the Buddha of nirvana.

As for elixir,
It is the elixir of the human heart.
As for dripping,
Our hearts melt into space.

As for elixir,
It is an unceasing vision of the force.
As for dripping,
We do not visualize our hearts.

As for cutting through samsara from start to end:

Samsara is the sorrow of our lust and hatred.
Samsara is the darkness that is not clear.
Samsara in the end is a muddy swamp.
Samsara is our eighty thousand sorrows.

For this,
We need a method to cut through from start to end.

Our start is unchanging.
It is all-encompassing.
An ending is a subject that changes.
Our start is a great and universal station.
An ending is a Dharma that is apparent and is possible.

Our start is beyond speech, thought, and discussion.
An ending is a complication of the intellect.

Our start is unborn.
An ending is when a delusion that is unborn arises.

Our start is non-duality.
An ending is when dualistic visions arise in our understanding.

Our start is a great equality.
An ending is when many different positions and preferences arise.

Our start has nothing to stop or to work on,
Nothing to reject or accept.
As ending is when stopping and developing,
Rejection and acceptance,
Arise.

Our start has no delusion or non-delusion.
An ending is the arising of many kinds of delusional visions.

Our start has no clear divisions or accounting.
An ending is the arising of clear divisions and accounting.

Our start has nothing to teach and no act of teaching.
An ending is the arising of something to teach and an act of teaching.

Our start has neither anything to exemplify
Nor any act of exemplification.
An ending is the arising of something to exemplify
And an act of exemplification.

As for the characteristics of what we call a start,
It is unborn, unchanging, and insubstantial.
It is beyond exemplification.
It is beyond speech, thought, and discussion.

An ending is when light and flickering rays of awareness
Arise within the memories and ideas in our minds.
Our knowledge awakens our luck,
And is carried off in the fog.
We make up thoughts that have the names
Of being and non-being.
Then we are not aware of what is,
While we are aware of what is not.

We do not know the purpose for our lives.
We do not meet our mother.
We do not take our own place.
We do not cut through delusion.

For these reasons,
We enter the doorways
Of ignorance and delusion.

We repeatedly enter
The three ways of our delusions.
We experience the sorrows of the six classes of living beings.

In the three realms,
What we take in,
What we hold onto,
Our fantasies,
Cravings,
Delusional visions,
Our clinging to two truths,
Stopping and starting,
Strife,
Practice,
Rejection,

Acceptance,
Our collective ideas:
These are inconceivable!

We cannot speak of them!
These are our knowledge of the end.

That is what he said.

This is Chapter Forty-One: Putting the Start and End of Samsara into Context.

THE JEWEL THAT CUTS THROUGH STARTING AND ENDING AT THE ROOT

Then Vajrasattva said these words
To the All Good:

How do we cut through and slice off
Starts and endings?

That is what he asked.

Our teacher gave instruction to the audience:

A Tha 'Ba' Yis Siddhi 'Guya A Ā!

We use the words: "Cut through"
To cut through the ropes of the nets
Of starting and ending.
I teach that this is a core upadeśa instruction that is great.

Vajrasattva,
Take this into your thought!

The rays of our awareness melt
Into an experience of majestic light.
When we have nothing to join or part from
We cut through complications.

Our aware sentience of flickering memories
Is an experiential radiance.
We use the majestic wisdom of self-awakening
To overcome the blinding darkness of our ignorance.

The body of the Dharma
Arises from out of a clear and radiant space.
The three realms and the three worlds
Are primordially Buddhas.
The six classes of living beings
Cut through their delusions at the root.

At the door of our dawning
We use a pristine wisdom
To cut through the doorways
Of the wheels of darkness
At the root.

We cut through complications
By having no nirvana.

We cut through complications
By having nothing to name.

We cut through complications
By having nothing to discuss.

We cut through complications
By having no eternity.

We cut through complications
By having nothing to think about.

We cut through complications
By having nothing substantial.

We cut through complications
By having no awareness.

We cut through complications
By having no flickering.

We cut through complications
By having no divisions.

We cut through complications
By having no accounting.

We cut through complications
By having nothing to negate or prove.

We cut through complications
By having nothing to accept or to reject.

We cut through complications
By having nothing to take in or hold onto.

We cut through complications
By having nothing to do or seek.

We cut through complications
By having nowhere to travel.

We cut through complications
By having no reason to work.

We cut through complications
By having nothing to put down.

We cut through complications
In a magnificent primordial realization.

We cut through complications
In the majesty of our own place.

We cut through complications
In the magnificence of experiential living.

We cut through complications
In a magnificent primordial abiding.

We cut through complications
In a majestic self-radiance.

We cut through complications
In a magnificent self-awakening.

We cut through complications
In a great self-clarity.

We cut through complications
In a magnificent shining radiance.

We cut through complications
In the great and shining deeps.

We cut through complications
By having nothing to do with our thoughts.

We cut through complications
By having nothing to settle in our minds.

We cut through complications
By having nothing to contrive with our intellects.

We cut through complications
By not being corrupted in our ideas.

We cut through complications
By not being mistaken and not being contrived.

We cut through complications
Of something to be generated and any act of generation.

We cut through complications
By not splitting and not boiling.

We cut through complications
By not taking things in and having nothing to hold onto.

We cut through complications
By having nothing to grow or shrink.

We cut through complications
By being beyond all causes and conditions.

We cut through complications
By not looking where there is nothing to see.

We cut through complications
By not meditating where there is nothing to meditate.

We cut through complications
By not practicing where there is nothing to do.

We cut through complications
By not practicing where there is nothing to practice.

We cut through complications
By not rejecting where there is nothing to reject.

We cut through complications
By not attaining where there is nothing to attain.

We cut through complications
By settling with visions individually.

We cut through complications
By living by ourselves in the way that we live.

We cut through complications
When appearances and our minds are one.

We cut through complications
In the measure of our mind's fantasies.

We cut through complications
By the measure of the flickering in our thoughts.

We cut through complications
By the measure of what we experience with our awareness.

We cut through complications
By the measure of what we take in with our intellects.

We cut through complications
By the measure of what we think in our minds.

We cut through complications
Of memories, fantasies, attachments, and cravings.

The infinity of the apparent world
And the visions of samsara:
We do not investigate.
We do not practice.
We do not account for.
We cut through the complications of everything,
With no exceptions.

Our bodies are unchanging vajra bodies.
When we have the sorrows of birth, age, and death,
We use the eye of great wisdom
To awaken from the darkness of our ignorance.

We use a pristine wisdom that is clear and empty
To awaken from all our ideas about things to say.

As for the mother,
She uses an unceasing wisdom
To awaken everyone
To where what we take in and what we hold onto
Are non-dual.

As for the child,
He uses an unchanging knowledge
To awaken all those who hold to two truths.

We use our beginningless sense of thought
To awaken the apparent world
Into the dominion of the unborn.

We use our two hands,
Which are the pair of transmission and awareness,
To bring the Dharmas into a great circle.

We use our two feet,
Which are methods and knowledge,
To awaken those who grasp at dualities
Into the lack of any clear distinctions.
When there are no clear distinctions in the Dharmas,
We grow.

Everyone awakens into a dominion of equality.
When there is no accounting for the apparent world,
We grow.

We awaken from all our ideas
About taking things in and holding onto them.
We cut through complications.
In the space of the body of the Dharma
We grow.

We awaken from our preferred positions
And dualistic visions of ends and middles.
We have no preferences.
In the space of great bliss,
We grow.

A clear eye awakens
From the darkness of dense stupidity.
Our radiance is clear,
And in great wisdom
We grow.

We awaken from our sorrow
And the emotional problem of clinging to an I.
The wisdom of the great bliss that does not hold on
Grows.

That is what he said.

This is Chapter Forty-Two: The Jewel That Cuts Through Starting and Ending at the Root.

TEACHING THAT THE DRIPPING ELIXIR OF AMBROSIA IS OUR REWARD

Then Vajrasattva questioned our teacher,
The true mind of the All Good One:

What is the way to attain our reward?

So did he address him.

Then the true mind of the All Good
Entered the samadhi in which jewel light melts into us.

He got up from it.
Then the King of Teachers
Spoke to the audiences
With these words:

In my yoga of the Universal Ti,
There is no attaining or non-attaining of any reward,
But in the unmoving true nature of our hearts
The dripping elixir of ambrosia
Is explained to be our reward.

Vajrasattva,
Take this into your understanding!

The great treasury
That is the basis for all things
Is the expansive space of the body of the Dharma.
It was not generated by any cause.
It is not destroyed by any conditions.
Its essence is unchanging.
Its true nature is uncontrived.
It has no name.
It has nothing to say.
There is also no basis for its binding.

It has nothing to speak of.
It has nothing to discuss.
There is no real basis for its exemplification.
It has no awakening.
It has no growth.

There is no real basis for its body.
It has no ends.
It has no middle.
It is entirely free from any positions or boundaries.

It has no happiness.
It has no sorrow.
It is completely beyond the experience of sorrow.

A true nature of this sort
Is the true nature that is the basis for our reality.
The way things appear
Is characterized by rays,
But the essence of our existence
Is arising out of nothing.

We hold things that do not exist
To be.
We hold Dharmas that do not exist
To exist.
We hold the impermanent to be permanent.
We hold things that are non-dual
To be dualities.
We hold our sorrows to be happiness.

For such things as these
We hold what does not exist to exist,
And we experience our sorrows
In the way that we dream.

The three realms of samsara come forth from this.
They come forth,
But they do not move away from the base.

This spacious space is a reality that does not move.
Our knowledge of the rays
In the way things appear
Melts into this.

All our speech, discussion, and collective ideas
Melt into this.
On investigation,
All the objects of our intellects
Melt into the base.
Everything that we take in or hold onto,
That we stop or encourage,
Melts into this dominion.

All the awareness and memory of our minds
Melts into space.
All of our mental practices and collective ideas
Melt into this dominion.
Our limbs that have the characteristics of children
Melt into their mother.

The way things appear to be rays
Melts into the space of our hearts.
In the base we separate
The indivisible mother and child of the force.

Moreover,
You may ask what these resemble,
As an analogy.

It is like an orphan meeting his mother.
It is like salt melting into water.
It is like a water bubble melting into water.
It is like a stream arriving at the sea.

It is like ice dissolving into water.
It is like a rain of honey falling on a lake.
It is like the colors of a rainbow
Melting into the sky.
It is like the clouds
Shining in the sky.
It is like the moon
Rising up in the water.
It is like mixing water with milk.

The way things appear in the dominion of our hearts
Melts into an analogy.
The force melts into the base.

In the beginning
There was primordial Buddhahood.
Reality meets its mother.
So our delusions are liberated into their own places.

The unborn holds its own place.
So we rise up from the space of our own hearts.

Our ideas are liberated into their own places.
So the unchanging turns out to be the body of the Dharma.

Our essence takes its own place.
So our radiant clarity is our embodiment of the Dharma.

Our true natures take their own places.
So our own radiance is the embodiment of pleasure.

Our compassion takes its own place.
So we are manifest embodiments of our own radiance.

The indivisible three bodies are one.
This is our own magnificent radiance.

The bliss of the four bodies is greater.
So the secret sky is the embodiment of our true experience.

The five bodies melt into a dominion
Where nothing happens.
So the clear dominion of our indivisibility

Is the embodiment of our true nature.

The reward for embodying the Dharma
Is our own mind.

When we understand that we have been present
On our own behalf
Through beginningless time,
The fields and domains of the Victorious Ones
With their five bodies
Are the best rewards.

That is what he said.

This is Chapter Forty-Three: Teaching that the Dripping Elixir of Ambrosia Is Our Reward.

TEACHING THAT THE BODY OF THE DHARMA IS A MAGNIFICENT AND CLEAR RADIANCE

Then Vajrasattva questioned the All Good himself
With these words:

What is a magnificent and clear radiance?

That is what he asked.

The teacher of our own minds,
The All Good,
Entered the equanimity of the samadhi
In which the clear jewel light is clear unto itself.

He got up from it,
And spoke these words:

The true nature of our hearts
Is unborn and does not change.
The three bodies are not created in our thought.
This is a magnificent and clear radiance.

The five bodies are not created in our thought.
This is a magnificent and clear radiance.

Appearances are not created in our thoughts.
This is a magnificent and clear radiance.

The body of the Dharma is not created in our thoughts.
This is a magnificent and clear radiance.

The body of pleasure is not created in our thoughts.
This is a magnificent and clear radiance.

The manifest body is not created in our thoughts.
This is a magnificent and clear radiance.

Indivisibility is not created in our thoughts.
This is a magnificent and clear radiance.

We do not reject ignorance with our intellects.
This is a magnificent and clear radiance.

We do not change.
This is a magnificent and clear radiance.

There is no birth or death.
This is a magnificent and clear radiance.

Emptiness is not created in our thoughts.
This is a magnificent and clear radiance.

Generative forces are not created in our thoughts.
This is a magnificent and clear radiance.

Nothing changes.
This is a magnificent and clear radiance.

There is no birth or death.
This is a magnificent and clear radiance.

We were not generated for any reason.
This is a magnificent and clear radiance.

We are not destroyed by any conditions.
This is a magnificent and clear radiance.

Our essence is unchanging.
This is a magnificent and clear radiance.

We do not visualize our own natures.
This is a magnificent and clear radiance.

There is nothing to negate or to prove about an object.
This is a magnificent and clear radiance.

There is no substance to the mind.
This is a magnificent and clear radiance.

Objects and minds are neither separate nor clear.
This is a magnificent and clear radiance.

We are not corrupted by ideas.
This is a magnificent and clear radiance.

We do not contrive with our intellects.
This is a magnificent and clear radiance.

We do not contemplate in our thoughts.
This is a magnificent and clear radiance.

We do not break and we do not boil.
This is a magnificent and clear radiance.

We do not accept and we do not reject.
This is a magnificent and clear radiance.

We do not reject and we do not promote.
This is a magnificent and clear radiance.

We have nothing to do and we have nothing to seek.
This is a magnificent and clear radiance.

We do not look where there is nothing to see.
This is a magnificent and clear radiance.

We do not meditate when we have no ideas.
This is a magnificent and clear radiance.

We do not practice when we have nothing to do.
This is a magnificent and clear radiance.

We do not protect where there is nothing to transgress.
This is a magnificent and clear radiance.

We do not strive where there is nothing to seek.
This is a magnificent and clear radiance.

We do not travel when there is nowhere to go.
This is a magnificent and clear radiance.

We are ourselves without working on it.
This is a magnificent and clear radiance.

All the visions of our fantasies
Are a magnificent and clear radiance.

The entirety of the apparent world
Is a magnificent and clear radiance.

That is what he said.

This is Chapter Forty-Four: Teaching that the Body of the Dharma is a Magnificent and Clear Radiance.

TEACHING THAT WHEN WE SETTLE WITHOUT CONTRIVANCE INTO OUR NATURAL STATE OUR REWARD IS TO BE SEIZED WITH RESOLVE

Then Vajrasattva questioned the All Good himself
With these words:

What is a great self-awakening?

So did he address him.

The teacher of the true mind,
The All Good,
Entered the equanimity of the samadhi
Is which the jewel light is a great self-awakening.

He got up from it,
And he said these words:

The body of the Dharma has the true nature
Of the spacious space of the sky.
We stamp it with the seal
Of an unchanging heart.

Who will be stained by any problems
There may be in our ideas and our naming things?
In the magnificent reality that does not move
We have no birth.

We do not change.
Our ideas are not realized.

Our reward is that we hold resolve.
You must understand things this way.
Those with problems are not realized.
This is a great self-awakening.

Our virtues do not change.
This is a great self-awakening.

Our ignorance is not realized.
This is a great self-awakening.

Our wisdom does not change.
This is a great self-awakening.

The three poisons do not succeed.
This is a great self-awakening.

The three bodies do not transfer or change.
This is a great self-awakening.

The five poisons do not succeed.
This is a great self-awakening.

Our wisdom has no joining or parting.
This is a great self-awakening.

Samsara does not succeed.
This is a great self-awakening.

Nirvana does not change.
This is a great self-awakening.

Our ideas are not realized.
This is a great self-awakening.

Reality does not change.
This is a great self-awakening.

What we take in and what we hold onto are not realized.
This is a great self-awakening.

Our lack of clinging does not change.
This is a great self-awakening.

Our clinging to dualities is not realized.
This is a great self-awakening.

Non-duality does not change.
This is a great self-awakening.

Our preferred positions are not realized.
This is a great self-awakening.

Our lack of any position does not change.
This is a great self-awakening.

The I and the self are not realized.
This is a great self-awakening.

Our selflessness is unchanging.
This is a great self-awakening.

Our attachment and clinging are not realized.
This is a great self-awakening.

Our lack of attachment does not change.
This is a great self-awakening.

We have nothing to do with strife or development.
This is a great self-awakening.

Our lack of strife does not change.
This is a great self-awakening.

Our works are not realized.
This is a great self-awakening.

Our lack of anything to do does not change.
This is a great self-awakening.

The things we observe are not realized.
This is a great self-awakening.

The lack of anything to see does not change.
This is a great self-awakening.

The things we meditate on are not realized.
This is a great self-awakening.

Our lack of meditation does not change.
This is a great self-awakening.

Our practices are not realized.
This is a great self-awakening.

Our lack of practice does not change.
This is a great self-awakening.

The things we attain are not realized.
This is a great self-awakening.

With nothing to realize we have no hope or fear.
This is a great self-awakening.

All of these things are natural for us all,
But they are not contrived by our intellects.
They do not shift with our thoughts.
They are not revealed by our awareness.
They are not attributed by our minds.

The way it has been from the beginning.
Is that our true experience is not corrupt.

The one that does not contrive reality
Is actually our own mind.
When we abide in majestic pervasion
The unchanging body of the Dharma is present.

As for the samadhi in which our awareness is not distracted,
And we give up our work,
It is that we do not change
From our own unique reality.
In the hollow interior of our dominion
We are a body that does not transfer or change.

We are a speech that is beyond
All utterance, discussion, and exemplification.
We enjoy a sentience that is aware of thought.
This is beyond being an object for the intellect.
We are a mind that does not even think of deceit or fraud.

We are uncontrived.
We are uncorrupted.
We are fresh.
We are truly self-sufficient.

Being at ease,
We do not move away from our heart's purpose.
We are inhabitants of a majesty
That is our own ordinary way.

The All Good One
Is a contemplation for the Victorious Ones.

That is what he said.

This is Chapter Forty-Five: Teaching that When We Settle Without Contrivance into Our Natural State Our Reward Is to Be Seized with Resolve.

OUR OWN MINDS ARE THE CLEAR SKY

Then Vajrasattva again questioned the All Good:

How is it that our own sentience is a clear sky?

So did he address him.

The teacher of the true mind,
The All Good,
Entered the samadhi in which the jewel light
Is a majestic clear sky.

He got up from it,
And he spoke to the audience
With these words:

The body of the Dharma is not a compounded thing.
It is a magnificent clear sky.

Our heart is not a compounded thing.
It is a magnificent clear sky.

The basis for all things is not a compounded thing.
It is a magnificent clear sky.

Reality is not a compounded thing.
It is a magnificent clear sky.

The unborn is not a compounded thing.
It is a magnificent clear sky.

The unchanging is not a compounded thing.
It is a magnificent clear sky.

Our own experience is not a compounded thing.
It is a magnificent clear sky.

Our lack of deceit is not a compounded thing.
It is a magnificent clear sky.

This is beyond our thinking intellects.
It is a magnificent clear sky.

This has no name,
And is beyond being an object for our understanding.
It is a magnificent clear sky.

That is what he said.

This is Chapter Forty-Six: Our Own Minds Are the Clear Sky.

TEACHING THAT REALITY IS A MAGNIFICENT SHINING DEEP

Then Vajrasattva questioned the All Good
With these words:

What are the shining deeps of reality?

So did he address him.

Then the true mind of the All Good
Entered the samadhi in which
All the expansions and contractions of jewel light
Melt into the space of reality.

He got up from it,
And spoke to the audience
With these words:

The substance of our reality
Is a meaningful way of living.
It does not turn out to be an object
For the eight collections of our consciousness.
It is a majestic shining deep.

It does not turn out to be an object for the eye.
It is a majestic shining deep.

It does not turn out to be an object for the ear.
It is a majestic shining deep.

It does not turn out to be an object for the nose.
It is a majestic shining deep.

It does not turn out to be an object for the tongue.
It is a majestic shining deep.

It does not turn out to be an object for the body.
It is a majestic shining deep.

It does not turn out to be an object for our thought.
It is a majestic shining deep.

It is not visualized.
It is beyond visualizations.
It is a magnificent shining deep.

It is beyond being an object for speech and discussion.
It is a magnificent shining deep.

That is what he said.

This is Chapter Forty-Seven: Teaching that Reality Is a Magnificent Shining Deep.

TEACHING THE TRUE NATURE OF THE UNIVERSAL TI

Then Vajrasattva questioned our teacher,
The All Good One:

What is the true nature of the Universal Ti?

That is what he asked.

Then our teacher,
The All Good One,
Entered the samadhi in which
There is no accounting for the jewel light.

He got up from it.
Then he gave instruction:

Atha Pata Tika Kalaya Siti A!

This is my yoga of the Universal Ti!

There are these three:

The analogy,
The meaning,
And the signs.

As for the analogy,
It is like the sky.

Reality is a beginningless sky of clarity.
From the beginning it has had no substance.
Being truly without substance
It is itself the many things.

A variety of things are exemplified
By way of a basis for discussion.
In the same way,
We may praise the reality of the sky,
But it will not become good.
We may revile it,
But it will not become bad.

We are liberated from both praise and blame,
From both good and evil.
We harbor no extremes or middles.
We have no color.
We do not harbor any negations of proofs.
We have nothing to reject or accept.

There are no clear differences
Between outer and inner,
Between taking up and putting down.
There is no accounting for objects and minds,
For samsara and nirvana.

In the same way,
In the true mind of the sky
Nothing is substantial.
Nothing is named.
It is beyond discussion.

There is no base.
There is no wind.
There is no flickering.
We harbor no colors.
We are beyond shapes.

This is not male or female.
It is not sexless.
We are liberated from the triad
Of masculine, feminine, and neuter.

Our true minds have a nature that is maternal.
We have no measure,
An are not to be taken by any measure.

There is no appearance.
There is no investigation.
Our thoughts do not move.
We have no shape.
We are beyond holding onto shapes.
We have no position.
We are beyond holding onto positions.

We have no number.
We have no counting.
We are beyond counting.

We have nothing to exemplify.
We are beyond exemplification.

We have no measure.
We are beyond being estimated.

We do not grow.
We are beyond shrinking.

We have no causes or conditions.
We have no adversaries.
There is no river of birth, age, sickness, and death.

There are no nations.
There is no attachment to any nation.
There are no places.
We do not hold onto being assigned a place.

Our thoughts and practices do not flicker.
There are no heroes.

There are no dualities.
We are beyond dualistic discussions.

That is what he said.

This is Chapter Forty-Eight: Teaching the True Nature of the Universal Ti.

A REAL TEACHING ON DRIPPING AN ELIXIR OF REPEATEDLY REFINED AMBROSIA

Then Vajrasattva addressed our teacher,
The All Good,
With these words:

I ask you to teach on
The repeated refining of ambrosia.

That is what he said.

The true mind of our teacher,
The All Good,
Entered the samadhi in which
The jewel light is clear by itself.

He got up from it,
And he spoke these words:

A La La Api Thim!
All our contemplations of the Dharma
Are brought together into one!

Regarding the holy instructions
That are the inner heart of our purpose,
There is no basis for anything.
We are beyond any names there may be
For the basis of all things.

There is no body of the Dharma.
We are beyond being taken by any body of the Dharma.

There is no ignorance.
We are beyond working toward wisdom.

There are no doors of delusion.
We are beyond clearing up the doors that arise.

There are no three times.
We are beyond working toward the three bodies.

There are no five poisons.
We are beyond working toward the five bodies.

We do not use our intellects
To give up the evil ideas of sentient beings.

We do not use our intellects
To work on our desire for Buddhahood.

The sorrows of samsara are not evils that are to be rejected.
With our desire for the bliss of nirvana
We accomplish nothing.

We do not use our intellects to contrive this.
This is beyond the intellect.

We have nothing to work on in our thoughts.
This is beyond our workings.

We have no thoughts about our minds.
This is beyond being an object of thought.

We are not bound by nominal words.
We do not turn back.

We are beyond all cravings for permanence.
We do not put things into systems.

Even though there may be resemblances
We are beyond being put into a system,

Or putting things into systems.

You may ask why this is so.

The measure of our flickering,
The measure of our complexity,
The measure of our openness,
The measure of our giving,
The measure of our receiving,
The measure of our discussion,
The measure of our thought,
The measure of our memory,
The measure of our awareness,
The measure of our feelings,
Our craving for permanence,
Our dualistic visions,
Our clinging to our attachments,
Our objects and our mins:
Each and every one of these things
Is in fact our own mind.

As for the mind,
It is not anything at all.

It is not anything.
It is self-awakening.
It is self-radiant.
It becomes itself.

It is radiant itself.
It is a clear sky.
It is a shining deep.
It is self-fulfilling.
It grows by itself.

It is ordinary.
It is our own way.
It is not contrived.
It is spirit.
It is relaxed.
It is easy.
It is present when we are free
From development and strife.

The circle brings us all together.
Our complete perfection is totally clear.
Our lack of clinging is our embodiment of the Dharma.
A great wisdom arises within us.
Our inner spirit is a secret road.

We live without damming our river.
This is a contemplation for the All Good Victorious Ones.
We use the clarity that comes from the space of our hearts
To brilliantly abide in the experience of the unborn.
We melt into an experience of the unspeakable.

That is what he said.

From the Kissing of the Apparent World, this is Chapter Forty-Nine: A Real Teaching on Dripping an Elixir of Repeatedly Refined Ambrosia.

THE FOUR KINDS OF CERTAINTY

Then Vajrasattva questioned the All Good himself
With these words:

What are the four kinds of certainty?

That is what he asked.

Our teacher spoke to the audience
With these words:

It is certain that our views do not change.
It is certain that our meditation does not move.
It is certain that our practice does not crave for attachments.
It is certain that our reward has no hope or fear.

Those are the four kinds of certainty.

That is what he said.

This is Chapter Fifty: The Four Kinds of Certainty.

TEACHING THE THREE KINDS OF NOTHING

Then Vajrasattva questioned the All Good himself
With these words:

What are the three kinds of nothing?

That is what he asked.

Our teacher spoke to the audience
With these words:

In the way we see things
There is nothing to hold onto.
Our spiritual beliefs are nothing.

Nothing arises in our thoughts.
We have nothing to meditate on.

Nothing is born in our experience.
Nothing ends.

That is what he said.

This is Chapter Fifty-One: Teaching the Three Kinds of Nothing.

THE NINE KINDS OF SOMETHING

Then Vajrasattva questioned the All Good himself
With these words:

What are the nine kinds of something?

That is what he asked.

Our teacher spoke to the audience
With these words:

A view is something.
Nothing is something.

For those who have no meditation
Nothing is something.

For those who are sure of their practice
Nothing is something.

For those who protect samaya
Nothing is something.

For those who seek good works
Nothing is something.

For those who travel on pathways
Nothing is something.

For those who study on levels
Nothing is something.

For those who cling to the upadeśa instructions in their spirits
Nothing is something.

For those who are working toward rewards
Nothing is something.

That is what he said.

This is Chapter Fifty-Two: The Nine Kinds of Something.

TEACHING THE NINE KINDS OF ABSENCE

Then Vajrasattva questioned the All Good himself
With these words:

What are the nine kinds of absence?

That is what he asked.

Our teacher gave instruction to the audience:

In our minds,
Substances are primordially absent.

In our minds,
Things to exemplify are primordially absent.

In our minds,
Things to visualize are primordially absent.

In our minds,
Things to discuss are primordially absent.

In our minds,
Colors are primordially absent.

In our minds,
Bindings are primordially absent

In our minds,
Letters are primordially absent.

In our true minds,
Thoughts are primordially absent.

In our true minds,
Things to do with our thoughts are absent.

That is what he said.

This is Chapter Fifty-Three: Teaching the Nine Kinds of Absence.

TEACHING THE SIX THINGS THAT DO NOT CHANGE

Then Vajrasattva questioned the All Good himself
With these words:

What are the six things that do not change?

So did he address him.

Our teacher gave instruction to the audience:

Because it does not transfer or change,
Reality does not change.

Because it has no birth or death,
Reality does not change.

Because it has no birth or ending,
Reality does not change.

Because it is beyond our thinking,
Reality does not change.

Because it is beyond our visualizations,
Reality does not change.

Because it is beyond our intellects,
Reality does not change.

That is what he said.

This is Chapter Fifty-Four: Teaching the Six Things that Do Not Change.

A FINGER POINTING TEACHING ON SEEING THE BODY OF THE DHARMA NAKEDLY

Then Vajrasattva questioned the All Good himself
With these words:

What is it to see the body of the Dharma nakedly?

So did he address him.

Our teacher gave instruction to the audience:

When we awaken
From all our deceitful and fraudulent ideas,
Without any contemplation,
We see the body of the Dharma nakedly.

When there is nothing for us to do with our bodies
Without any striving
We see the body of the Dharma nakedly.

When we have no reason to talk about or discuss things
With our voices,
Without any discussion,
We see the body of the Dharma nakedly.

That is what he said.

This is Chapter Fifty-Five: A Finger Pointing Teaching on Seeing the Body of the Dharma Nakedly.

TEACHING THE FOURTEEN RESOLUTIONS

Then Vajrasattva questioned the All Good himself
With these words:

What are the fourteen resolutions?

That is what he asked.

Our teacher gave instruction to the audience:

When our views go beyond words
We are seized with a resolve of shining radiance.

When our meditation goes beyond contemplation
We are seized with a resolve that is unchanging.

When our practices have no strife or development
We are seized with a resolve where we have nothing to do.

When we do not leave behind the meanings that we understand
We are seized by the resolve of samaya.

From the beginning there has been nothing to seek.
So we are seized by the resolve of good works.

From the beginning there has been nothing to study.
So we are seized by a resolve that is balanced.

From the beginning there has been nowhere to go.
We are seized by the resolve of the path.

From the beginning there has been nothing to work on.
We are seized by a resolve for development.

From the beginning there has been nothing to take in.
We are seized by a resolve for the upadeśa instructions.

We are not separated.
So we are seized by a resolve for knowledge.

There is nothing for us to acquire.
So we are seized by a resolve for a reward.

We have nothing to hold onto.
So we are seized by a resolve for a vehicle.

Our true natures are settled.
So we are seized by a resolve for samadhi.

We do not pray for something else.
We are seized by the resolve of the Universal Ti.

That is what he said.

This is Chapter Fifty-Six: Teaching the Fourteen Resolutions.

TEACHING THE SIX KINDS OF SETTLING

Then Vajrasattva questioned the All Good himself
With these words:

What are the six kinds of settling?

That is what he asked.

Our teacher gave instruction to the audience:

How do we settle our own vision of the way we appear?
It is settled that appearances are actually natural.
It is settled that appearances and minds
Are actually inseparable.
It is settled that our five doors are delusional.
It is settled that we have no dualistic thoughts to hold onto.
It is settled that there is no accounting for
Our cutting through complications.

That is what he said.

This is Chapter Fifty-Seven: Teaching the Six Kinds of Settling.

BRINGING OUR CONTEMPLATIONS INTO ONE ALL AT ONCE

Then Vajrasattva questioned the All Good himself
With these words:

How are we to bring together the contemplations of the Sugatas?

That is what he asked.

Our teacher gave instruction to the audience:

I take it that the eighty-four thousand vehicles
Are brought together into a single contemplation.
This brings together the contemplations
Of the Victorious Ones of the three times.

They are brought together in an unspeakable experience
All at once.
We bring the contemplations of the Buddhas
Together in the unborn
All at once.

We bring together our contemplations on realities
In the unchanging
All at once.

We bring together our contemplations of the holy Dharmas
Into an absence of attachment and clinging

All at once.

We bring together our contemplation of the upadeśa instructions
Into an absence of craving and clinging
All at once.

We bring together our contemplations on yogas
Into an absence of taking things in and holding onto them
All at once.

We bring together our contemplations on the oral lineage.
They are brought together in an experience
In which the Dharma and our minds are blended.

We bring together our contemplations on Dharma practices.
We bring them together in the experience
Of having no struggle, strife, or anything to do.

We bring together our contemplations on our views.
We bring them into an absence of spiritual beliefs,
All at once.

We bring together our contemplations on our meditations.
We bring them into an experience
Where we have no cravings and we have no deceit.

We bring together our contemplations on our practices.
We bring them into an experience
Where there is no attachment, craving, or anything to do.

We bring together our contemplations on our rewards.
We have no hope.
We live by ourselves.
We have no fear.
We are brought together in the experience
Of having no thought or prayer.

All our needs are brought together into one.
The one comes together in the experience of our own minds.

Our own minds come together in their lack of substance.
Our lack of substance comes together
In an experience that we do not visualize.

We come together in the experience of being beyond
Speech, contemplation, and discussion.

We are brought into an experience of the unborn
All at once.

That is what he said.

This is Chapter Fifty-Eight: Bringing Our Contemplations into One All at Once.

TEACHING THE INSTRUCTIONS FOR THE UNIVERSAL TI

Then Vajrasattva questioned the All Good himself
With these words:

What are the instructions for the Universal Ti?

That is what he asked.

Our teacher gave instruction to the audience:

In the experience of having nothing to say
Our memories and understandings are decimated.

In the experience of the unchanging
We melt into the measure of our existence.

What is our melting?
It is the body of the Dharma.

The body of the Dharma
Is actually beyond any exemplification.

We have no reason to talk about
What it means to be beyond.

We do not give any name
To what it means to be beyond.

We have no reason to desire
What it means to be beyond.

We do not abstain from the things that we desire,
In any way.

We do not visualize a reason for our desire
Of any kind.

However things may appear,
Those who crave for what they want
Have no letters for their proper meaning.

Their not having them
Is something they do not exemplify.

There is no binding of their absence.
There is no greatness to their absence.
There is no duality in their absence.
There is nothing to reject or accept in their absence.
There is nothing to negate or prove in their absence.
There is no clear division to their absence.
There is no accounting for their absence.

No matter how things may appear
They do not cease.
We have no grasping.
So we do not visualize things.
This absence is an absence that limits our vastness.
This absence is an absence of falling into any position.

That is what he said.

This is Chapter Fifty-Nine: Teaching the Instructions for the Universal Ti.

THE HEART'S WAY OF LIVING

Then Vajrasattva questioned the All Good himself
With these words:

What is our way of living in the Universal Ti?

That is what he asked.

Our teacher gave instruction to the audience:

Concerning the yoga of the Universal Ti
Of the Great Perfection,
We do not work toward anything at all.
We do not abandon the universe.
We are not under any limitations
Due to falling into a position.

We agree with everyone.
We are especially noble.
We are not anything at all.
We are the Bodhicitta.

From our base we are not contrived.
We are spontaneously realized.
We are ordinary in our own way.
We are self-radiant.
Our hearts are spontaneously realized.
We live as embodiments of the Dharma.

Anything may arise from nothing at all.
It may arise,
But it is our minds that arise.
We are perfect in ourselves.

That is what he said.

This is Chapter Sixty: The Heart's Way of Living.

TEACHING THAT THE BUDDHA POINTS HIS FINGER AND WE SEE NAKEDLY

Then Vajrasattva questioned the All Good himself
With these words:

What does the Buddha point his finger at?

That is what he asked.

Our teacher gave instruction to the Audience:

Our Buddhahood has been realized from the beginning
In our minds.
We are already realized.
If we are not distracted from our purpose
We do not need to seek Buddhahood
From anyone else.

All the Dharmas are gathered in our minds.
To have no thoughts in our minds
Is Buddhahood.

All the Dharmas are realized from out of our minds.
Our own minds are unborn Buddhas.
All the Dharmas are gathered in our minds.
Our own minds are unspeakable Buddhas.
All the Dharmas are gathered in our minds.

Our own minds are Buddhas that have nothing to work on.

We awaken from deceit, strife, negating, proving,
Working, and seeking.

We grow to be uncontrived,
Having nothing to do,
And free from complications.

It is said that when we do not think
We do not contrive,
And we are not corrupt.
We are primordial Buddhas.

We awaken from mental practices,
Memories, ideas, and signs.
We grow into an absence
Of thought, awareness, and sentience.

We awaken from all our attachments,
Cravings,
And clinging.
We grow into a space of unchanging great bliss.

We have no methods
To intellectually contrive our struggle and strife.
The totality of the apparent world
Is gathered in our minds.

Our minds do not realize anything.
The primordial Buddha is pointing his finger.

For an analogy,
You must understand that you are in the sky.
The sky has no end, middle, or position.
It lives in its liberation from all conventionalities.

As for our understanding,
Our own minds do not cease.

The many things are perfect in their universal appearance.
There is a majesty in not rejecting things
And not developing them.

What this means
Is that reality has no birth.
It has no substance.
It is not to be discussed.
It has nothing to visualize.
We live in the space of our hearts.

That is what he said.

This is Chapter Sixty-One: Teaching that the Buddha Points His Finger and We See Nakedly.

TEACHING THAT WHATEVER WE DO THERE IS NO PROBLEM FOR WE ARE SELF-LIBERATED

Then Vajrasattva questioned the All Good himself
With these words:

If it turns out that this is so,
Is what we do for the karma of our work
A problem or not a problem?

That is what he asked.

Our teacher gave instruction to the audience:

The child of true name
Melts into the heart-mother.
By the indivisible recognition of the mother and the child
They attain the body of the Dharma.

Whatever they do to teach of this attainment
Is a space for the Dharma.

The Buddhas have virtues
That are not to be measured.

We may go,
But we will not stomach going into
The space of reality.

We may sit,
But we will not stomach
The experience of the unchanging.

We may eat,
But we will not stomach
The food of samadhi.

We may drink,
But we will not stomach
The elixir of the ambrosia of the heart.

We may be clothed,
But we will not stomach
Being clothed in the power of our blessings.

We may be enthroned,
But we will not stomach
The throne of the unchanging.

There may be a cushion,
But we will not stomach
The cushion of the insubstantial.

We may lay down,
But we will not stomach
Laying down in the space of our hearts.

We may sleep,
But we will not stomach
The space of great bliss.

We may be wealthy,
But we will not stomach
The precious jewel of our own minds.

There may be a nation,
But we will not stomach
That this is inconceivable.

There may be homes,
But we will not stomach

The very pure home that is the space of the sky.

We may live,
But we will not stomach
The life of the unchanging heart.

There may be a fortress,
But the fortress of great dhyāna meditation
Has no resistance.

There may be a mother,
But we will not stomach
The mother of non-duality.

There may be a child,
But we will not stomach
That he is a self-originating experiential radiance.

There may be an audience,
But the unceasing five bodies
Are the audience of our minds.

There may be a city,
But we will not stomach
That the city that is the basis for all things
Is universally encompassing.

That is what he said.

This is Chapter Sixty-Two: Teaching that Whatever We Do There Is No Problem for We Are Self-Liberated.

TEACHING
THE THREE KINDS OF INTRODUCTION

Then Vajrasattva questioned the All Good himself
With these words:

What are the three kinds of introduction?

That is what he asked.

Our teacher spoke to the audience
With these words:

Know that these three:
Water,
A fire crystal,
And the five doors
Are introductions that use analogies.

Know that these three:
The Dharma body,
The pleasure body,
And the manifest body
Are introductions of portent.

Know that these three:
Our own mind,
Reality,
And the wisdom of our awareness

Are introductions of signs.

That is what he said.

This is Chapter Sixty-Three: Teaching the Three Kinds of Introduction.

TEACHING THAT
ON RECOGNITION OF OUR BUDDHAHOOD
WE DO NOT NEED TO DO
ANY STRIFE OR PRACTICE

Then Vajrasattva questioned the All Good himself
With these words:

When we are introduced to Buddhahood in this way
Are we not seeking the contrivances of strife and practice?

That is what he asked.

Then our teacher spoke to the audience
With these words:

Our heart's true nature is to be a mother.
This does not change.
The force appears.

Many kinds of branch characteristics appear.
They appear,
But they do not move away from
The purpose of our way of living.

They are not boiled into anything else.
They melt into the space of the heart.
Once they melt,
Right when we understand that they are

Indivisible and unborn,
No matter what we may do,
We will turn out to be friends with reality.

When we give up all the karmas of our work
We must live in the experience of having nothing to do.
Abiding in the base,
We are uncontrived and spontaneously realized.

As for living in our own ordinary way,
We live in the space of the reality of our hearts.

Do not do it!
Do not enact the karma of striving!
Deceit and strife,
Negating and proving,
Rejecting and accepting:
They do not exist!

We live in a non-duality
For which there is no accounting.
In the way of living where we settle things directly,
We use a lack of settlement for our essence.
We use a lack of going
For our hearts.
We use what we ourselves are
To live in our own places.
We use a lack of anything to work on
To be primordially realized.

Due to our lack of preferences
We do not hope for anything else.

Moreover,
For what validation is it
That our own minds are without substance?

Delusional sentience will arise in any case,
And insubstantial things will arise in any case.
These two in their true essence are indivisible.
They are not different.
This is the body of the Dharma.

Our hearts have no substance,
And our awareness arises as yoga.
There is no difference between these two.
In the experience of reality
They are not different.
So this is reality.

Our essence is not to be seen.
We see a variety of characteristics.
There is no difference between these two
In the experience of reality.
They are not different.
This is the body of the Dharma.

Our way of living has no birth,
While thoughtful analysis has many kinds of birth.
There is no difference between these two.
In the experience of our way of living
They are inseparable.
They are one.
This is the body of the Dharma.

This being so,
We must understand things this way.
Our way of living has been primordially realized
From the beginning.
The levels and paths are primordially traveled.
This is a primordial study.

We have primordially attained
The reward for settling our karma.
Understanding this,
We take on the karmas of samsara.
We find the Buddha that we wanted
In ourselves.

This being so,
An all-encompassing insubstantial body
Is a body that has no body.
This is the best body.
We live like vajras.

As for our country,
Our reality is a home in the sky.
The father and mother of the All Good Mother
Are friends in great bliss.
Their children are the experiential radiance
Of the circle of five wisdoms.

The gatherings of suns,
Moons,
Planets,
Stars,
Rainbow colors,
And water moons
Are playful ornaments
Of our own unceasing force of reality.

That is what he said.

This is Chapter Sixty-Four: Teaching that on Recognition of Our Buddhahood We Do Not Need to Do Any Strife or Practice.

THE WAY TO MAINTAIN A RESOLUTE UNDERSTANDING

Then Vajrasattva questioned the All Good himself:
With these words:

When our reality is seized by numbering things,
How are we to have resolve?

That is what he asked.

Our teacher gave instruction to the audience:

When you have the resolve
That is an understanding of the Universal Ti,
At that very moment you will have this kind of resolve.

We awaken from the darkness of ignorance
While there is no time for our awakening.

The sun of wisdom rises,
While there is no time for it to rise.

Our own minds are clearly embodiments of the Dharma.
We open the door to the arising of awareness
While there is no time in which to open it.

We hold onto three kinds of memories,
While there is no time to hold on.

We perfect the karmas of samsara,
While there is nothing to perfect.

We abandon the deeds of the world,
While there is no time to abandon them.

We are freed from the chains
Of taking things in and holding onto them,
While there is no time to be freed.

We get out from the mud of our emotional problems,
While there is no time to get out.

We realize the three bodies within ourselves,
While there is no time to realize them.

The reality of our wisdom grows,
While there is no time for it to grow.

We take reality into ourselves,
While there is no time to take it in.

We cut through our delusions at the root,
While there is no time to cut through them.

We awaken from our attachments and cravings for ideas,
While there is no time to awaken.

We liberate the five poisons into their own places,
While there is no time to liberate them.

We understand that our heart embodies the Dharma,
While there is no time to understand this.

There is no place for our hopes.
There is no place to fall into fear.
The Buddhas of the three realms
Cut through the roots of the six classes of living beings.

We cut through the door
Of birth, age, sickness, and death.

We cut through the ropes of the net.
We overwhelm the three worlds.
The apparent world is sealed and supported.

This is the contemplation of the Buddhas of the three times.

That is what he said.

This is Chapter Sixty-Five: The Way to Maintain a Resolute Understanding.

EXPLAINING THE DEFINITION OF CLEANSING AND FULFILLMENT

Then Vajrasattva questioned the All Good himself
With these words:

Please explain the meaning of the cleansing and fulfillment of enlightenment.

That is what he asked.

Our teacher gave instruction to the audience:

As for cleansing,
We cleanse what we take in,
Both externally and internally.

As for fulfillment,
We are fulfilled in our great indivisibility.

As for cleansing,
We cleanse our collective understanding of the five doors.

We do not change.
We do not practice.
We are fulfilled without counting anything.

As for cleansing,
We cleanse our inner ideas.

As for fulfillment,
We are directly fulfilled
As we cut through complications.

As for cleansing,
We cleanse both what we take in
And what we hold onto.

As for fulfillment,
We are directly fulfilled
Without taking anything in
Or holding onto anything.

As for cleansing,
We cleanse our ideas about signs.

As for fulfillment,
We are fulfilled without any signs.

As for cleansing,
We cleanse permanence, change,
And the measure of our craving.

As for fulfillment,
We are fulfilled within an unspeakable space.

As for cleansing,
We cleanse the five poisons and the three poisons.

We are fulfilled in the five bodies
And the five kinds of wisdom.

As for cleansing,
We cleanse our collective ideas,
However many there may be.

As for fulfillment,
We are fulfilled in a magnificent lack of ideas.

That is what he said.

This is Chapter Sixty-Six: Explaining the Definition of Cleansing and Fulfillment.

EXPLAINING THE DEFINITION OF A MIND HERO

Then Vajrasattva questioned the All Good himself
With these words:

Please explain what it means to be a mind hero.

That is what he said.

Our teacher gave instruction to the audience:

As for the mind,
It is sentience in its correct meaning.

As for a hero,
He is a hero at what it means to be non-dual.

As for the mind,
It is a sentience of what it means to be unborn.

As for a hero,
He is heroic at what it means to be unceasing.

As for the mind,
It is a sentience of something that has no birth.

As for a hero,
He is heroic at being without transfer or change.

As for the mind,
It is a sentience of both samsara and nirvana.

As for a hero,
He is heroic at a magnificent non-duality.

As for the mind,
It is the sentience of an unchanging experience.

As for a hero,
He does not practice and has no attachment or craving.

As for the mind,
It is a sentience of there being no object or mind.

As for a hero,
He has no good or evil,
Nothing to negate or prove.

As for the mind,
It is a sentience of reality as our mother.

As for a hero,
He is heroic in the indivisibility of a mother and her child.

As for the mind,
It is sentience in unchanging space.

We are heroic
In the unspeakable space of great bliss.

That is what he said.

This is Chapter Sixty-Seven: Explaining the Definition of a Mind Hero.

EXPLAINING THE MEANING OF SELF-ORIGINATION

Then Vajrasattva questioned the All Good himself
With these words:

Please explain what it means to be self-originating.

That is what he asked.

Our teacher gave instruction to the audience:

Our hope for a beginning for ourselves
Is the basis of our existence.
As for our origination,
Does only the mind exist?
Or is there a base?

As for the self,
It is an insubstantial and all-encompassing base.

As for our origination,
It is the wind that abides in the base.

As for the self,
It is only a thought and is a basis for being deceived.

As for our origination,
Our origin is a trifling event.

As for the self,
The basis of all things is universally pervasive.

As for our origination,
We arise in five self-evident lights.
This is the mandala of our own light.

As for our origination,
We arise as rays from out of the light.
Our own rays have the true nature of being gods.

As for our origination,
It is in the five ways that knowledge appears.

As for the self,
It is a primordial knowledge.

As for our origination,
We are not aware of the meanings of our lives.

For this reason,
We say that ignorance is a delusion.
Our own ignorance is the doorway to our delusions.

As for our origination,
An awareness of thought arises in our minds.
There are three ways that we delude ourselves.

As for our origination,
We arise in the three realms of samsara.

As for the self,
It is our own mind.

As for our origination,
We arise as eighty thousand collective understandings.

As for the self,
It is the mind of samsara that does not understand.

As for our origination,
We arise with eighty thousand emotional problems.

That is what he said.

This is Chapter Sixty-Eight: Explaining the Meaning of Self-Origination.

TEACHING THE NINE KINDS OF MIRRORS

Then Vajrasattva questioned the All Good himself
With these words:

What is the shining mirror of our own mind?

That is what he said.

Our teacher gave instruction to the audience:

A heart has the true nature of a mother.
It does not move and it does not change,
But it is explained to be a shining mirror of jewels.

Vajrasattva,
Take this into your thought!

There are the mirror that is present by itself in appearances,
The mirror of self-arising awareness,
And the mirror of the basis of all things that has no complications.
These are the outer mirrors.

As for the teaching on the inner mirrors,
There are the mirror where fantasy visions appear,
The mirror of empty awareness,
And the mirror of the mind that is the basis for all things.

As for the teaching on the secret mirrors:
There are the mirror of sentient appearances,

The mirror in which our awareness of thought does not flicker
And we brilliantly understand the purpose of our hearts,
And the mirror of the unborn mind.

That is what he said.

This is Chapter Sixty-Nine: Teaching the Nine Kinds of Mirrors.

TEACHING THREE WORDS OF INSTRUCTION

Then Vajrasattva questioned the All Good himself
With these words:

Please teach us the three words
That are the instructions of the All Good.

That is what he asked.

Our teacher spoke to the audience
With these words:

You must understand that every appearance
Of signs in any external objects
Is a delusion.

Cut through the ropes of complication
In all your experiences of mental practice
And the flickering of aware memories!

Use the seal of the non-duality
Of experiential radiance
And unchanging self-liberation
For your attainment!

In the experience of being free from
The eight limitations from complicating things
And the eight Dharmas
We live as unborn embodiments of the Dharma

In the experience of a dominion
That does not speak, discuss, or change.

I the All Good have three words of instruction:

Come into the center of the heart of Vajrasattva!

That is what he said.

This is Chapter Seventy: Teaching Three Words of Instruction.

TEACHING THE FOUR KINDS OF CERTAINTY

Then Vajrasattva questioned the All Good himself
With these words:

What are the four words that are certain?

That is what he asked.

The All Good One spoke these words:

It is sure that the king of views
Has no spiritual beliefs.

It is sure that the king of meditations
Has nothing that must be produced.

It is sure that the king of practices
Has no work or quest.

It is sure that the king of rewards
Has no hope or fear.

That is what he said.

This is Chapter Seventy-One: Teaching the Four Kinds of Certainty.

TEACHING THE SIX KINDS OF HIGHER SEEING

Then Vajrasattva questioned the All Good himself
With these words:

What are the six kinds of higher seeing?

That is what he asked.

Our teacher gave instruction to the audience:

When we do not recognize any view
We have no position.
This is a higher seeing.

When we have no ideas about changes in our meditation
Our contemplations are not deceptive.
This is a higher seeing.

When our practice has nothing to be done
It is a contemplation of Buddhahood.
This is a higher seeing.

When our samaya have nothing to protect
We contemplate having no problems.
This is a higher seeing.

When our good works have no ulterior motives
We contemplate having nowhere to go.
This is a higher seeing.

When our reward is that we have nothing to work on
We live alone without hope.
This is a higher seeing.

That is what he said.

This is Chapter Seventy-Two: Teaching the Six Kinds of Higher Seeing.

TEACHING THE TEN WAYS OF BEING BEYOND

Then Vajrasattva questioned the All Good One:

What are the ten ways of being beyond?

That is what he asked.

The All Good One gave instruction:

When our views have no scripture
They are beyond words.

When our meditation is without thought
It is beyond the intellect.

When our practices have nothing to be done
They are beyond the pathways of samsara.

When our samaya have nothing to protect
And nothing to transgress
They are beyond protection.

When our good works have no ulterior motives
We have nothing to do.
We are beyond experiencing things.

When we do not travel any roads
We have nowhere to go.
We are beyond experiencing things.

When we do not study the levels
We have nothing to study.
We are beyond experiencing things.

Our transmission is unmistaken.
We are beyond those transmissions that use words.

Our upadeśa instruction is to not hold on.
We do not cling.
We are beyond experiencing things.

Our rewards are primordially present.
Our thoughts are prayers.
We are beyond thought.

That is what he said.

This is Chapter Seventy-Three: Teaching the Ten Ways of Being Beyond.

TEACHING REALITY WITH SYMBOLS

Then Vajrasattva questioned the All Good himself
With these words:

How are we to use symbols to exemplify our homes and our bodies?

That is what he asked.

Our teacher said these words to the audience:

We may damage the purity of the empty sky,
But we will get something.
By wreaking damage on the empty sky
The great rivers descend in an unbroken stream.
It is because there is no break in the stream of the great rivers
That we are like revolutionary kings who protect their own wealth.

Memories do not arise.
We live in the space of reality.
We may be distracted,
But reality is not distracted.
This is the dominion of the Dharma.

That is what he said.

This is Chapter Seventy-Four: Teaching Reality with Symbols.

A SYMBOLIC TEACHING ON THE FIVE POISONS, THE FIVE BODIES, AND THE FIVE WISDOMS

Then Vajrasattva questioned the All Good himself
With these words:

What is the symbolic Dharma
In which the five bodies are the five poisons?

That is what he asked.

Our teacher gave instruction to the audience:

In the cathedral of unobstructed total clarity
There lives the King who is the one God.
He is surrounded by four men
Who are great ministers of power.

The King controls the four men who are ministers.
As he controls these four men
They become four bodies.

The King is the embodiment of the unchanging Dharma.
The four men are the four kinds of wisdom.

One man is the wisdom of the dominion of the Dharma.
In the density of the dark house of ignorance
There lives the blind woman of ignorance,

Whose King is a heaping hatred.
He enters into competition with the high.
He curses and hates the low.
He is attached to the measure of his meetings,
And in other ways
Is for his family a master who rejects
The three realms of samsara.

He savors the experience
Of the sorrows of birth, age, sickness, and death.
When he wants to turn away from these sorrows
He opens up his understanding of the darkness.
He attains a wisdom that is clear.

He opens the eyes of ignorance
And the sun of wisdom dawns.
He cuts through hatred at the root.
The King of the heaps is systematically destroyed.
Pride destroys itself.
Jealousy does not even have a name.

There are three thousand Buddhas
Who do not wander through the three realms.
We cut through the four rivers at the root.
The four bodies are the four wisdoms.

That is what he said.

This is Chapter Seventy-Five: A Symbolic Teaching on the Five Poisons, the Five Bodies, and the Five Wisdoms.

PUTTING REALITY INTO ORDER

Then Vajrasattva questioned the All Good himself
With these words:

What is the meaning of the Bodhicitta?

That is what he asked.

Our teacher gave instruction to the audience:

By negating appearances we do not stop them.
So then,
Do we stop them, or what?

Appearances are substantial.
So there are no clear divisions between objects and minds.
By looking for our true mind we will not see it.

Well then,
Do we see them, or what?

The self-radiance of emptiness and its clarity
Are from the beginning without duality.
By working toward non-duality
We will not succeed.

Well then,
Do we work on things, or what?

The non-duality that we create
And that we work toward
Is a compounded Dharma of our intellects.
By seeking for Buddhahood
We will not find it.

We then,
Do we seek, or what?

It is simply our own minds.
It is not possible that we find it anywhere else.
Once we understand our way of living,
We do not meditate on any misunderstandings at all.
It is sure that this is the Vajra All Good One.

In the same way that we understand meanings,
We use a knowledge that we understand.
There is nothing to be meditated on in this.
As objects for our ideas, minds, thoughts, and intellects.

That is what he said.

This is Chapter Seventy-Six: Putting Reality into Order.

TEACHING THE HEART
THAT EMBODIES THE DHARMA

Then Vajrasattva questioned the All Good himself
With these words:

Please explain the purpose of our hearts.

That is what he asked.

The All Good One gave instruction:

A heart is not a compounded thing.
A heart is unborn and unchanging.
A heart is an insubstantial embodiment of the Dharma.
A heart is a solitary Buddha.
A heart is an unchanging reality.
A heart is an unchanging authenticity.
A heart is a stainless clear light.
A heart is an uncompounded basis for all things.
A heart is a pile of jewel light.

As an analogy,
Butter can melt into one thing in our mouths.
When we condense it through four measures,
There is the heart of the butter.

In the same way,
All of the Dharmas may also be brought together into one.

This is our heart.

That is what he said.

This is Chapter Seventy-Seven: Teaching the Heart that Embodies the Dharma.

EXPLAINING THE DEFINITION OF THE BODY OF THE DHARMA

Then Vajrasattva questioned the All Good himself
With these words:

What is the traditional explanation for the body of the Dharma?

That is what he asked.

Our teacher spoke to the audience
With these words:

The body of the Dharma is not substantial.
The body of the Dharma is beyond
Being an object for our visualizations.
The body of the Dharma has no causes or conditions,
No transfer or change.
The body of the Dharma has no strife, projection,
Work, or quest.
The body of the Dharma is beyond being a topic of discussion.
It is not to be exemplified with words or letters.

It encompasses us all with compassion,
But we do not recognize it.
It is beyond the extremes of strife and practice,
Rejection and acceptance.
We do not develop any body of the Dharma.
Our own minds are embodiments of the Dharma.

This is Chapter Seventy-Eight: Explaining the Definition of the Body of the Dharma.

CONDENSING AND TEACHING THE UPADEŚA INSTRUCTIONS

Then Vajrasattva questioned the All Good himself
With these words:

What are the summary upadeśa instructions?

That is what he asked.

Our teacher gave instruction to the audience:

I will explain the upadeśa instructions
For the three kinds of gathering.

The true nature of our hearts does not move.
Our limbs use the force of our awareness
To give names to things.
The entirety of the eighty-four thousand vehicles
Is gathered into the experience
Of my yoga of the Universal Ti.

Even the eighty-four thousand doorways of the holy Dharma
Are explained to be gathered into the experience
Of having no attachment or clinging.

The eighty thousand branches of the collection of merit
Are gathered into a great compassion.

E Ma Ho!
This instruction on the three kinds of gathering
Cuts through the three poisons at the root.
It overwhelms the three realms.

The three realms of samsara do not exist.
We realize the three bodies within ourselves.
We do not travel any three levels.
We go to the level of Buddhahood.
We do not reject the three realms.
They turn out to be fields for the three bodies.

Instructions of the heart
That teach things this way
Are not seen by any looking.
We melt into the unchanging dominion of our own minds.

We do not use any meditation
To meditate on it.
We melt into an experience in which
Our understandings and thoughts do not flicker.

We do not use any practices to practice this.
We melt into an uncomplicated experience
In which we have nothing to do with attachment or craving.

We do not work toward any reward.
We live by ourselves without hope.
In decisive unity,
We melt into the space
In which the three bodies are indivisible.

This instruction on the three gatherings
And four meltings
Cuts through the three realms at the roots.
It cuts through the abyss of the six classes of living beings.

Vajrasattva,
Hold this in the center of your heart!

Prahe Vajra will come later on.
Teach him these instructions that are meaningful!
This is not the time

To teach them to anyone else.

You may ask what the validation for this is.

Many are deceived by the demons of samsara.
Many are ensnared in taking things in and holding onto them.
Many crave for lust and hatred.
Many are stuck in hopes and fears.

For these reasons they are not fit recipients.
This Dharma is not for them.

It is also certain
That for those who take this into their experience
The three bodies will arise within themselves.

That is what he said.

From the Latter Tantra on Kissing the Apparent World while Dripping an Elixir of Ambrosia to Cut through Samsara from Start to Ending, this is chapter Seventy-Nine: Condensing and Teaching the Upadeśa Instructions.

A Pa Ra | Guhya | Dharmma Kāya A!

THE LATTER OF THE LATTER TANTRA ON KISSING THE APPARENT WORLD WHILE DRIPPING AN ELIXIR OF AMBROSIA TO CUT THROUGH SAMSARA FROM START TO END

TEACHING THE WAY OF SEEING OF THE UNIVERSAL TI

This yoga of the Universal Ti
Is the heart of the teachings.
It is said to be the universal ancestor
Of all the vehicles.
It is said to be the highest peak of the nine stages.
It is said to be the executioner of makers of views.
It is said to be an antagonist for the makers of meditations.
It is said to be a demon for the makers of practices.
It is said to be a broom for the makers of projects.

This yoga of the Universal Ti
Is the king of the vehicles.
Those who view things as having two truths
Do not see this.

Those who contrive things into a duality of objects and minds
Do not see this.

Those who view things as either to be taken in or to be held onto
Do not see this.

Those who practice the three kinds of purity
Do not see this.

Those who connect their views and practices into pairs
Do not see this.

Those who view a duality of birth and ending
Do not see this.

Those who view their methods and knowledge
Do not see this.

Those who view their dominions and wisdom
Do not see this.

Those who believe that everything is the body of the Dharma
Do not see this.

Those who position the views of others behind them
Do not see this.

Those who actually crave their own views
Do not see this.

Those who are ensnared by taking things in
And holding onto them
Do not see this.

Those who are ensnared by negations and proofs
Do not see this.

Those who are ensnared by rejection and acceptance
Do not see this.

Those who use the eye of Atiyoga
Are the seers.
At the moment we see,
Recognition will appear,
No matter what.

At the moment we are absent,
Thusness will appear,
No matter what.

At the moment it appears
We know the face of thusness.
The totality of samsara and nirvana
Will be liberated into its own place.

In this,
We use the core of the instructions
When we need to be correct.

This instruction is inseparable from
The All Good himself.

Vajrasattva,
Hold it well within your thoughts!

That is what he said.

This is Chapter Eighty: Teaching the Way of Seeing of the Universal Ti.

TEACHING THE HEART BLOOD OF THE UNIVERSAL TI

Vajrasattva addressed him again:

Please teach the upadeśa instructions for the Universal Ti.

Then our teacher,
The All Good,
Gave instruction to the audience that had gathered:

This is the upadeśa instruction
For the Universal Ti of the Yang Ti:

I do not teach any duality of truths.
I will explain the upadeśa instructions for a great relaxation.

Refute dualistic truths!

I will explain the instructions
That come from the dominion of the sky.

In your heart,
Which is the experiential radiance of the body of the Dharma,
Do not think about work in your thoughts!
Know that your own radiance is your own mind.
Do not think thoughts in your mind!
Do not think in intellectual contrivances!

Know that your own mind is a Buddha!
Do not use your awareness to give things names!

I do not teach about strife or strivers.
I do not teach about crafts or craftsmen.

Do not think about holding or a holder!
Do not think about visualizations or visualizers!
Do not make up any view or viewer!
Do not think about meditation or a meditator!
Do not think about practice or a practitioner!
Do not think about projects or a projector!
Do not think about protection or a protector!
Do not think about travel or a traveler!
Do not think about happiness or one who is happy!
Do not think about being or one who is!
Do not think about jumping or a jumper!
Do not think about clarity or one who is clear!
Do not think about raising or one who raises!
Do not think about being serious or one who is serious!
Do not think about places or any placer!
Do not think about being together or anyone who is together!

One who hopes or one who fears:
Do not hold onto either hope or fear!
Negating and proving,
Rejection and acceptance:
These are Dharmas of dualistic clinging.

I,
The All Good,
Do not explain them.

The body of the Dharma,
The body of pleasure,
And the manifest body,
The Buddha,
Dharma,
And the five bodies:
We have no reason to believe
In what they seem to be.

Do not make things up in your thoughts!
Give up your work!
Do not work!
Do not enact the karma of strife!
Abide in an experience of having no thought,
That does not change!

In a meaningful way of living,
Where appearances and emptiness are indivisible,
Settle yourself into a vision of uncontrived awareness.

In a spacious space
Of a reality we do not think about,
Settle yourself in the radiant experience
Of a mind that remembers
That it has nothing to meditate on.

If the All Good One
Has not contemplated or meditated something,
What would Vajrasattva meditate about it?

The view that has nothing to see
Is especially noble.
This is the great samadhi
That we are not to meditate on.

The practice that has nothing to be practiced
Is especially noble.

The body of the Dharma projects nothing.
Our delusion is our own.

That is what he said.

This is Chapter Eighty-One: Teaching the Heart Blood of the Universal Ti.

TEACHING THE DEFINITION OF THE BASIS OF ALL THINGS

Then Vajrasattva again questioned the All Good:

What is the purpose for the basis of all things?

So did he address him.

The All Good One gave instruction:

As for all,
It is the apparent world of samsara and nirvana.
As for the base,
It is the Bodhicitta.

As for all,
It brings together the forms
Of those who are born and live.
As for the base,
It is the basis for the origination of the mind.

As for all,
It is what we call the Dharmas
That happen and that appear.
As for the base,
It is what we call the basis for our beginnings.

That is what he said.

This is Chapter Eighty-Two: Teaching the Definition of the Basis of All Things.

TEACHINGS ON THE UNMISTAKEN BUDDHA

Vajrasattva again questioned him:

What is an unmistaken Buddha?

So did he address him.

The All Good One gave instruction:

The essence of an unmistaken Buddha
Is that we will not realize Buddhahood
By working toward it,
For Buddhahood is primordially realized in our minds.

If you do not get distracted
Away from what it means
That you are already realized,
You do not need to do any practices.

Sit up straight!
Observe your spontaneous realization!

When we look for it,
We do not even see one thing.
We see the face of its absence.
We awaken from the ignorance
That is samsara's darkness.

We spread open the door
To the arising of an awareness of wisdom.
We awaken from what causes
Our clinging to a self,
And our emotional problems.

We grow a very pure wisdom
That does not cling.
We spread open the door
To the dawning of an awareness of wisdom.

That is what he said.

This is Chapter Eighty-Three: Teachings on the Unmistaken Buddha.

NIRVANA THAT IS UNMISTAKEN AND SURE

Vajrasattva questioned him again:

What is the unmistaken nirvana
Where we leave behind our sorrows?

So did he address him.

The All Good One gave instruction:

As for sorrow that is unmistaken and sure,
In the space that is the basis for all things
And is the origin of our births,
We leave it behind.

The knowledge of her branch children
In the space of the heart-mother
Is left behind.

Our visions of the force
And the ways its characteristics appear,
In the dominion of the sky-space of emptiness
Are left behind.

All our cravings to bind the visions of our minds
In the reality of the Bodhicitta
Are left behind.

The doubts that appear in our intellects,
In the space of the sky that is the basis of all things
Are left behind.

The substance of our ignorance
Is in our awareness
Left behind.

The substance of what appears
Is in emptiness
Left behind.

All our dualistic visions
Are in non-duality
Left behind.

All our grasping at a self
Is without grasping
Left behind.

All our positions and preferences
Where there are no positions
Are left behind.

All our cravings and attachments
Where there are no cravings
Are left behind.

The sorrows of the three realms of samsara
In the space of nirvana
Are left behind.

Sentient beings with their bad ideas and self-clinging
In the dominion of the great bliss of the Buddhas
Are left behind.

That is what he said.

This is Chapter Eighty-Four: Nirvana that Is Unmistaken and Sure.

PUTTING OUR TRUE MINDS INTO ORDER WITHOUT MISTAKE

Then Vajrasattva questioned the All Good himself
With these words:

What is our own unmistaken mind?

The All Good One gave instruction:

The true nature of an unmistaken mind
Is a sentience that is without contrivance.
It is fresh.
It is our own way.
It is our soul.
Our true minds are free from any
Clinging to a self.

Our Buddhahood is a non-dual shining radiance.
Our true minds are liberated from visions
That would bind us.
This is an unmistaken and very pure wisdom.

We awaken from our intellectual engagements
And the prayers in our thoughts.
Our true minds have no prayer in our thought.

From Kissing the Apparent World while Dripping an Elixir of Ambrosia, this is Chapter Eighty-Five: Putting Our True Minds into Order Without Mistake.

A SUMMARY TEACHING ON THE WAYS THE MIND APPEARS

Then Vajrasattva questioned the All Good himself
With these words:

What is the way in which the mind appears?

That is what he asked.

The All Good One gave instruction:

The ways in which the mind appears are infinite.
Both samsara and nirvana
Are in fact ways that the mind appears.

Buddhas and sentient beings
Are ways that the mind appears.

The vessel and contents of the apparent world
Are ways that the mind appears.

The gathered forms of those who are born and live
Are ways that the mind appears.

The eighty-four thousand
Are ways that the mind appears.

The vehicles of the nine stages
Are ways that the mind appears.

Understanding and misunderstanding
Are ways that the mind appears.

Awareness and ignorance
Are ways that the mind appears.

Everything is non-dual.
There are no clear differences.

From out of the ignorant delusions of our intellects
Things appear to be dual.
When we use our knowledge to understand
Our true natures will be entirely balanced.

The appearances of our minds have infinite divisions,
But when we know that we are equal
We are equal to all the Buddhas.

That is what he said.

This is Chapter Eighty-Six: A Summary Teaching on the Ways the Mind Appears.

THE WAY WE BRING TOGETHER THE WAY THINGS APPEAR TO OUR MINDS

Then Vajrasattva asked:

How are we to bring the ways things appear into unity?

So did he address him.

The All Good One gave instruction:

An infinite variety of things
Are brought together in our minds.

The things we look at and the act of seeing
Are brought together in our minds.

The things we meditate on and the act of meditation
Are brought together in our minds.

The things we practice and the act of practicing
Are brought together in our minds.

The things that we develop and the act of developing
Are brought together in our minds.

The things we protect and the act of protection
Are brought together in our minds.

The things we strive for and the act of striving
Are brought together in our minds.

From the very beginning,
They have been brought together in this way.
As an analogy,
This is like the tributary waters of the ocean.
They come from the sea and they are gathered into the sea.
This is not something that is brought together by working on it.

As an analogy,
We have been brought together like this.

That is what he said.

From the Tantra on Kissing the Apparent World, this is Chapter Eighty-Seven: The Way We Bring together the Way Things Appear to Our Minds.

TEACHING INSTRUCTIONS THAT ARE UNMISTAKEN AND SURE

Then Vajrasattva questioned the All Good himself
With these words:

What is an instruction that is unmistaken and sure?

That is what he asked.

The All Good One gave instruction:

This is an instruction that is unmistaken and sure!

Come into the experience
Where we have nothing to talk about or discuss:
The Bodhicitta that is not to be exemplified!

Come into the experience that is beyond the intellect:
The Bodhicitta that is not to be taught!

Come into the experience where there is nothing to be observed:
The Bodhicitta that is not to be seen!

Come into the experience of having nothing to meditate on:
The Bodhicitta that is not to be contemplated!

Come into the experience of having nothing to do or seek:
The Bodhicitta that is not to be practiced!

Come into the experience
Where there are no hopes or fears to project:
The Bodhicitta that is not to be developed!

Come into the experience
Of a magnificent absence of complications:
The Bodhicitta that is not complicated.

That is what he said.

This is Chapter Eighty-Eight: Teaching Instructions that Are Unmistaken and Sure.

LIBERATING THE FIVE POISONS INTO REALITY

Vajrasattva again questioned him:

How will the five poisons be liberated in our minds?

That is what he asked.

The All Good One gave instruction:

Regarding the liberation of the five poisons in our minds,
To be dense is our teaching on reality.
To be dark is the darkness over Dharmas that have names.
For these reasons,
Our own minds are stupid:
Dense and dark.

Our desire is a desire for the unborn body of the Dharma.
Our attachment is an attachment to the space of great bliss.
This being so,
Our own minds are lusty:
Desirous and attached.

Our spite is a spite for the dominion of our own minds.
Our hatred is a hatred for the Dharmas of samsara.
For these reasons,
Our own minds are hateful.

The I is the unborn Bodhicitta.
Victory is winning the war of samsara.

For these reasons,
Our own minds are proud.

A dangerous road is a road
To the dominion of the unchanging.
A narrow passage is a passage
Through the five kinds of attachment and hatred.
For these reasons,
Our own minds are jealous.

The five poisons are the unborn Bodhicitta.

That is what he said.

This is Chapter Eighty-Nine: Liberating the Five Poisons into Reality.

LIBERATING THE FIVE ELEMENTS INTO OUR MINDS

Then Vajrasattva asked:

How are we to liberate the five elements in our minds?

That is what he asked.

The All Good One gave instruction:

As for liberating the five elements into our minds:

Space is a space that has no birth.
The sky is a sky that has no ending.
The Bodhicitta has neither birth nor ending.
For these reasons,
Our own mind is the sky.

As for the earth,
It is the foundation for our sentience,
The basis of all things.
All of the many things are born and do arise,
But the true nature of reality
Is to be hard and stable.
This being so,
Our own mind is earth.

We use the great fire of the Bodhicitta
To burn the fire-wood of the five poisons,
Which are our emotional problems.
For this reason,
Our own mind is also fire.

Reality is a water that is not without moisture.
When we condense things into non-duality,
We are also water.

We use the great wind of our self-originating force
To sweep our eighty thousand emotional problems
With a broom.
Our ideas are carried on the wind.
For these reasons,
Our own mind is also the wind.

The five elements,
With no exceptions,
Are perfected in our minds.

That is what he said.

This is Chapter Ninety: Liberating the Five Elements into Our Minds.

LIBERATING DIRECTIONS AND BOUNDARIES IN OUR MINDS

Then Vajrasattva questioned the All Good himself
With these words:

How are we to liberate extremes, middles,
Positions, and boundaries
Into our minds?

That is what he asked.

The All Good One gave instruction:

As for the way in which positions and boundaries
Are perfected in our minds,
The body of the Dharma is unchanging and stable.
So the Bodhicitta is also the middle.

Wisdom dawns from out of the space of our hearts.
The Bodhicitta is the direction of the East.

Our clinging to the attachments and hatreds
That are our emotional problems
Is South.
The Bodhicitta is the direction to the South.

The names of our ideas,
However many there may be,

Set into the unborn dominion of the non-conceptual.
The Bodhicitta is the direction to the West.

Our negating and proving
What we take in and what we hold onto
In our emotional problems
Is our learning.
The Bodhicitta is the direction to the North.

The border between the East and the South
Is unborn.

The border between the South and the West
Is unending.

The border between the West and the North
Is non-dual.

The border between the North and the East
Is liberated into its own place.

The above and the below are non-dual.
There are no clear differences.
The upward direction
Overwhelms those of the inferior vehicles.
The downward direction is a fulfillment
That is pervasive and encompassing.

For these reasons,
The directions and boundaries
Are liberated in our minds.

That is what he said.

This is Chapter Ninety-One: Liberating Directions and Boundaries in Our Minds.

TEACHINGS ON COLOR

Then Vajrasattva questioned the All Good himself
With these words:

How are we to liberate colors into our minds?

So did he address him.

The All Good One spoke these words:

Our taking things in and holding onto them
Are not stained by any filth.
This is white.

Our virtues with none excepted
Are the source of all things.
This is yellow.

We bring our visions together under our control.
This is red.

Reality is unchanging.
This is black.

Our self-origination is spontaneously realized.
This is green.

The five kinds of color
Are liberated in the Bodhicitta.

That is what he said.

This is Chapter Ninety-Two: Teachings on Color.

LIBERATING MEN INTO THEIR MINDS

Vajrasattva questioned him again:

How will men be liberated in their minds?

That is what he asked.

The All Good One gave instruction:

As for men being liberated in their minds,
A man is a man in his self-originating wisdom.
A hero is a hero in his great and total clarity.

A man is a man
In the self-radiance of his own awareness.
A hero is a hero
Who destroys himself and awakens himself.

A man is a man
In the knowledge that he understands.
He has awakened from the darkness of his ignorance.
So he is a hero.

That is what he said.

This is Chapter Ninety-Two: Liberating Men into Their Minds.

LIBERATING WOMEN INTO THEIR MINDS

Then Vajrasattva asked:

How will women be liberated into their minds?

That is what he asked.

Our teacher gave instruction to the audience:

To protrude is to protrude from out of the Dharmas of samsara.
Its absence is the absence of the black darkness of ignorance.
For these reasons,
A woman is the Bodhicitta.

To protrude is the protruding of all our emotional problems.
We have no attachment or hatred,
No dualistic clinging,
And nothing to negate or prove.
For these reasons,
Women are liberated in their minds.

So he spoke.

This is Chapter Ninety-Four: Liberating Women into Their Minds.

PERFECTING YOGA IN OUR MINDS

Vajrasattva questioned him again:

How do we perfect yoga in our minds?

That is what he asked.

The All Good One gave instruction:

Regarding the way in which we perfect yoga
In our minds:

In general,
There are four kinds of yoga.
There is the yoga that attains a great transmission,
The yoga that is a perfection of our great force,
The yoga that is a practice of devotion,
And the yoga that is a husk.
These are the four.

Regarding the yoga of attaining a great transmission,
The unborn transmission of the All Good One
Is Vajrasattva's heart contemplation.
Prahe Vajra of Orgyan received it.

Regarding the yoga of perfecting our great force,
We perfect the forces that have no birth or death.
We also perfect the empowerment
Into the word of the Victorious Ones.

Regarding the yoga that is a practice of devotion,
We are connected for the sake of the words of the holy ones.

There is the so-called: "Husk yoga."
We enjoy and are attached to
The five kinds of attachment and hatred.
Yogas that are holy are not impoverished.

As for yoga in its correct meaning,
Our nature is a nature that is unborn and is unchanging.
Joining is our joining into the space of our hearts,
Our nature is natural in itself
As we abide at base.

Joining is joining in the space of reality.

That is what he said.

This is Chapter Ninety-Five: Perfecting Yoga in Our Minds.

THE PRISTINE FIVE DOORS

Vajrasattva questioned him again:

What is it to be pristine in our five doors?

So did he address him.

The All Good One gave instruction:

Regarding pristine wisdom in our five doors:

The wisdom that is neither clear nor darkened
Is the pristine consciousness of the eye.

The wisdom that has no birth or ending
Is the pristine consciousness of the ear.

The wisdom that has no obstructions
Is the pristine consciousness of the nose.

The unchanging Bodhicitta
Is the pristine consciousness of the tongue.

The Bodhicitta that has no birth or destruction
Is the pristine consciousness of the body.

The five doors are perfected in the Bodhicitta.

That is what he said.

This is Chapter Ninety-Six: The Pristine Five Doors.

UNSTOPPING SELF-EVIDENCE

Then Vajrasattva questioned the All Good himself
With these words:

What is unceasing wisdom?

So did he address him.

The All Good One gave instruction:

When appearances do not stop
The dominion of the Dharma is self-evident.
When awareness does not stop
Our wisdom is self-originating.

The outer and inner are not two things.
They are inseparable.

This is Buddhahood.

That is what he said.

This is Chapter Ninety-Seven: Unstopping Self-Evidence.

TEACHING THE WAY THAT THE THREE GROUPS IN THEIR TRUE SIGNS ARE PERFECTED IN THE YOGA OF THE UNIVERSAL TI

Vajrasattva questioned him again:

How are the three sections of true signs perfected?

That is what he asked.

Our teacher gave instruction to the audience:

Of these,
The Auditors' way of perfection
Is to listen,
For they listen to the meaning of the unborn,
And to hear,
For they quickly attain awareness.

What we take in and what we hold onto
Are non-dual.
There are no clear differences.
For these reasons,
Auditors are perfected in their own minds.

As for a self,
It is an embodiment of a self-radiant Dharma.
As for victory,

They are victorious over both attachment and hatred.
The Bodhicitta has no duality of negation and proof.
For these reasons,
The Self-Victorious are perfected in their own minds.

As for Sutras,
They are the Sutras of the outer vehicles.

As for groups,
They are enumerations of the mind.

As for cleansed,
They are cleansed in the space of fulfillment.

As for the mind,
We are sentient of an unchanging purpose.

As for a vehicle,
Our vehicles are eighty-four thousand.

As for a hero,
We are heroic in the yoga of the Universal Ti.

For these reasons,
The Sutra Group is perfected in their own minds.

That is what he said.

This is Chapter Ninety-Eight: Teaching the Way that the Three Groups in Their True Signs Are Perfected in the Yoga of the Universal Ti.

THE THREE SECTIONS OF THE OUTER TANTRAS ARE PERFECT

Vajrasattva questioned him again:

How are the outer Tantras of the Secret Mantra perfected?

That is what he asked.

The All Good One gave instruction:

In the space of our hearts we do not change:
This is Kri.
As for Ya,
It is a Ya that has no birth.
Their vehicle is stable and does not change.
Outer purity, inner purity, and secret purity:
The vehicle of the Kriya is perfected in our minds.

As for U,
It is the unborn.
As for Pa,
It is the unending.
With an upward view and a downward practice
There is no birth or ending.
The Upa are perfected in the Bodhicitta.

As for Yo,
It is the space that is the basis for all things,

With no exceptions.
As for Ga,
We melt into the space
Of the way things appear.
Our birth and ending are not a duality.
There are no clear distinctions.
The community of the thirty-five gods
Are perfected in the reality of the Bodhicitta.

The three sections of external Tantras
Are perfected in our minds.

That is what he said.

This is Chapter Ninety-Nine: The Three Sections of the Outer Tantras Are Perfect.

TEACHING THE WAY IN WHICH THE MAHĀYOGA IS PERFECT

Vajrasattva questioned him
With these words:

How are the three sections of the inner Tantras perfected?

Our teacher gave instruction to the audience:

As for Ma,
It is the mother that is our heart's purpose.
As for Hā,
It is the child that is a vision of the force.
The communities of the gods
Are her unending children.

As for Ma,
It is the unborn Bodhicitta.
As for a child,
It is a method of vision.

Yoga is non-dual.
There is no accounting for it.
The forty-two are perfected in our minds.

That is what he said.

This is Chapter One Hundred: Teaching the Way in which the Mahāyoga Is Perfect.

TEACHING THE WAY IN WHICH THE ANUYOGA IS PERFECT

Vajrasattva questioned him again:

How is the Anuyoga perfect?

So did he address him.

The All Good One gave instruction:

As for A,
It is the unborn Bodhicitta.
As for Nu,
It is unceasing wisdom.

As for Nu,
The apparent world is in the dominion of the Dharma.
As for A,
It is unborn wisdom.

Our dominion and our wisdom are not two things.
Our reality is perfected in the Bodhicitta.

That is what he said.

This is Chapter One Hundred One: Teaching the Way in which the Anuyoga Is Perfect.

THE ATI IS PERFECTED IN OUR MINDS

Vajrasattva questioned him again:

How is the Atiyoga perfect?

The All Good One gave instruction:

Regarding the way in which the Atiyoga is perfect:

As for A,
It is the space of an unborn heart.
As for Ti,
It is stable and unchanging.
As for Yo,
It is a general summary of our vehicle.
As for Ga,
It is the unchanging dominion of the Dharma.

Our vehicle is the Great Perfection.
The Great Perfection is perfected in the Bodhicitta.

As for Perfection,
The apparent world of samsara and nirvana
Is perfect.
As for Great,
It is a greatness that has no rival.

The Great Perfection is perfected
In the sentience of our hearts.

That is what he said.

This is Chapter One Hundred Two: The Ati is Perfected in Our Minds.

THE PERFECTION OF THE KARMAS OF SAMSARA

Here is the *Pa Sa Sva Tva I Li I Dharmma A Yoga!*

Then Vajrasattva addressed the All Good himself
With these words:

How is it that all the vehicles
With no exceptions
Are perfected in the vehicle of the Universal Ti?

So did he address him.

Then our teacher,
The All Good,
Entered the samadhi in which
The symbolic union of the jewel light is not revealed.

He got up from it,
And he spoke these words:

This is my yoga,
The Universal Ti.

Everyone is completely perfected in this.
In the vision of the force of our hearts
Our bondage, craving, names, and words
Are perfected.

The birth and shaking of the apparent world,
The dualistic vision of samsara and nirvana,
Are perfected.

The origin of the birth of all things
Perfects the seeds of samsara.

We are not held by any creator.
The karmas of samsara are perfected.

By working toward success we will not succeed.
Our thoughts, prayers, hopes, and fears
Are perfect.

The outer and inner,
Negations and proofs,
Rejection and acceptance,
Taking in and holding on:
They are perfect!

That is what he said.

This is Chapter One Hundred Three: The Perfection of the Karmas of Samsara.

EVERYONE IS PERFECTED IN THE YOGA OF THE UNIVERSAL TI

Then Vajrasattva asked:

How are the eighty-four thousand perfected?

So did he address him.

The All Good One gave instruction:

The eighty-four thousand vehicles
Are also perfected in my yoga of the Universal Ti.
The views, meditations, and practices
Of the nine stages of the vehicles
Are finally perfected.

Our mandala, empowerment, and samaya propitiation
Are perfect.

Our views, trainings, and the Auditor rules of discipline
Are perfect.

The stages, paths, and six perfections
Are perfect.

Our ten levels, prayers, aspirations, hopes, and fears
Are perfect.

Our blessings, realizations, feasts, and tormas
Are perfect.

Our worship and praise,
The cleansing of our regrets,
And our removal of obstructions
Are perfect.

Our awareness has no clear divisions.
It is perfect.

The world has no birth.
It is perfect.

Our dualistic thoughts have nothing to take in
Or to hold onto.
We are perfect.

Our awareness is perfected in its own magnificent radiance.
Our mental understandings are perfected
In a magnificent self-destruction.
Our intellectual bonds are perfected
In a magnificent self-destruction.
Objects and minds are perfected
In that there is no accounting for them.

The outer and inner are perfected in their lack of duality.
Our tsatsas, coins, butter lamps,
Tormas of offering, food, and water tormas
Are perfect.

All of our prayers and aspirations are perfect.
Our knowing contemplations
And every measure of our understanding
Are perfect.

Everyone is perfect
In the yoga of the Universal Ti.

That is what he said.

This is Chapter One Hundred Four: Everyone Is Perfected in the Yoga of the Universal Ti.

TEACHING THE WAY IN WHICH THE UNIVERSAL TI IS PERFECTED IN OUR MINDS

Vajrasattva questioned him again:

How do we perfect the Universal Ti in our minds?

So did he address him.

Our teacher gave instruction to the audience:

As for Universal,
It is everything,
With nothing left out.
As for Ti,
It turns out to be the space of our own hearts.

As for Universal,
It is our thought, awareness, sentience, and ideation.
As for Ti,
It turns out to be the space of our own hearts.

As for Yo,
There are no clear distinctions or accountings for it.
As for Ga,
It is the space of the reality of our hearts.

For these reasons,
The Great Vehicle is overwhelming.

This being so,
The Universal Ti is perfected in our own minds.

That is what he said.

This is Chapter One Hundred Five: Teaching the Way in which the Universal Ti Is Perfected in Our Minds.

TEACHING THAT BY AN UNDERSTANDING OF THE UNIVERSAL TI WE WILL UNDERSTAND EVERY DHARMA

Vajrasattva again questioned him:

By knowing the yoga of the Universal Ti
Will we come to know all of the Dharmas?

So did he address him.

Our teacher gave instruction to the audience:

When we understand the knowledge
Of the Universal Ti
We will understand all the Dharmas,
None excepted.

When we know the Universal Ti
We know an infinity of vehicles.

When we understand the Universal Ti.
We understand every view.

When we realize the Universal Ti
We realize every siddhi.

When we ponder the Universal Ti
We ponder the weakness in our own vehicles.

We arrive at the level
Of the Buddha that we were praying for
In our thoughts.

Moreover,
As an analogy,
You must know it is like this:

From the summit of supreme brilliance
We can see all the mountain ranges.

When we observe the ocean
We see all the channels of water.

When we cut the roots from the trunk
The branches will dry.

When a single pit is hollow inside
Everything is empty.

From out of our experience of the sky
The four great elements are also clear.

If a single olive rots,
They all rot.

When we see both sun and moon
All the planets and stars will be clear.

When we know there is one gold,
We ponder that everything is unchanging.

When we find a precious jewel
It will bring us everything we need and want.

When we have a single brocade
We have many kinds of silk.

When we hold to the king of vehicles,
The Universal Ti,

We will take hold of an infinity of vehicles,
With none excluded.

When we understand one word
We will understand all words.

When we understand one meaning,
We are the lords of all good things.

That is what he said.

This is Chapter One Hundred Six: Teaching that by an Understanding of the Universal Ti We Will Understand Every Dharma.

TEACHING THE WAYS THAT WE ATTAIN REWARDS FOR THE UNIVERSAL TI

Then Vajrasattva asked:

How are we to attain any reward
For the Universal Ti?

So did he address him.

Our teacher gave instruction to the audience:

Among the rewards for the yoga of the Universal Ti,
We observe a view where there is nothing to see.
We see the Bodhicitta,
Which is a reality where there is nothing to see.

There is no time in which we see it.
It is insubstantial.
It is a radiant self-awakening.

We meditate on a meditation
Where there is nothing to meditate on.
So we pacify the markings of our ideas,
In which there is nothing to pacify.

We involve ourselves in objectives
For which there is nothing to be done.

We succeed in all of our karmas,
Which are the deeds that we do.

We project ourselves into a reward
For which there is nothing to work toward.

We attain a spontaneous realization of the three bodies,
Where there is nothing to be attained.

We will actualize our own minds
Where nothing is done quickly.

We awaken from the darkness of ignorance,
While there is no time in which we awaken.

The sun of wisdom dawns,
While there is no time for any dawning.

We grow from out of the space of our hearts,
While there is no time for growing.

We attain the experiential radiance
Of the body of the Dharma
While we do not strive or practice.

We also teach about the space of our hearts
While there is nothing to teach.

We have an unchanging resolve.
We stamp the apparent world with our seal.

From out of the space of the unborn
We attain the unchanging body of the Dharma.

Clear appearance has no substance.
It becomes a body of perfect pleasure.

The many things are non-dual.
This is the body of manifest compassion.

The three bodies are inseparable.
They are one.

This is the body of an unspeakable great bliss.

We are all indivisible.
This is a body that is like a vajra.

The five bodies are a reality
That we attain with the Bodhicitta.

We attain such things,
And this is also our hope.

That is what he said.

From the Tantra on Kissing the Apparent World While Dripping an Elixir of Ambrosia to Cut through Samsara from Start to End, this is Chapter One Hundred Seven: Teaching the Ways that We Attain Rewards for the Universal Ti.

TEACHING THE NAMES OF THIS KING OF TANTRAS

Then Vajrasattva questioned the All Good himself
With these words:

What are the signs for the time that is our time?

So did he address him.

Our teacher gave instruction to the audience:

I will explain the names of this king of Tantras.

The apparent world is united
In a space of non-duality.
So Kissing the Apparent World
Is the king of the Tantras.

The juice of reality controls
The demons that are our emotional problems.
The Ambrosia that Removes Illnesses
Is the king of the Tantras.

We drip an elixir of instructions
On the illness of samsara.
Dripping Elixir and Concocting Medicine
Is the king of the Tantras.

We cut through all the roots
Of the start and ending of samsara.
So the Big Chisel Razor
Is the king of the Tantras.

We pray for those on the dangerous pathways
Of the general vehicles.
Opening Our Understanding to Take the Dangerous Pathway
Is the king of the Tantras.

We open our understanding
To the views and meditations of the eighty-four thousand.
The Key to Delusion
Is the king of the Tantras.

The meanings of the names are like that
For a start.

That is what he said.

This is Chapter One Hundred Eight: Teaching the Names of this King of Tantras.

TEACHING THE SEAL OF BEQUEST AND SPECIFICS ABOUT FIT RECIPIENTS

Vajrasattva questioned him again:

To which people do you bequeath this Tantra?

So did he address him.

The All Good himself gave instruction:

Those whose preferred positions are few
And whose faith is great,
Those whose avarice is small
And whose ability to give is great,
Those whose emotional problems are small
And whose knowledge is great,
Those whose attachments and cravings are small
And whose samaya are great:
To these I bequeath this king of Tantras.

A Master's mind is in his heart.
He safeguards the upadeśa instructions
As if they were his life.
He protects the samaya scriptures
And is careful about the maturation of events.

For the sake of the holy Dharma,
He gives his body and life without hesitation.

He is not attached to jewels and such things:
The good things we desire.
He offers them without hesitation.

His intellect is great.
His intellect is spacious.
He is sharp.
To him do I transmit and bequeath
This king of Tantras.

Those who have no samaya
And whose compassion is small,
Those who have no knowledge
While their desires are great,
Those who have no thought for lineage
While they deceive their brothers and friends,
Those whose perseverance is small
While their attachments and hatreds are great:
Up until the time that they acquire this
Their faces will be connected in purity,
But as soon as they get it into their hands
They will sell it as merchandise.

Moreover,
Just before they die
They will be made to eat wet meat and blood.
After that,
They will both fall into hell.
Their sin is greater than that
Of moving poison through the ocean.

This being so,
Do not teach!
It is proper to be secretive.

This is not a Dharma
For those who are not fit recipients.

That is what he said.

From the Tantra on Kissing the Apparent World while Dripping an Elixir of Ambrosia to Cut through Samsara from Start to End, this is Chapter One Hundred Nine: Teaching the Seal of Bequest and Specifics about Fit Recipients.

TEACHING THE TIME THAT THE TEACHING WILL COME FORTH

Then Vajrasattva questioned the All Good himself
With these words:

There will come a time in the future,
A time when this Tantra will come forth.
What about that?

So did he address him.

Our teacher gave instruction to the audience:

At the time this king of Tantras comes forth
The teachings about our bodies and speech will have failed.
The blessings of the word of the Sugatas will have faded.
It will be a time for the spread
Of the teachings of the heart.
At that time,
This Tantra of mine will come forth.

When our home foundation is surrounded
By the trenches of war,
When the most venerable make disturbances among the ranks,
When monks work as businessmen,
When we stick knives beneath our Dharma robes,
When the most venerable ones take wives,
When the very venerable ones work at the concoction of poisons:

That is the time when this king of Tantras will come forth.

When most of the people wear black,
When our shoes and hats are made out of our hopes,
When humans survive by fraud and deceit,
We will not be free from our five kinds of attachment and hatred.

We will carry our views in our mouths.
We will not turn back our cravings.
We will say that the Buddha is now.
This is the time that the body of the Dharma
Will spread the Great Perfection.

When there is no merit in the Dharma,
That will be the time this king of Tantras will come forth.
When the Sugatas are not able to bless things,
When the elements are not able to treasure things,
When the dakinis are not able to care for the bequest,
When the intellects of those who are born and live
Are not able to care for the bequest:
That is the time when this king of Tantras will come forth!

That is what he said.

From the King of Tantras on Kissing the Apparent World while Dripping an Elixir of Ambrosia to Cut through Samsara from Start to End, this is Chapter One Hundred Ten: Teaching the Time that the Teaching Will Come Forth.

The King of Tantras on Kissing the Apparent World while Dripping an Elixir of Ambrosia to Cut through Samsara from Start to End in One Hundred Ten Chapters is finished.

The Master from Urgyan Padmasambhava
And the Tibetan translator Kawa Paltsek translated this.

They bequeathed it to the child of god Trisong Detsen.
Then it was hidden as a treasure of great price.

The Seal of Treasure!
The Seal of Hiding!
The Seal of Bequest!

Samaya!

TIBETAN MANUSCRIPT

Images from the rNying ma rgyud 'bum mTshams brag dgon kyi bri ma, National Library, Royal Government of Bhutan, Thimpu, 1982. 46 Vols. Volume 10, pp. 259-399.

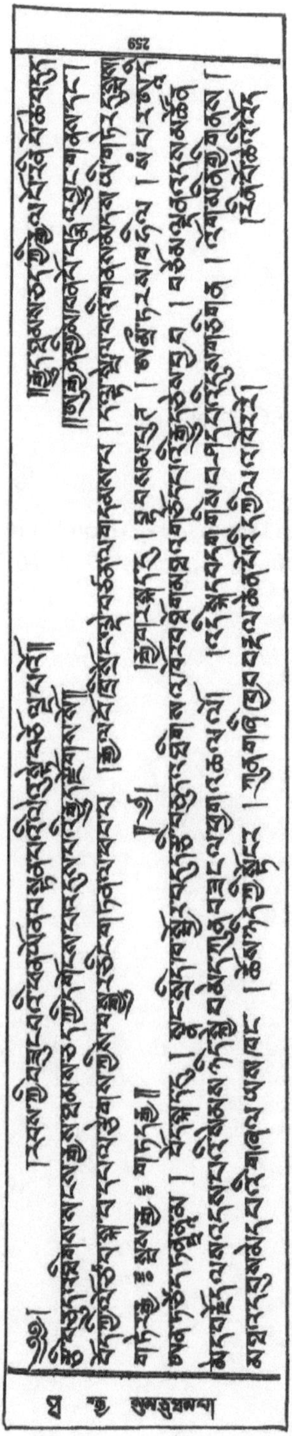

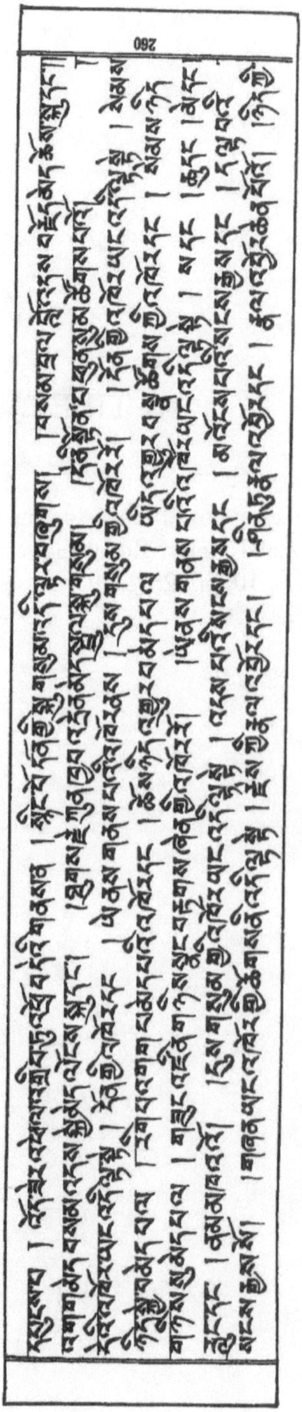

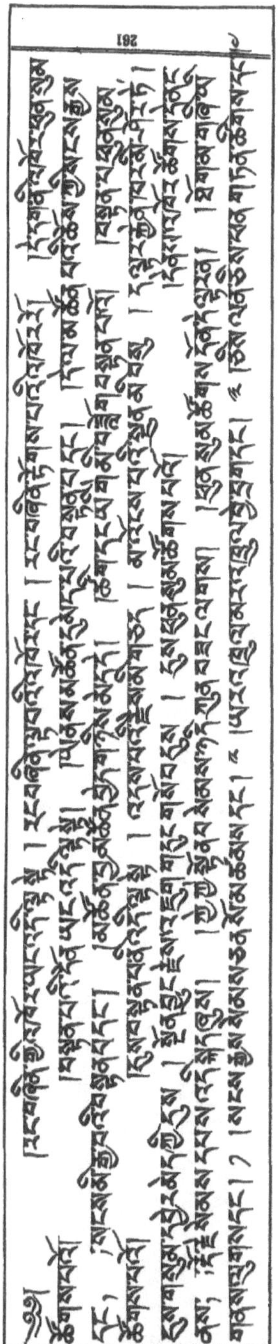

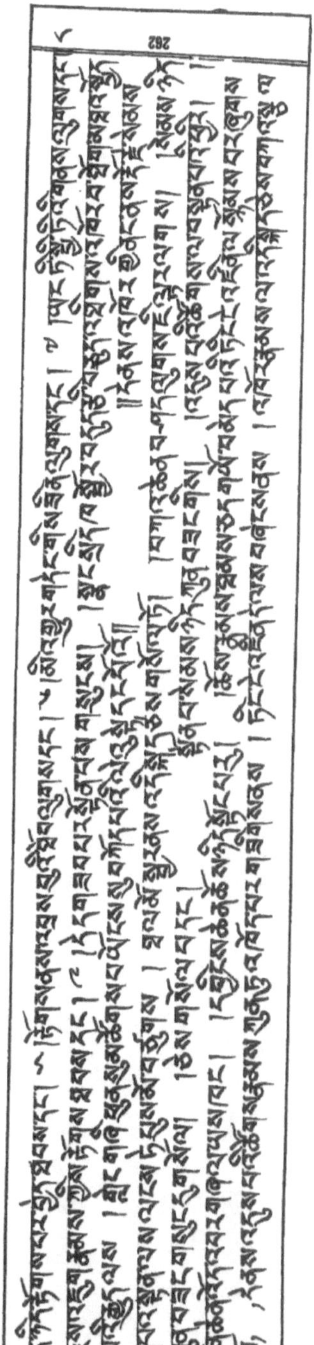

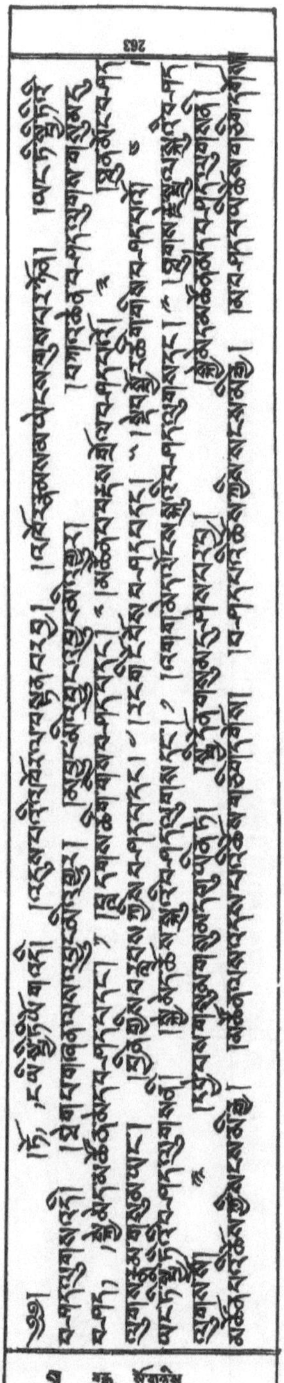

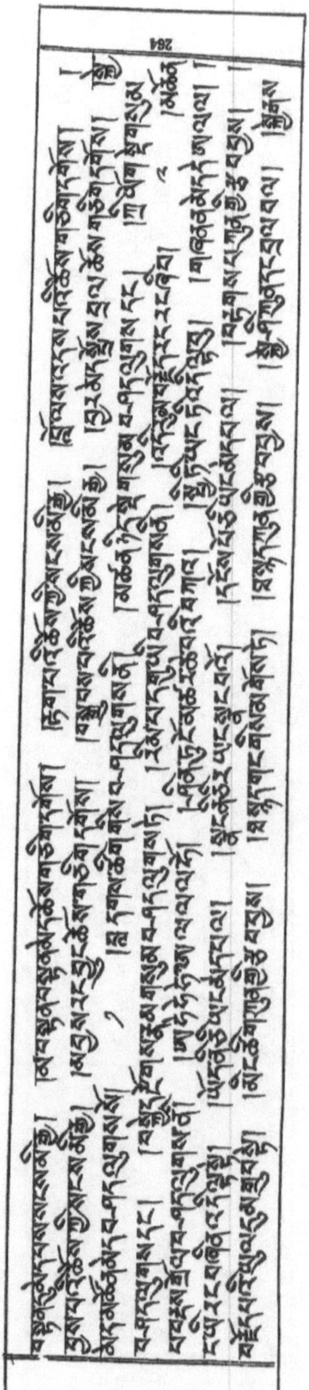

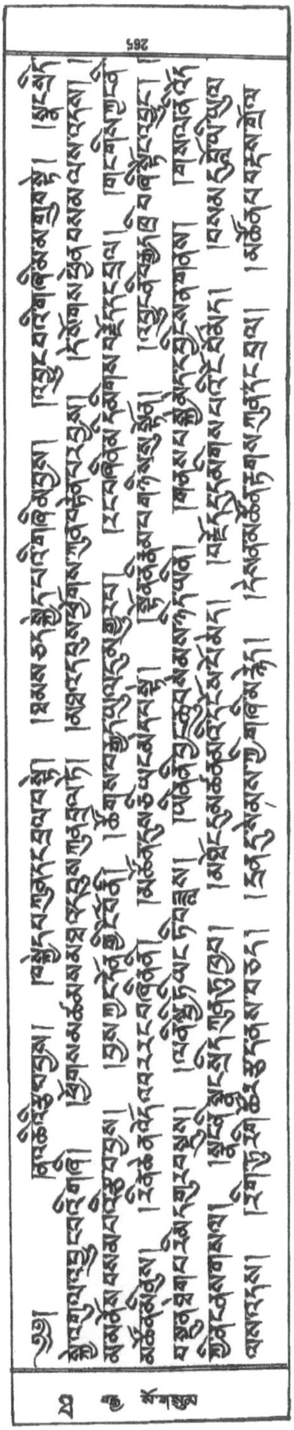

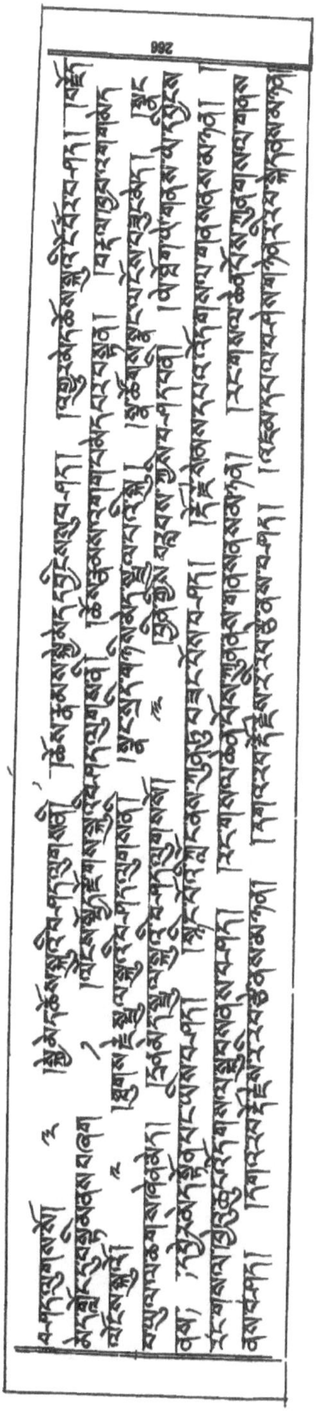

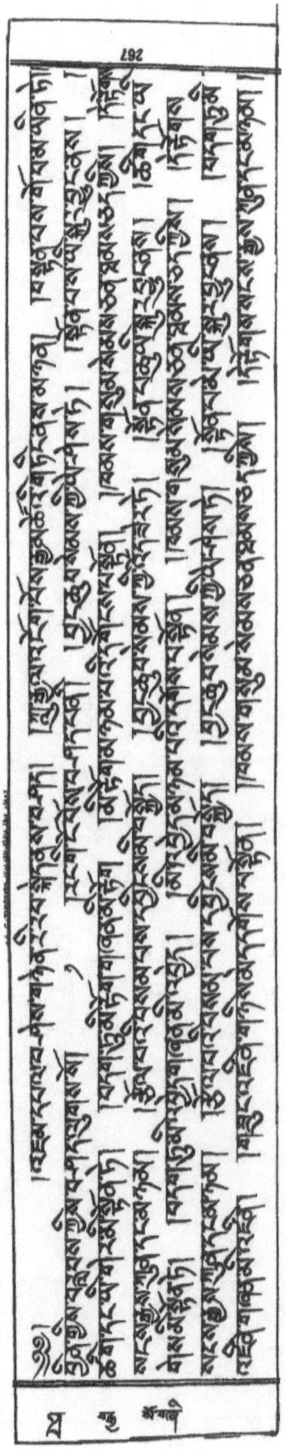

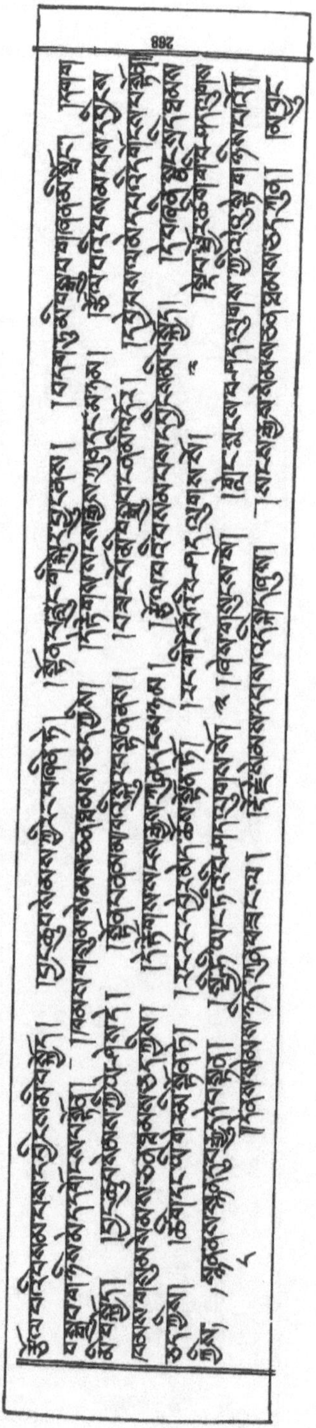

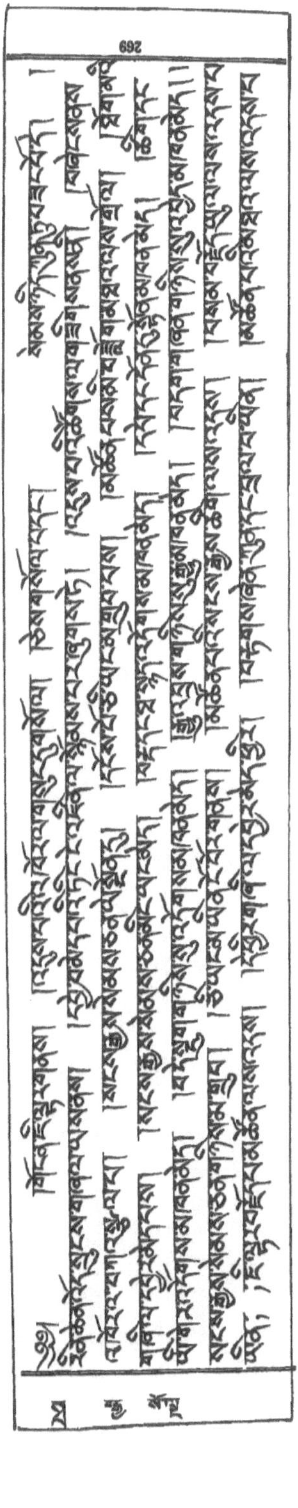

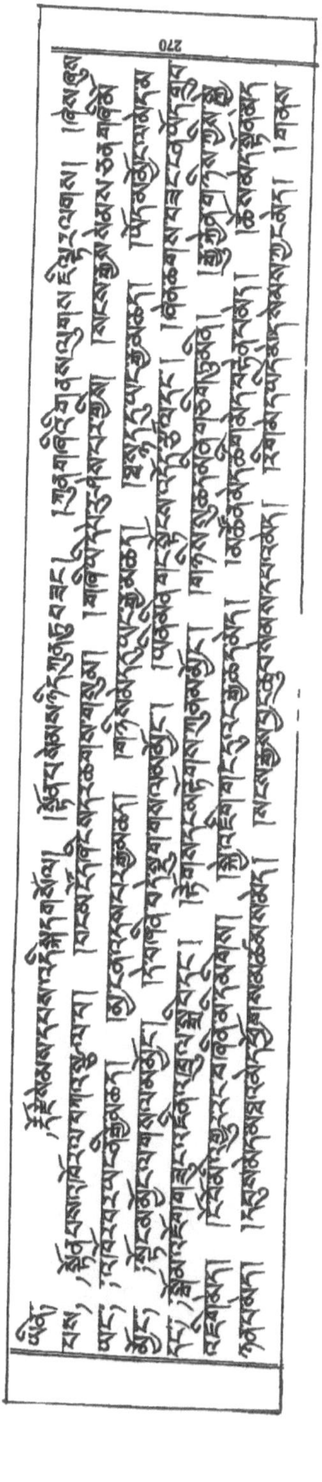

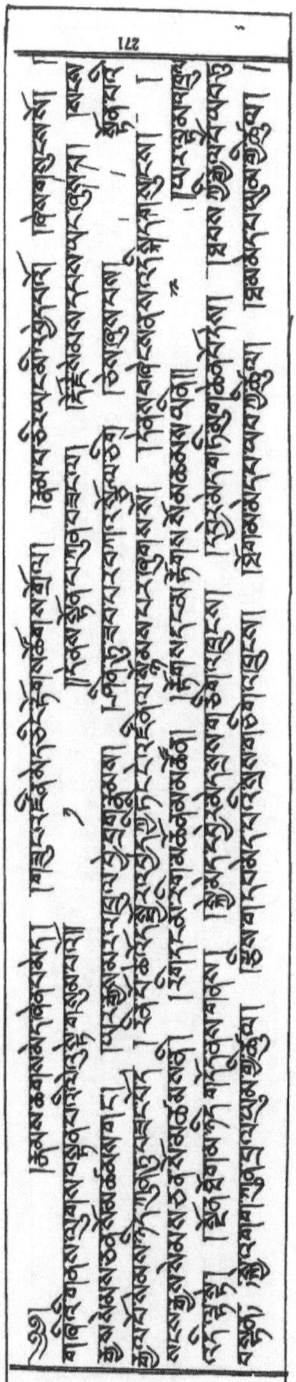

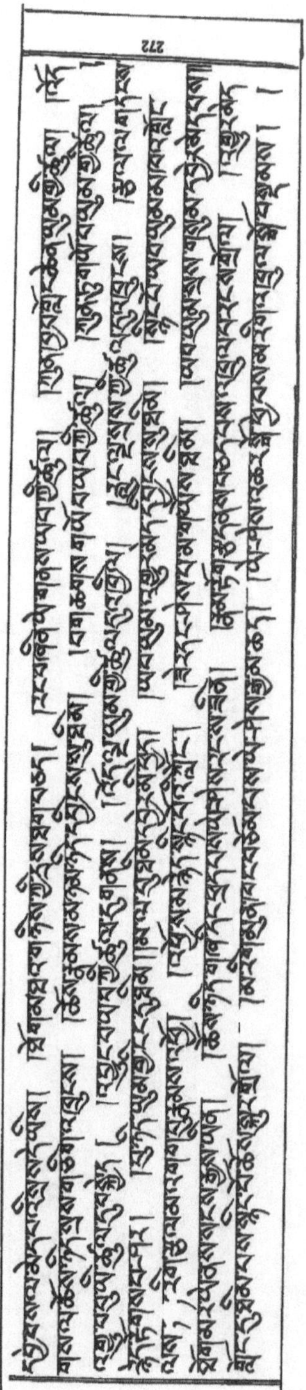

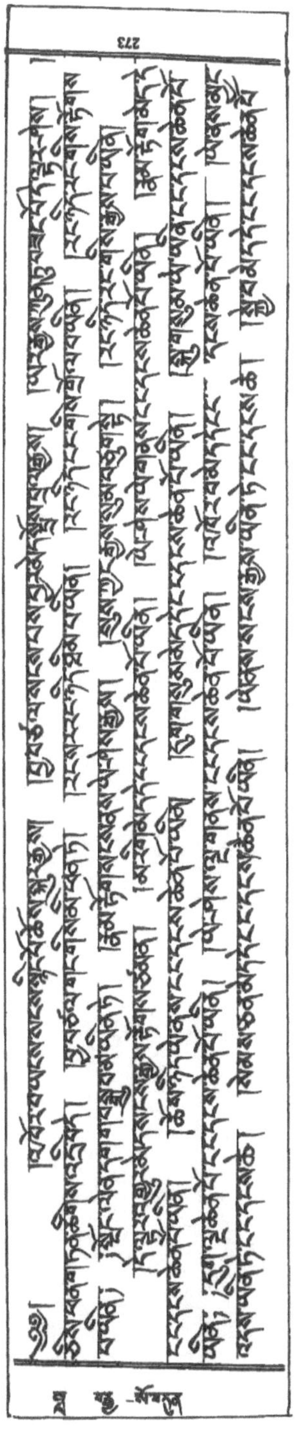

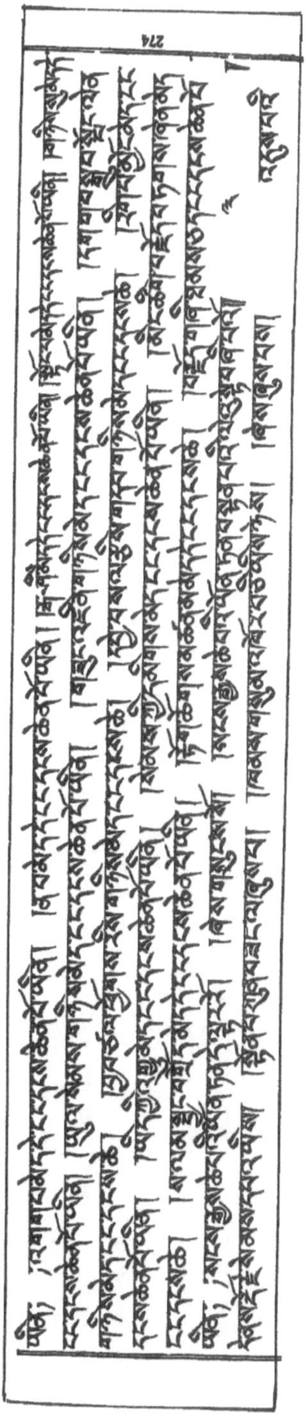

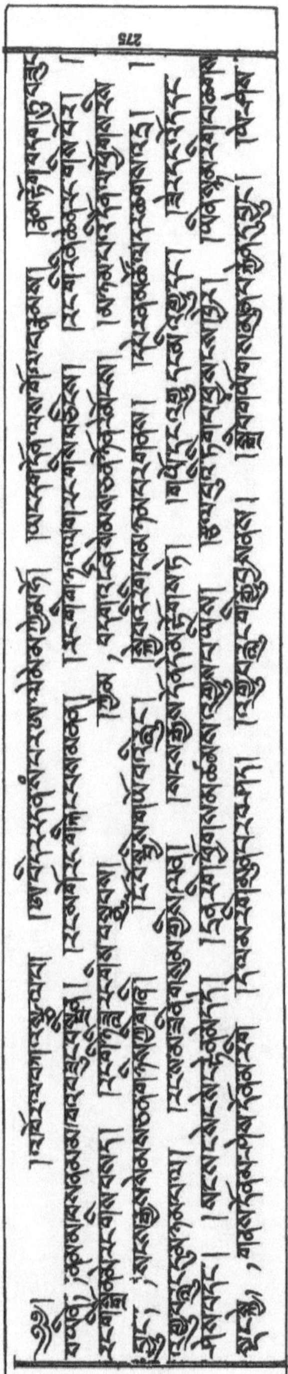
275

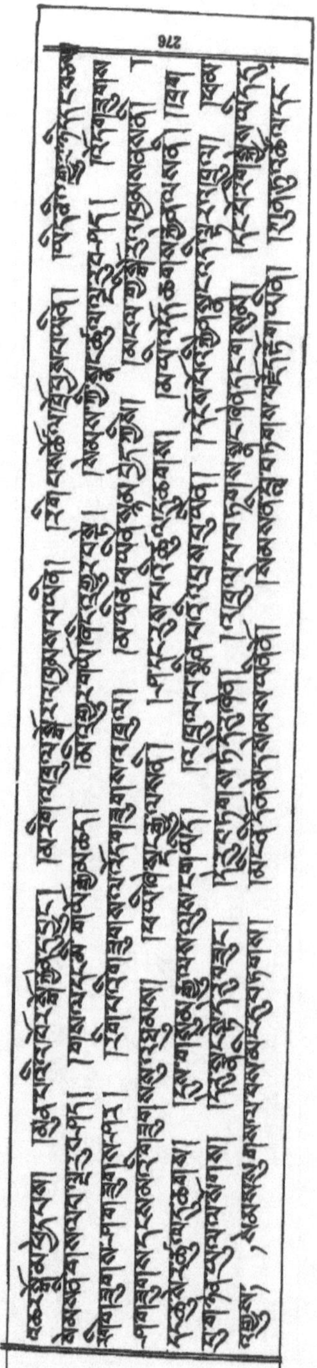
276

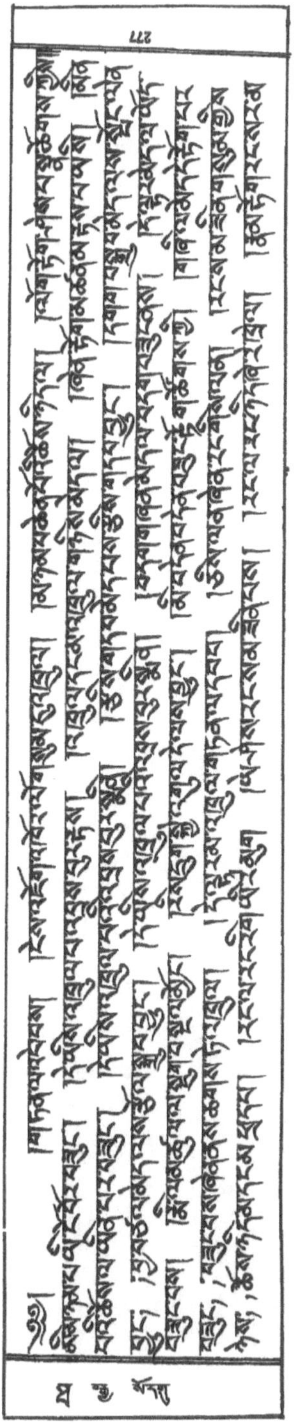

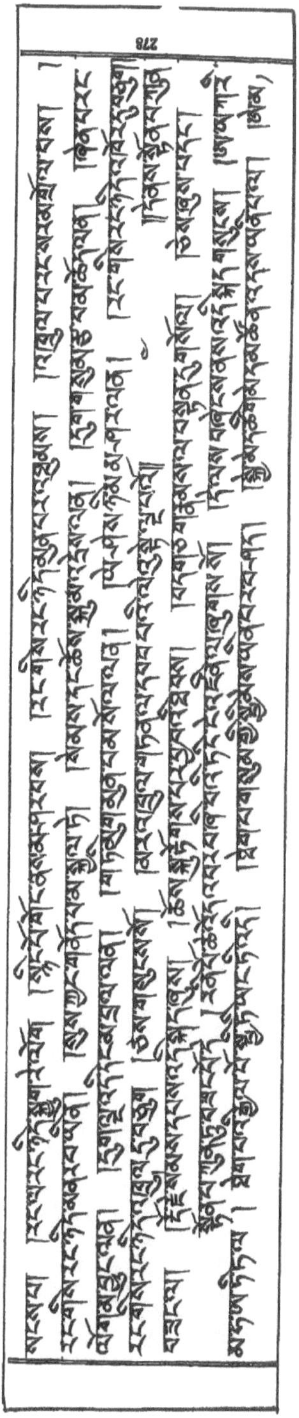

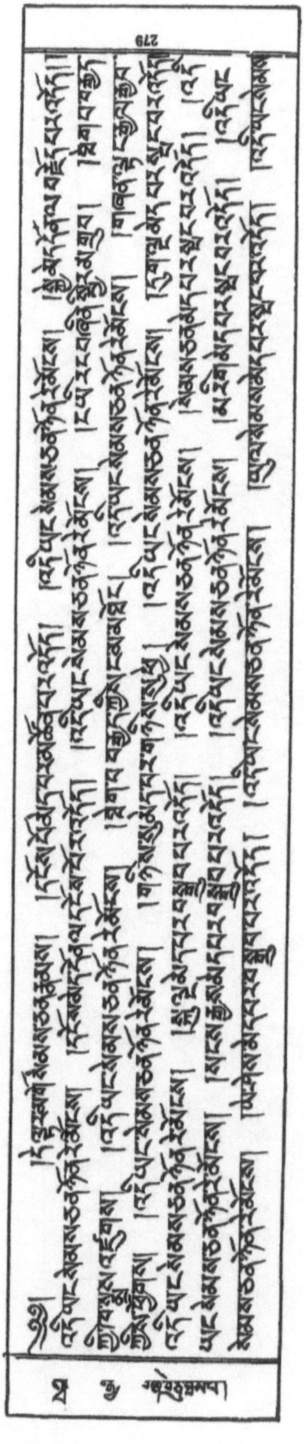

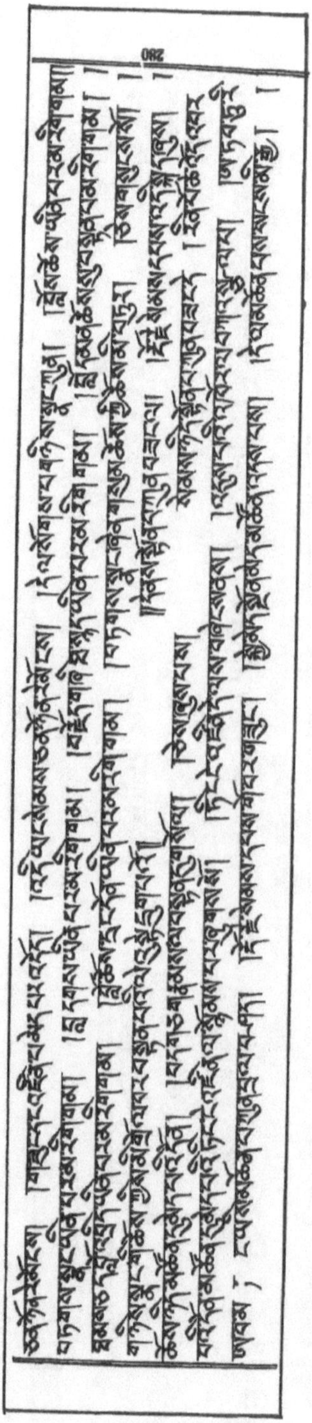

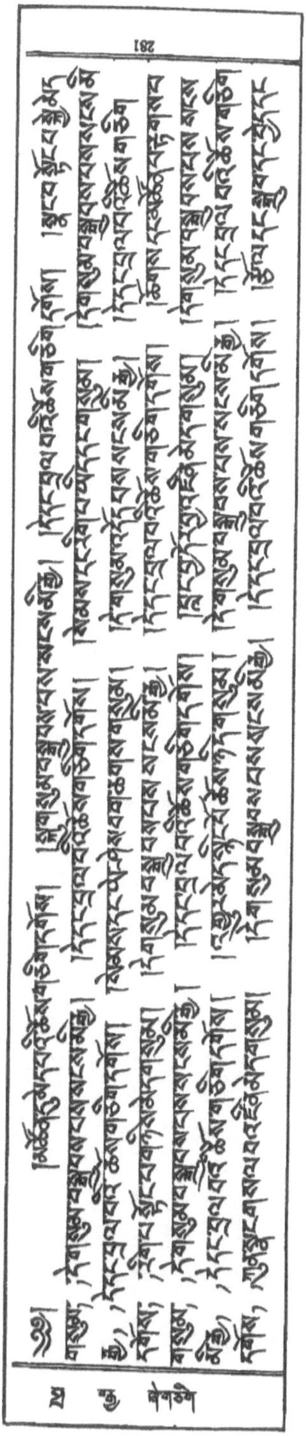

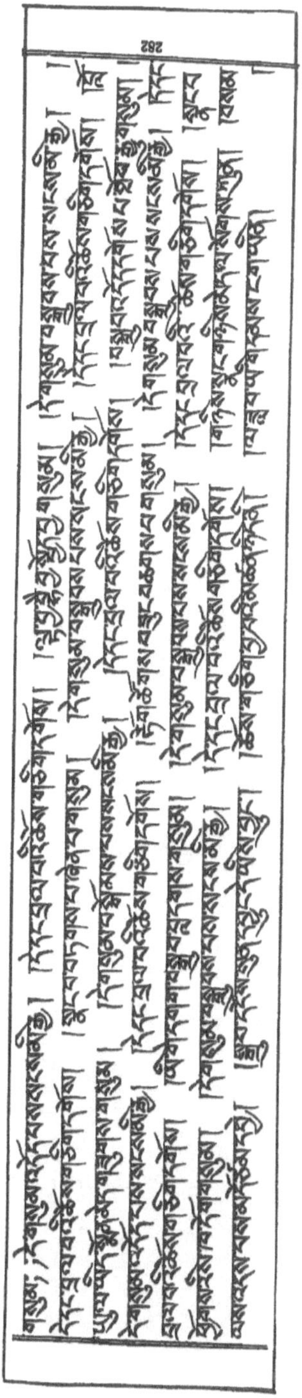

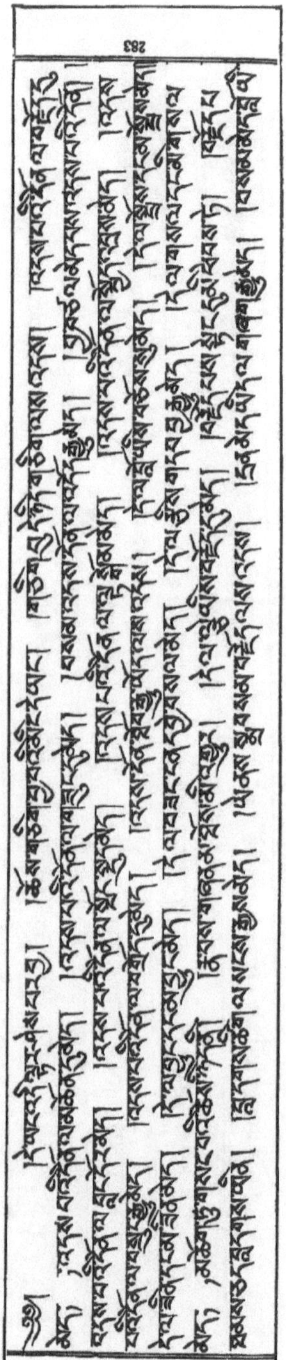

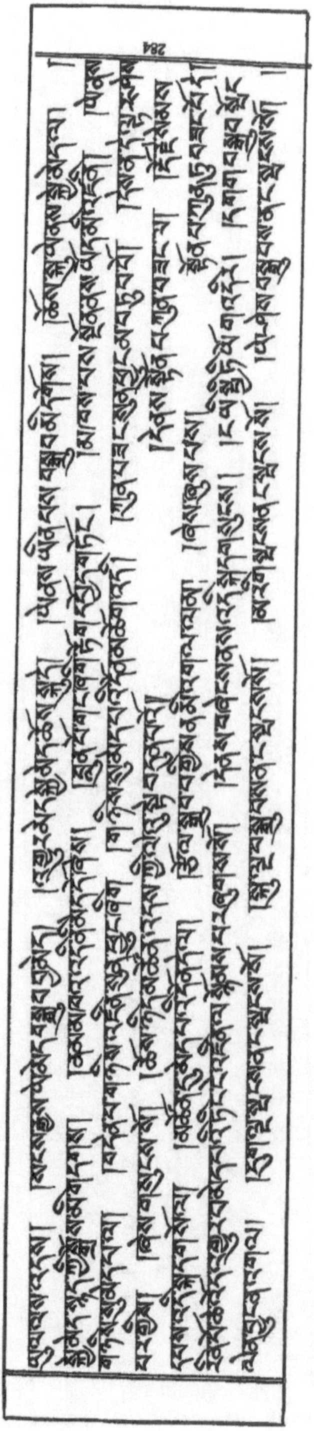

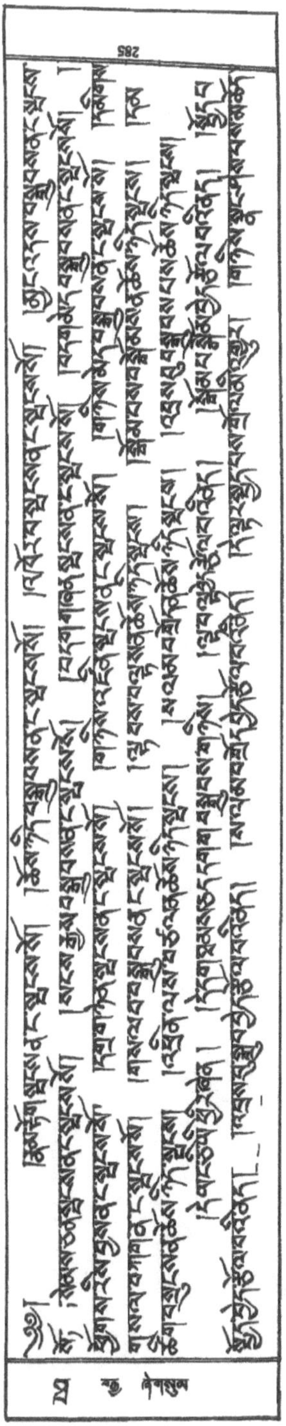

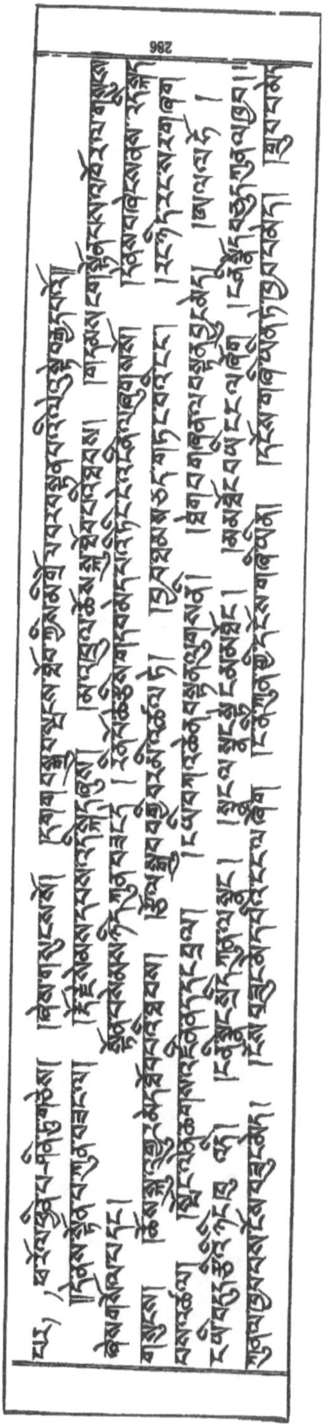

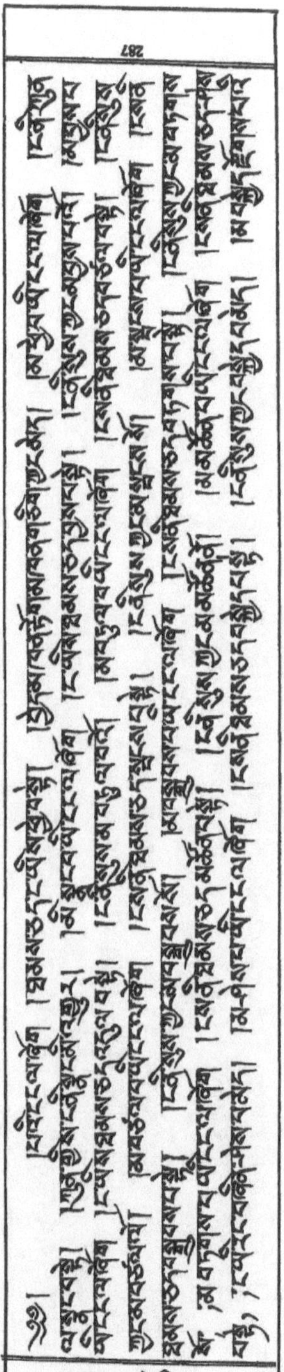

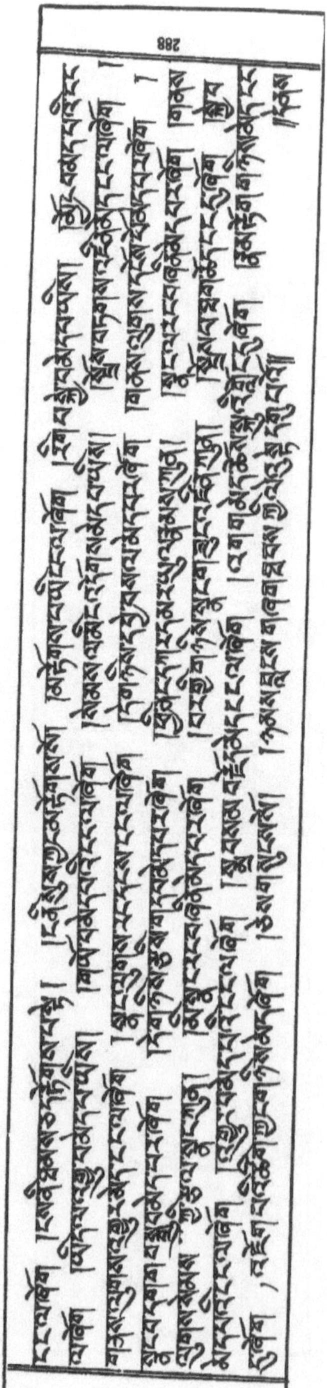

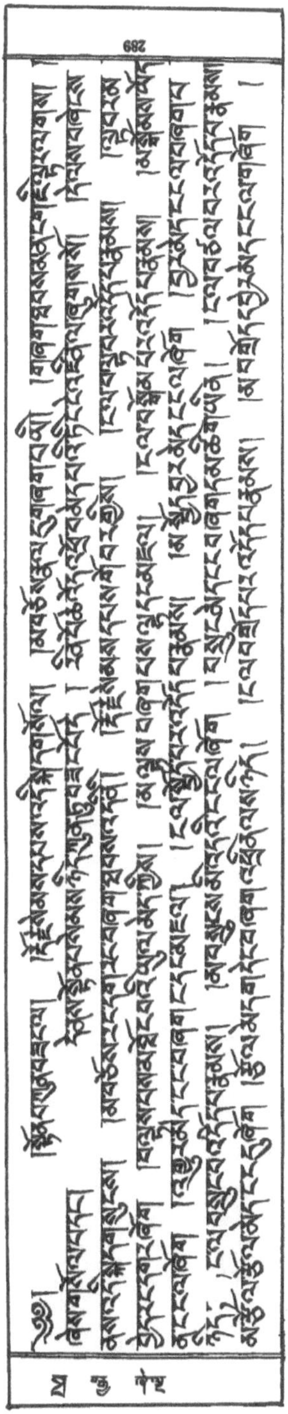

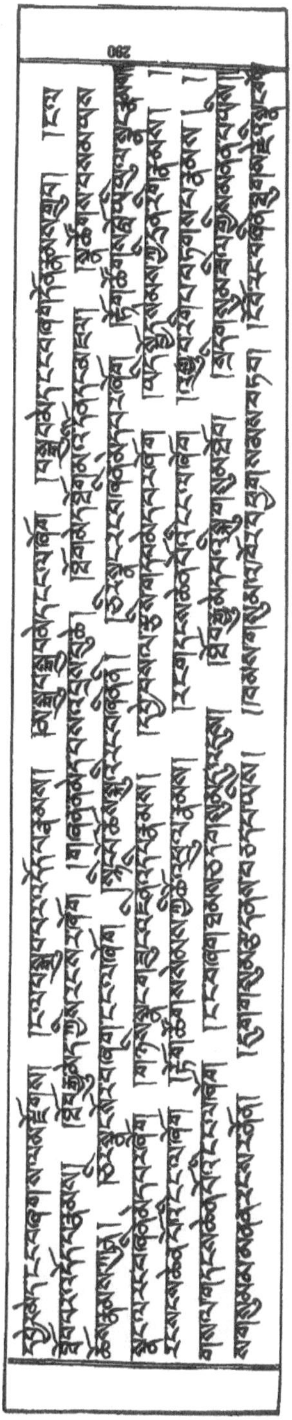

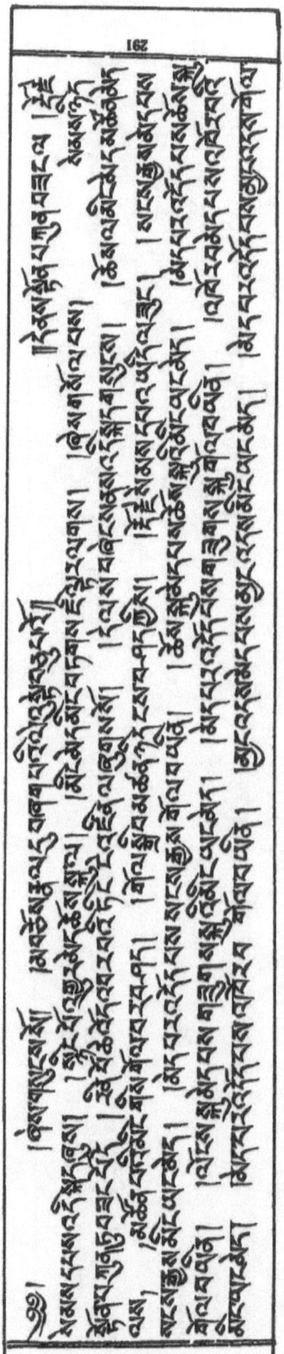

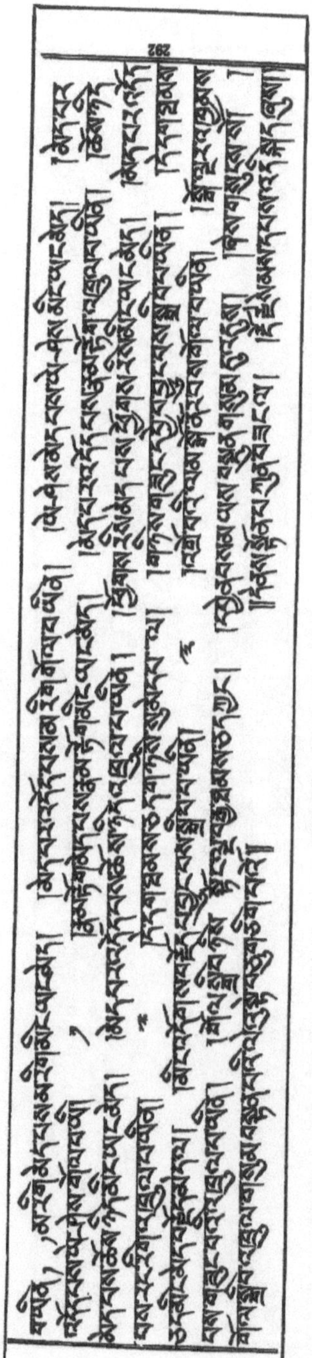

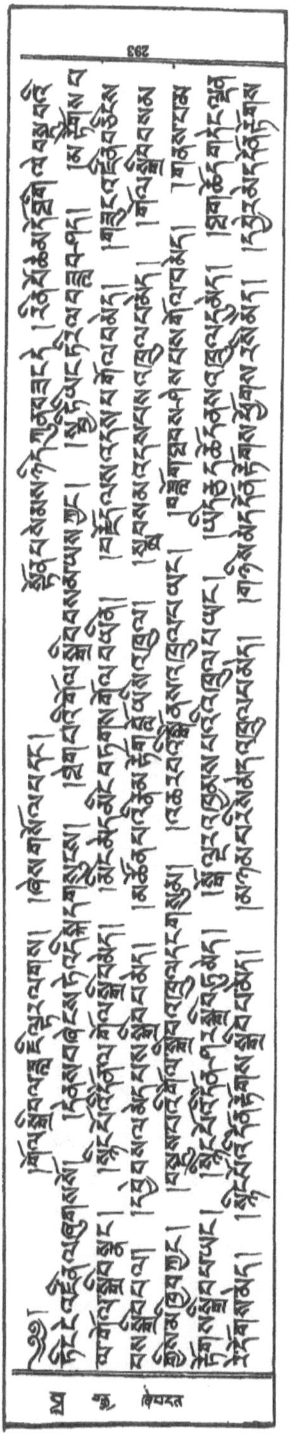

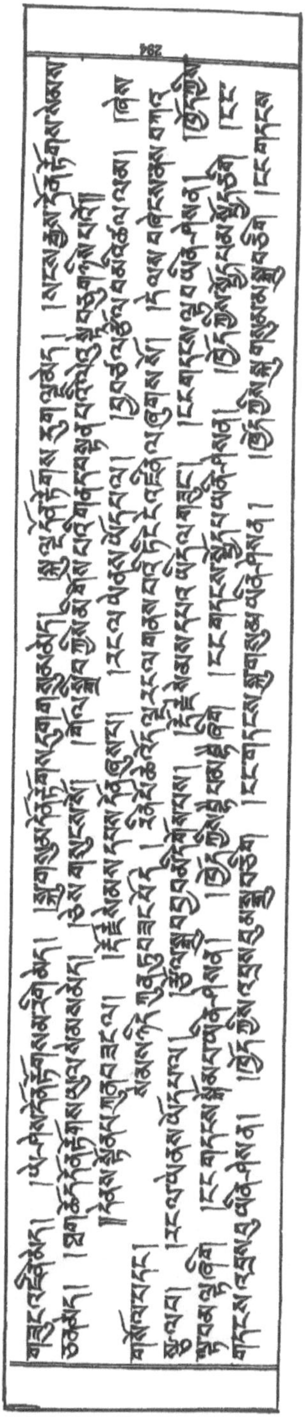

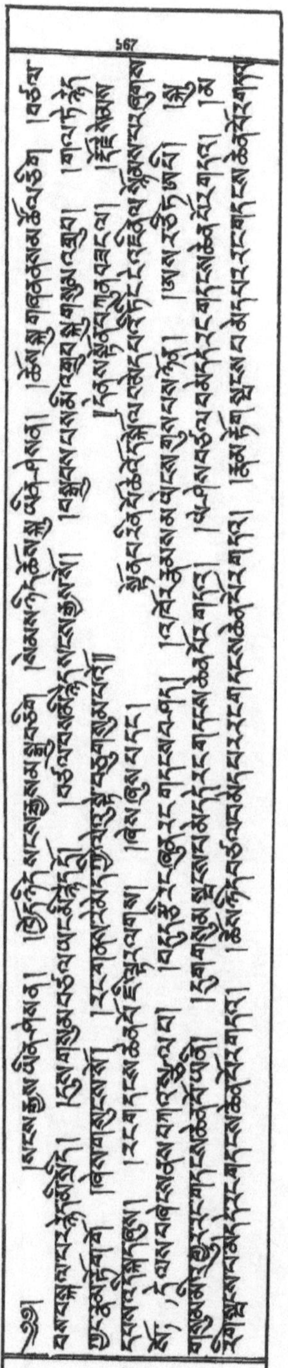

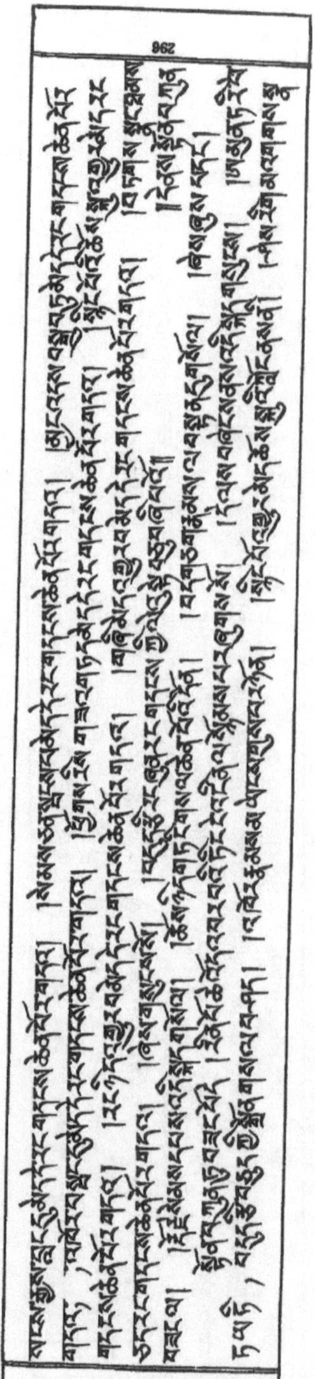

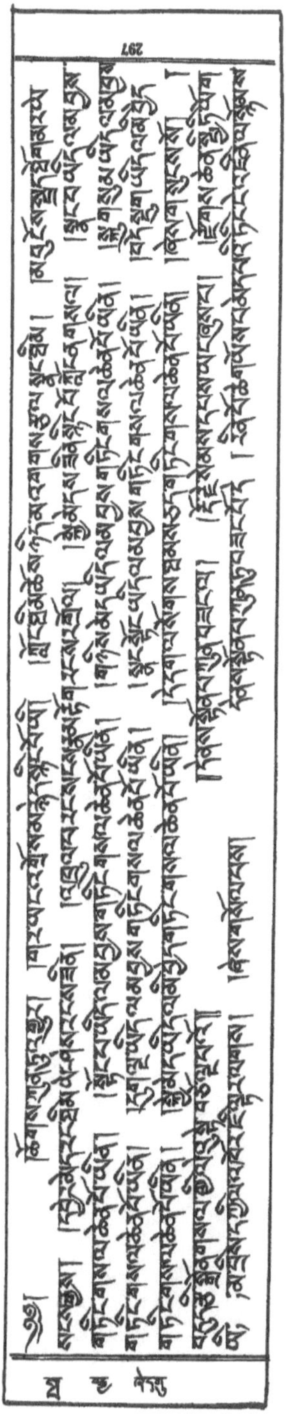
297

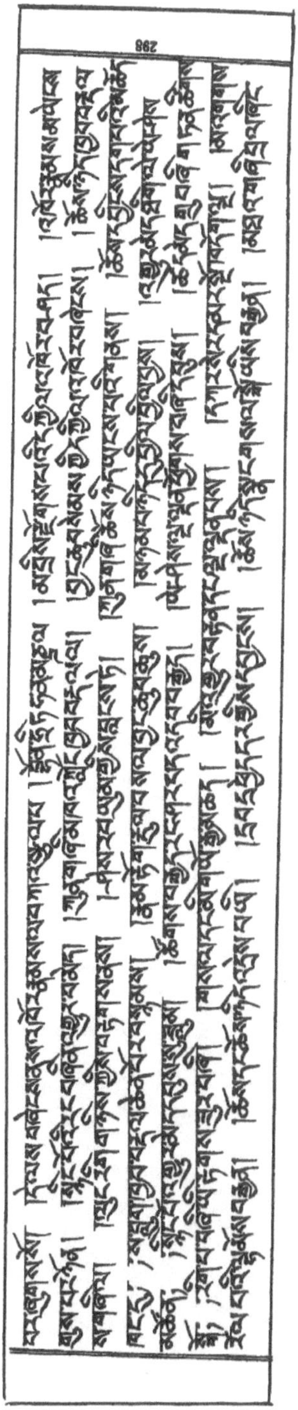
298

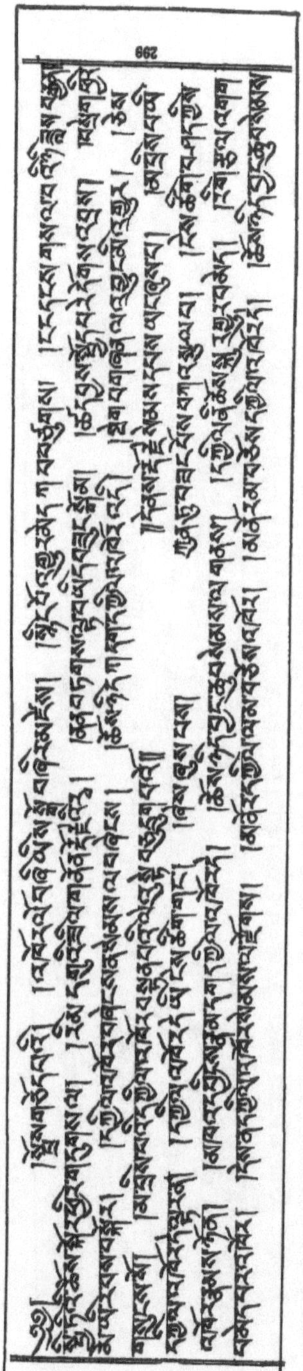

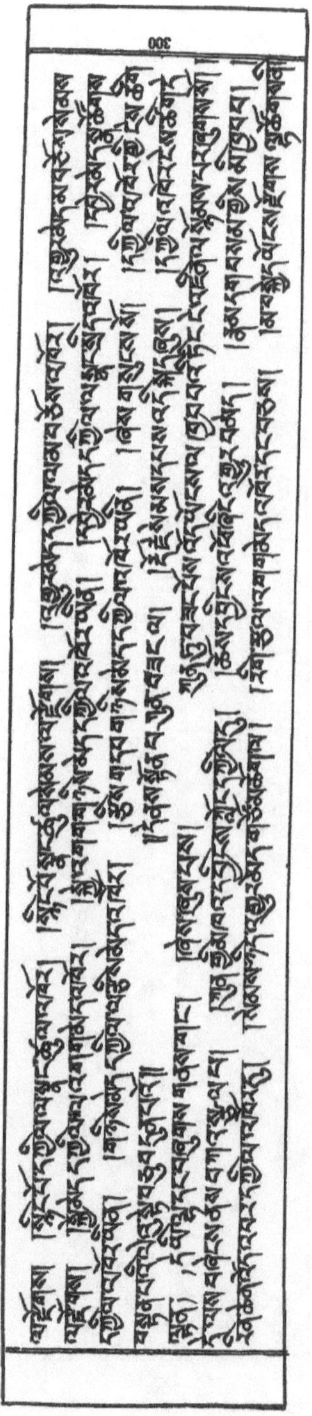

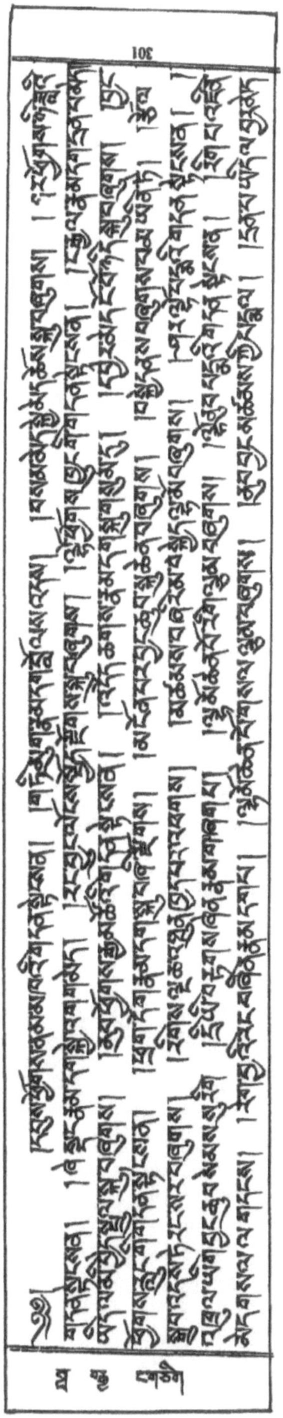

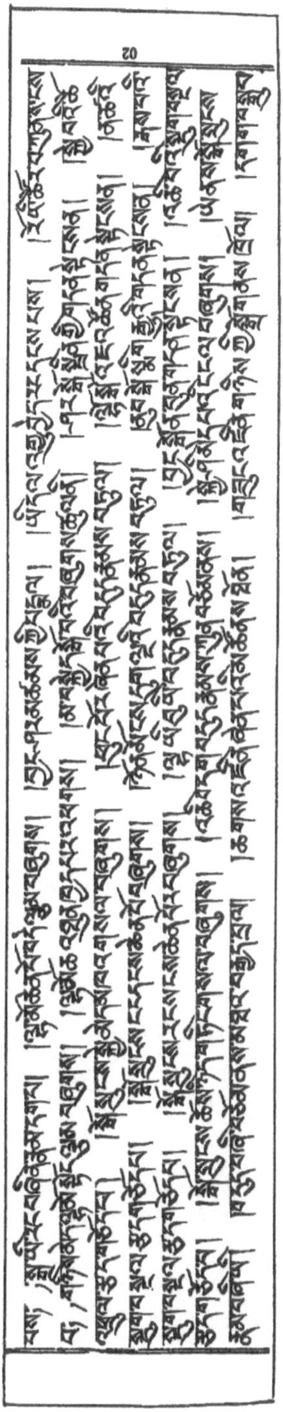

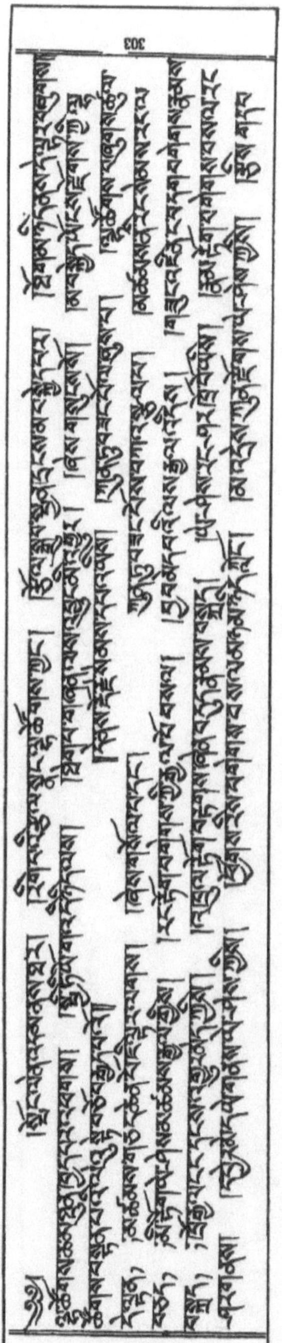

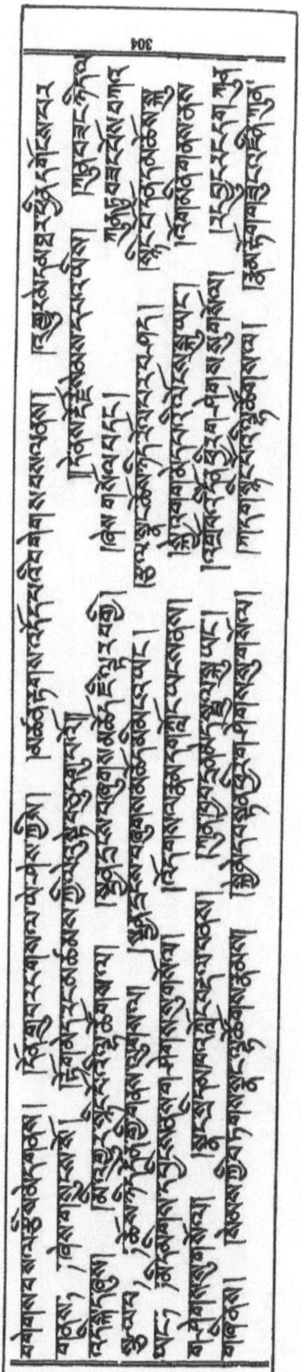

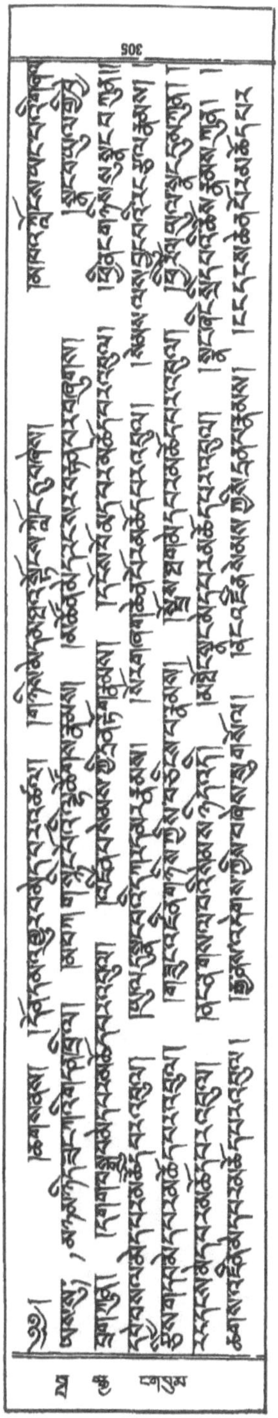

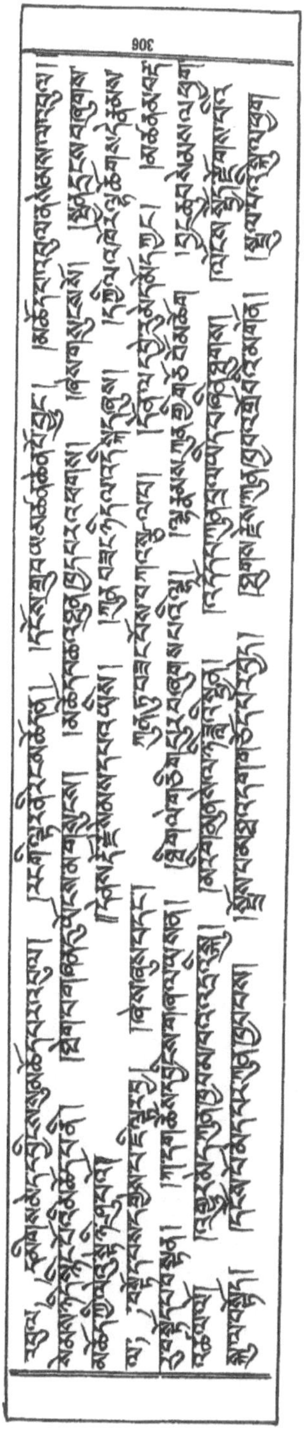

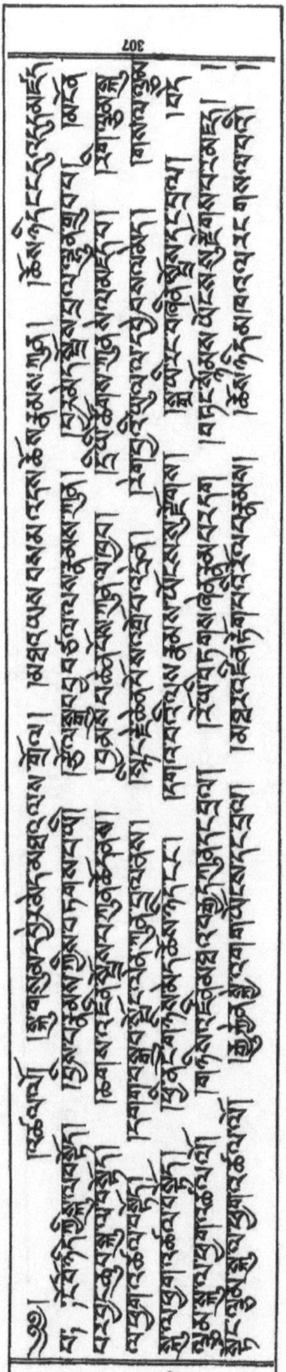

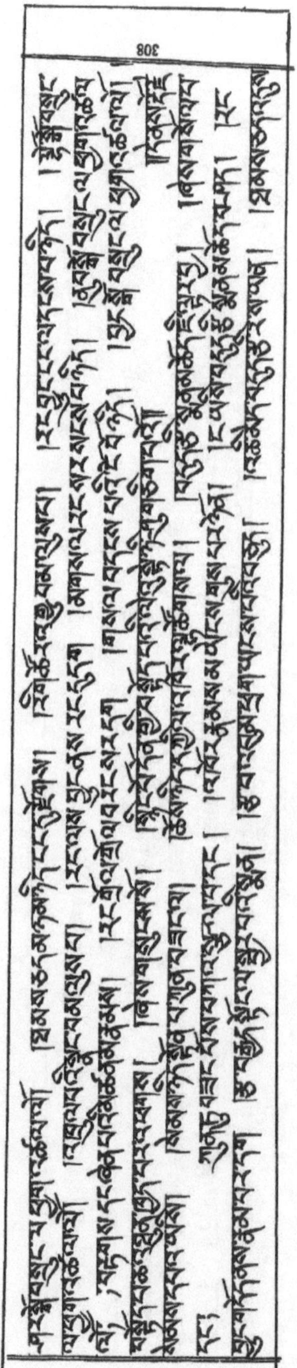

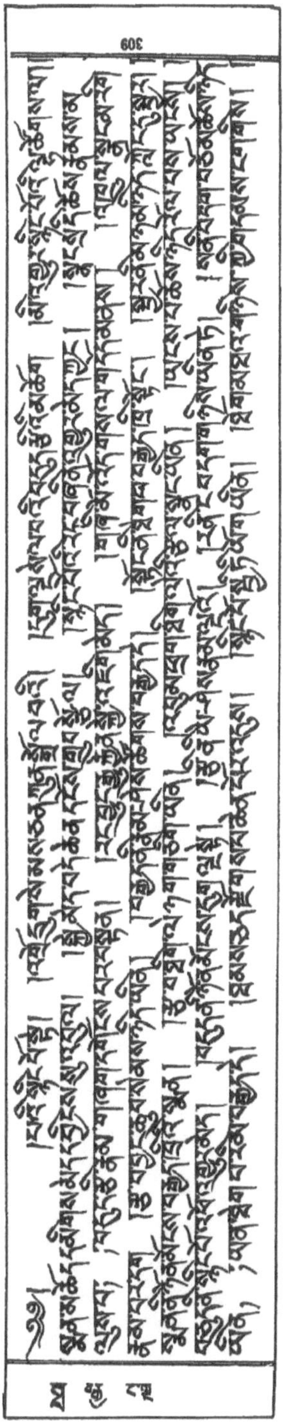

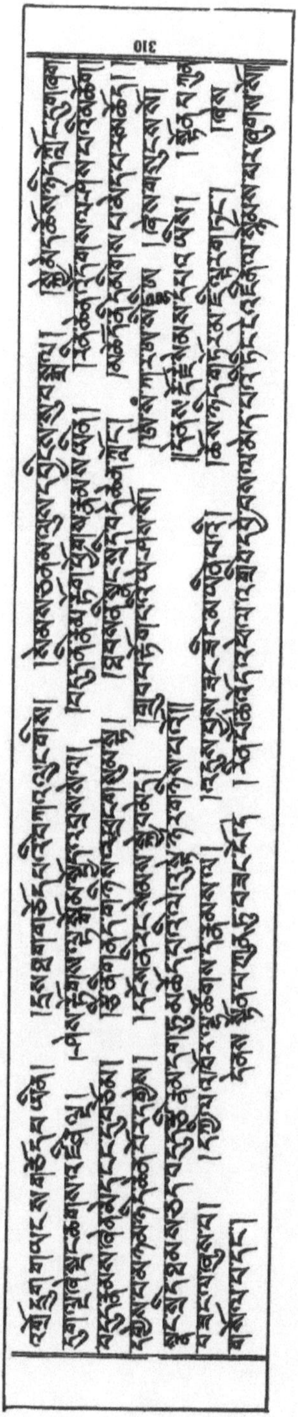

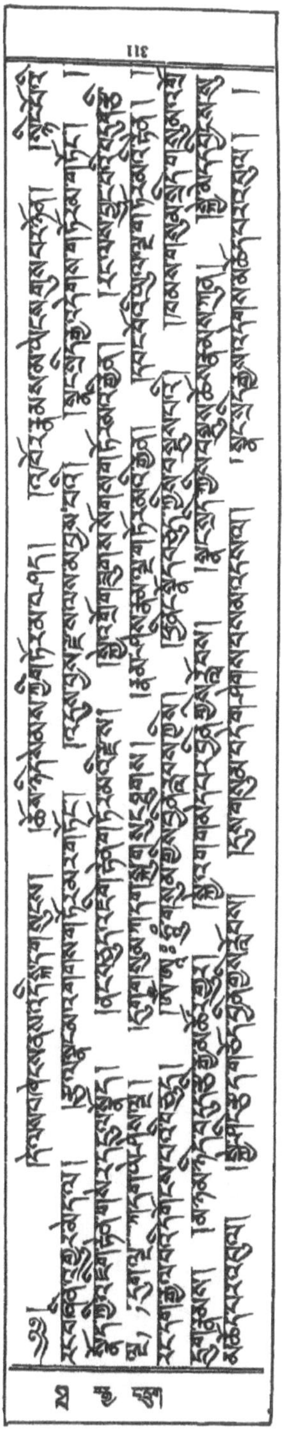

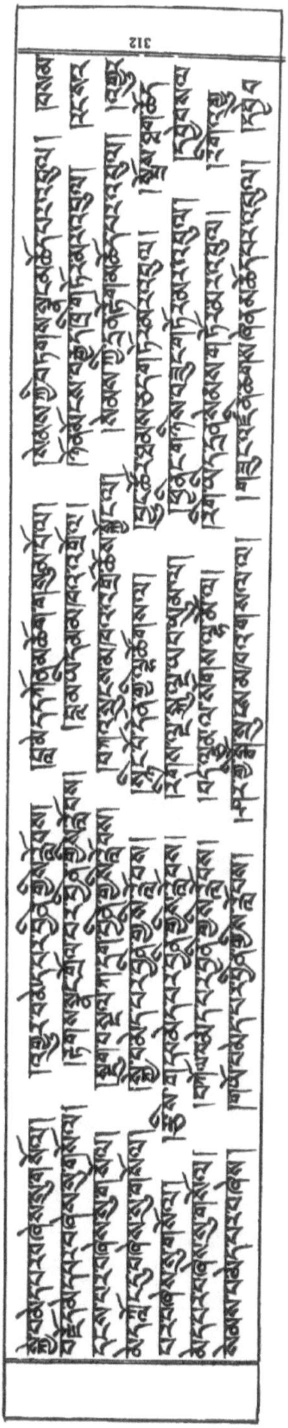

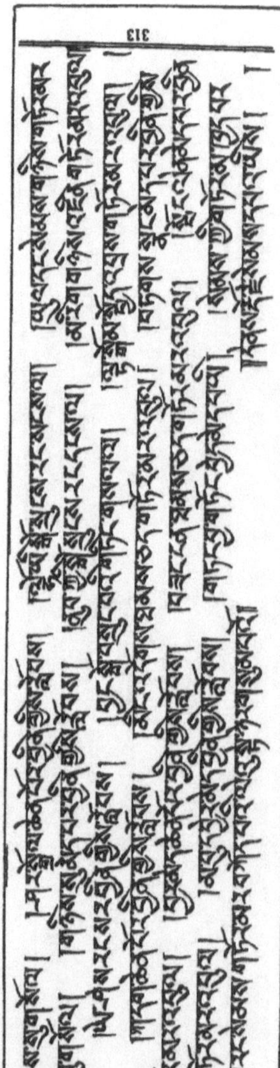

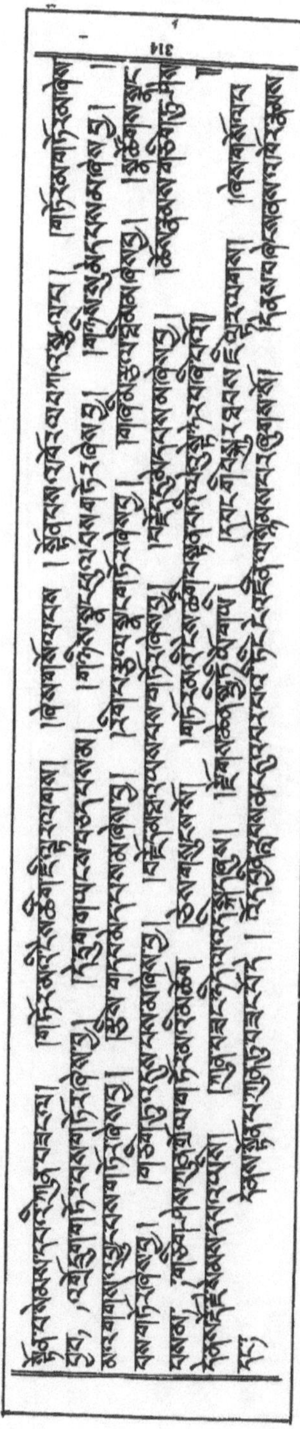

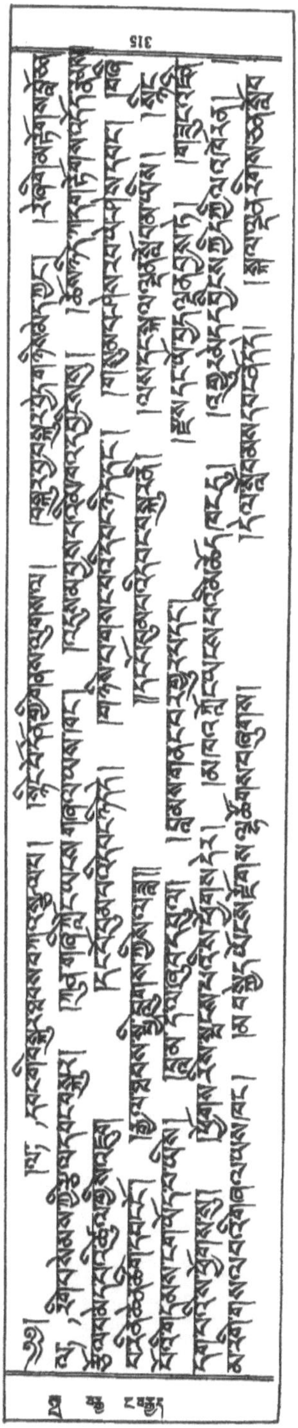
315

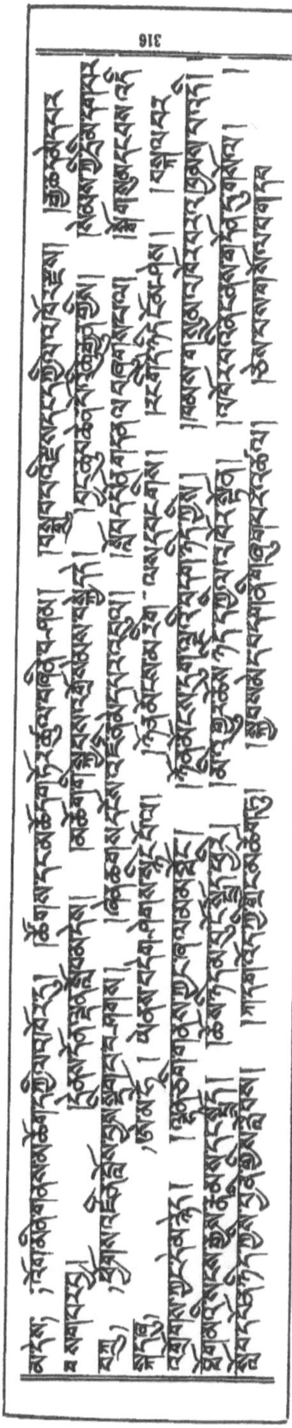
316

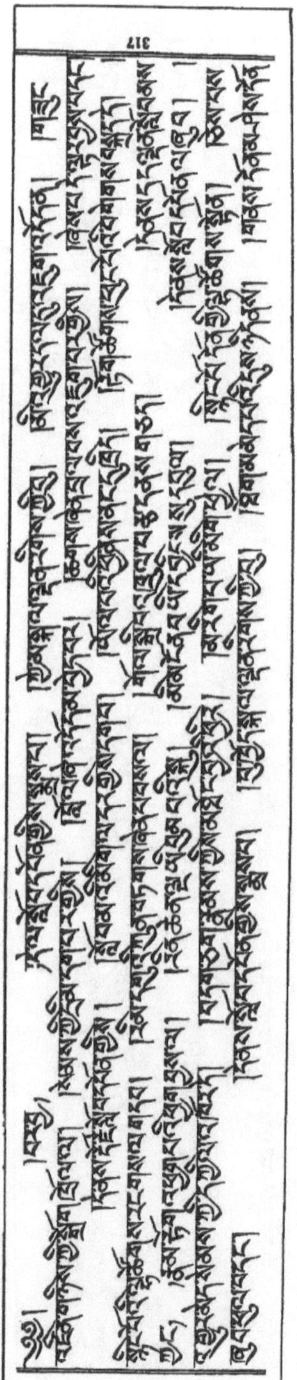

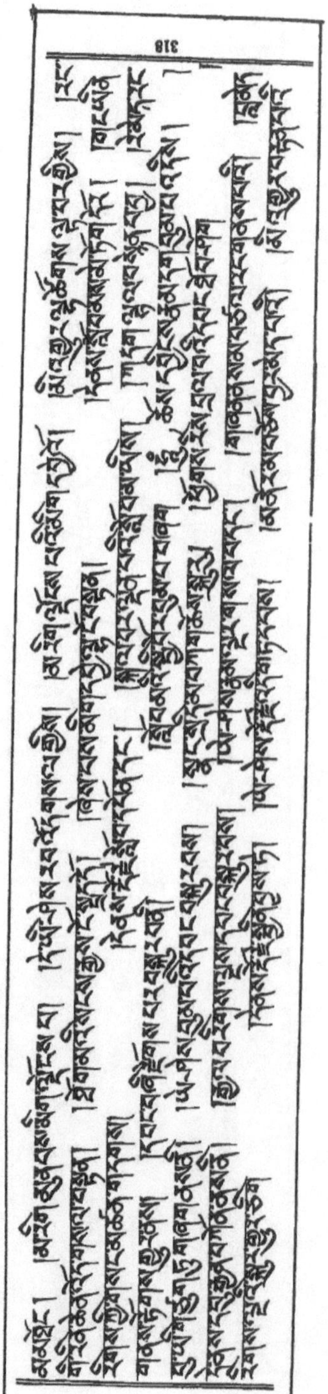

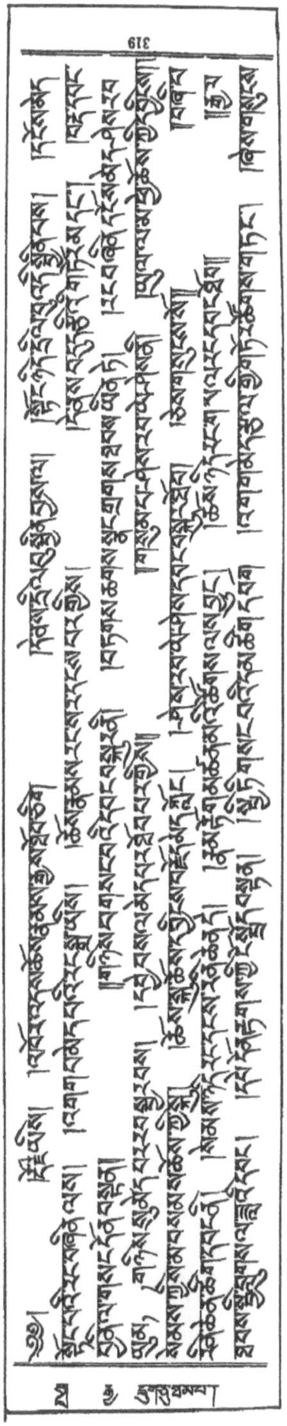

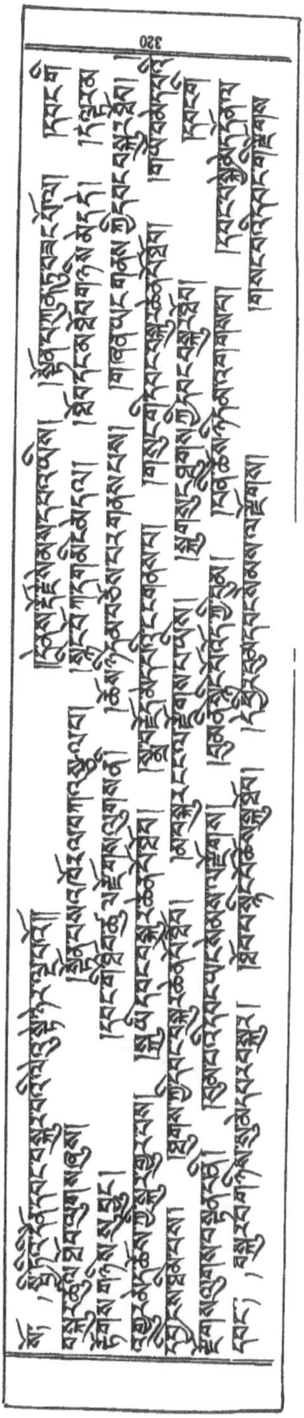

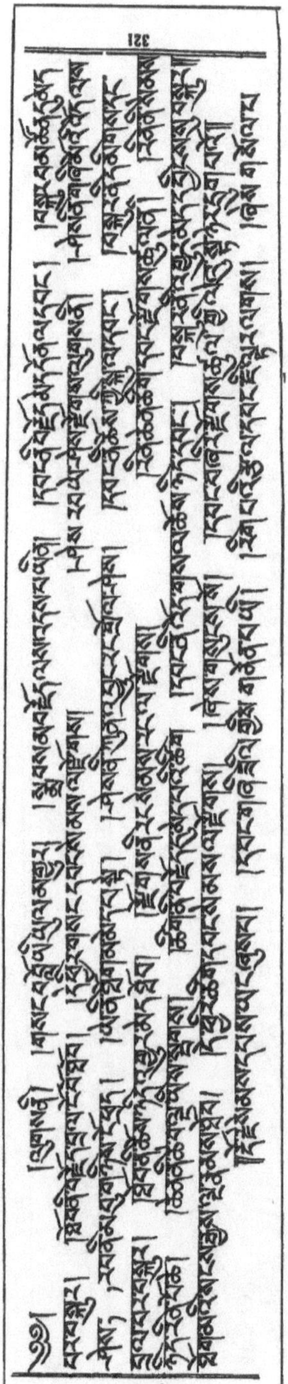

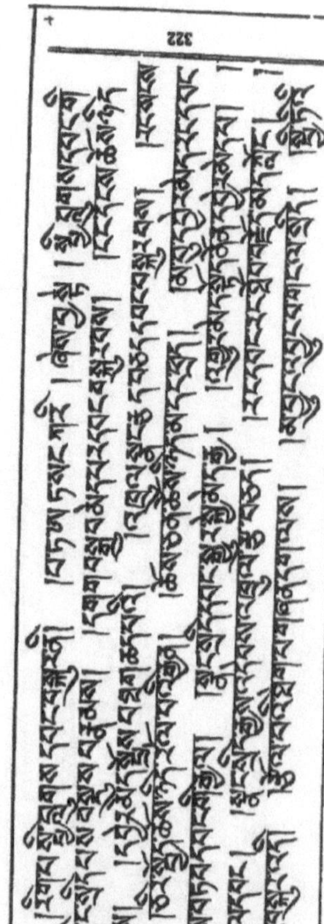

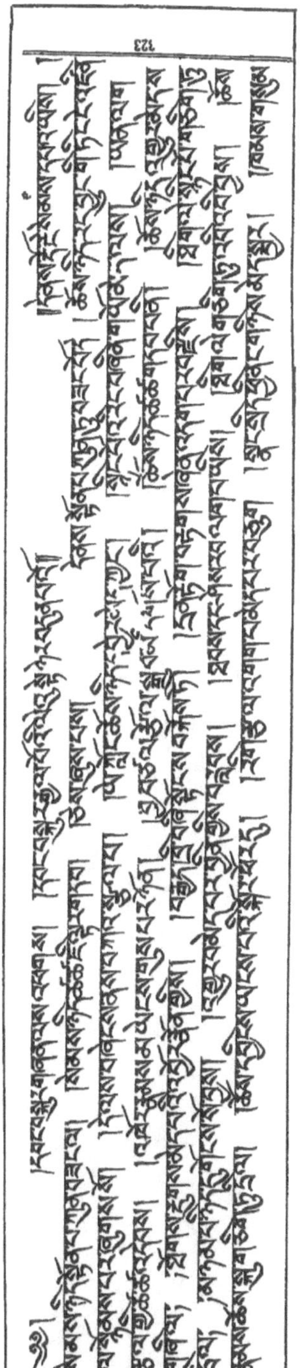

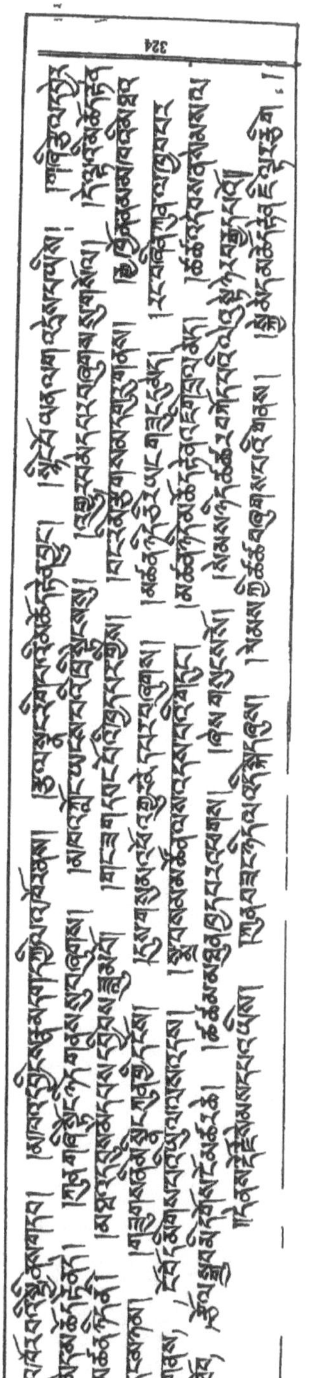

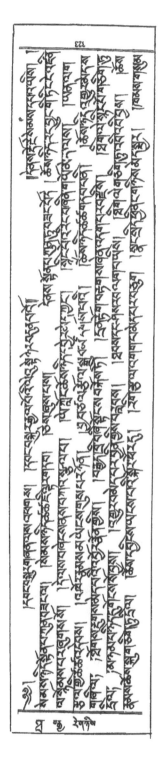

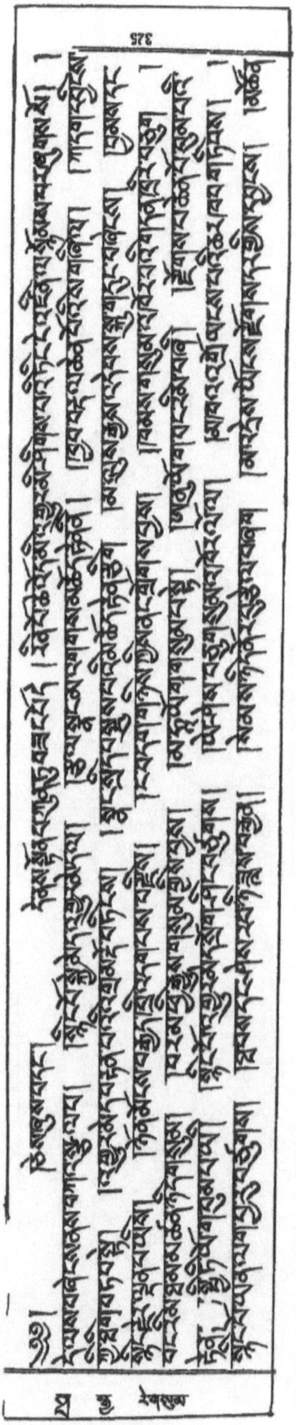

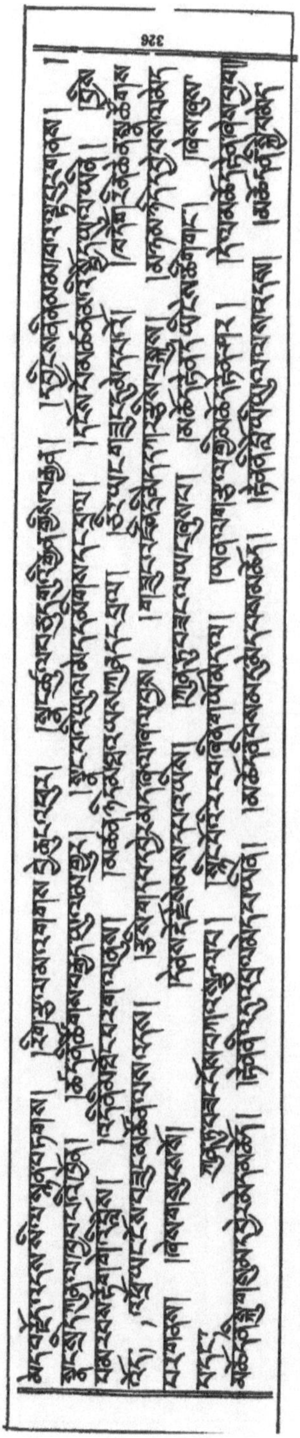

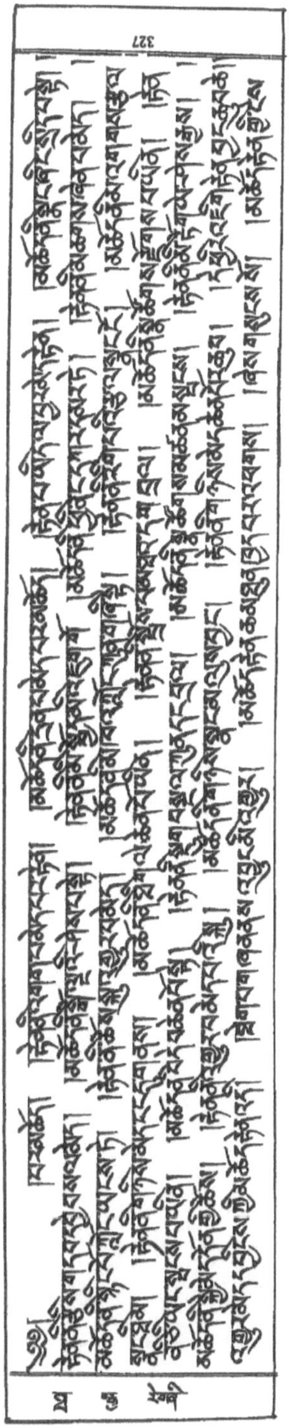

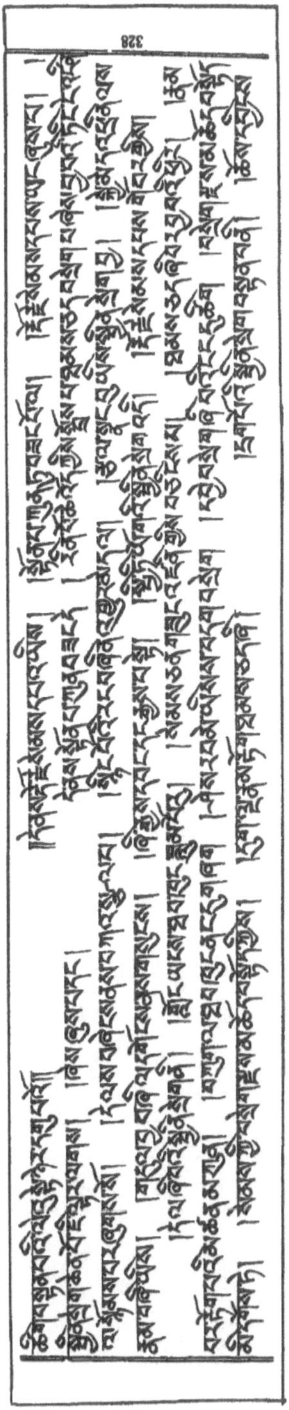

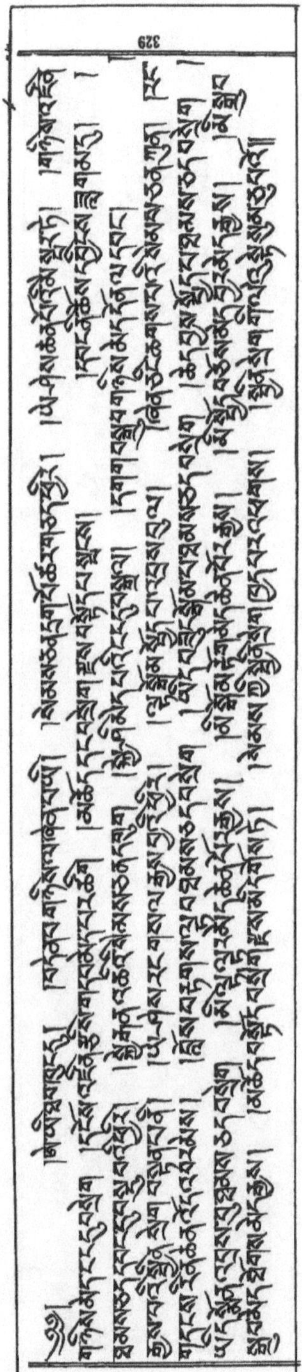
329

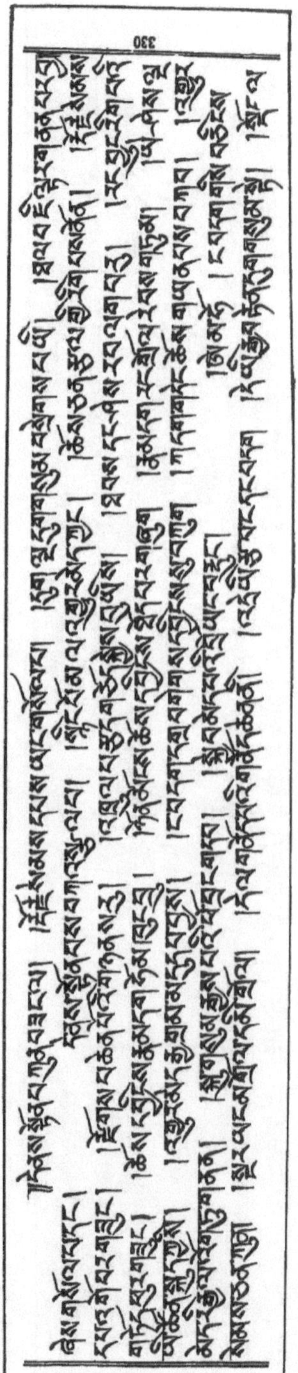
330

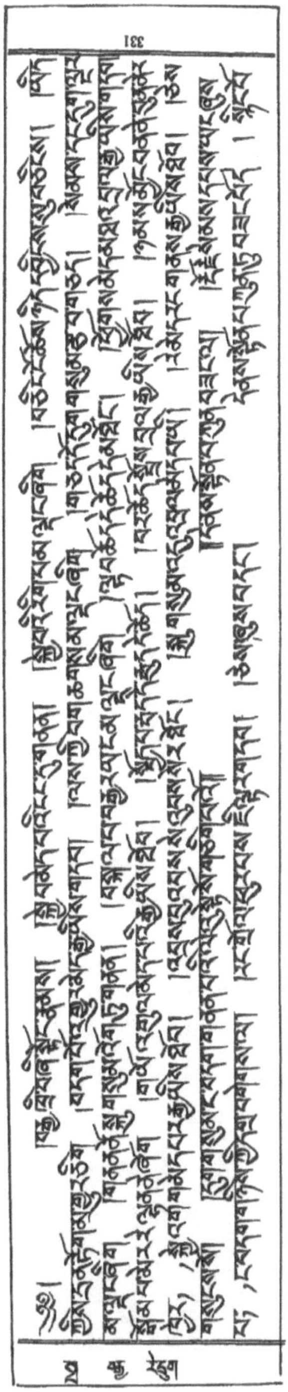

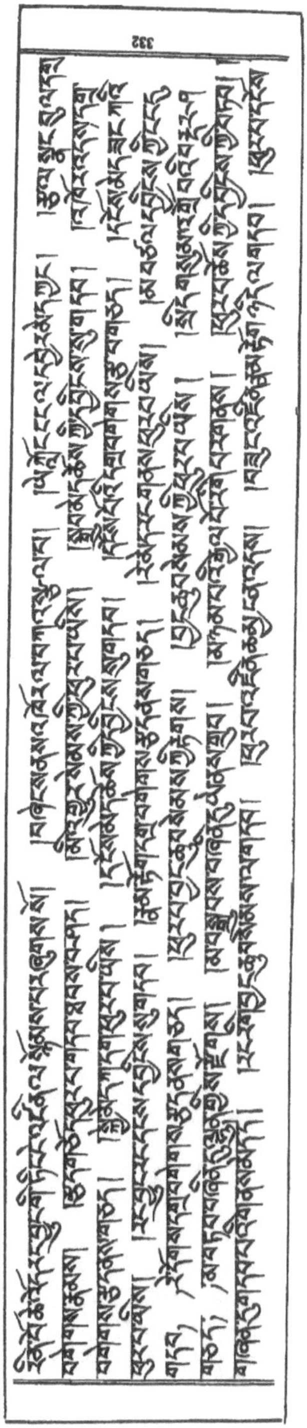

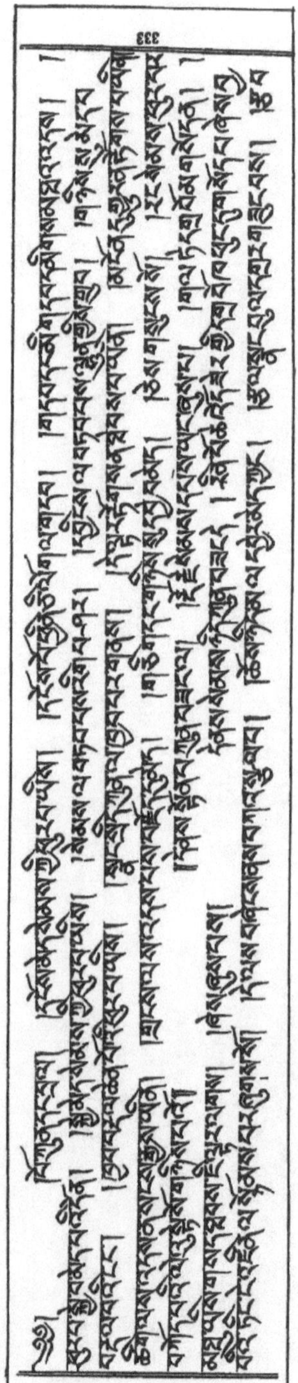

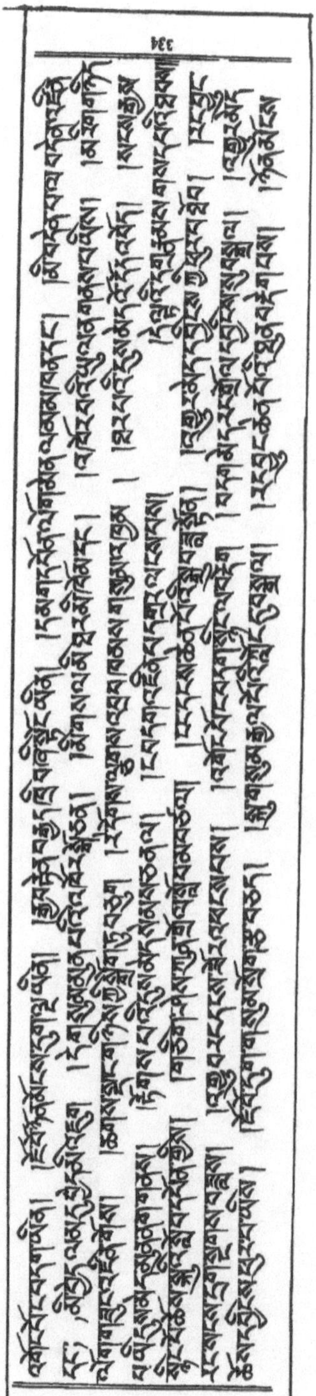

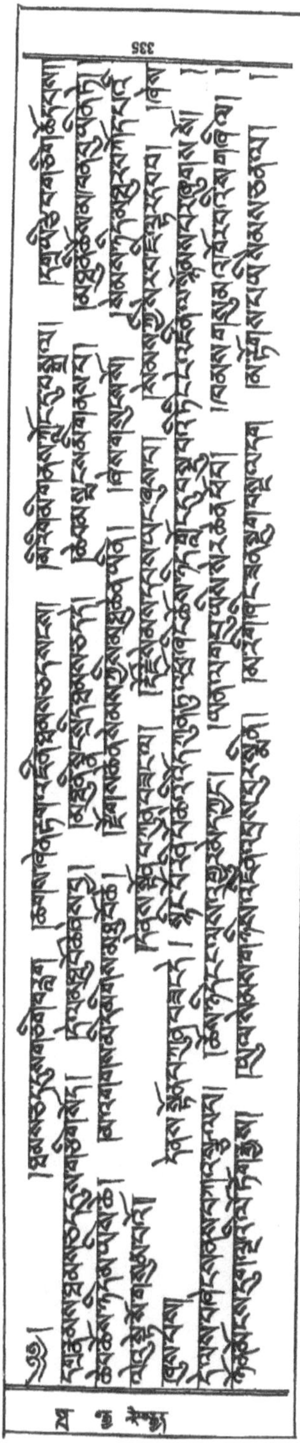

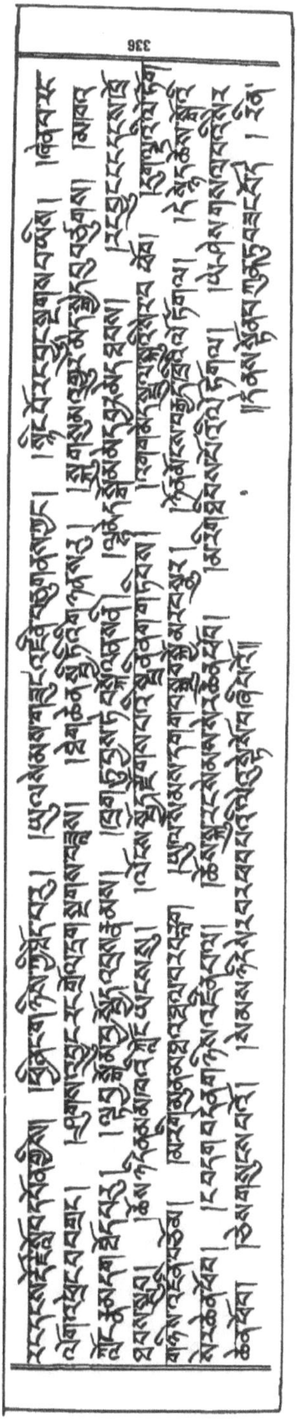

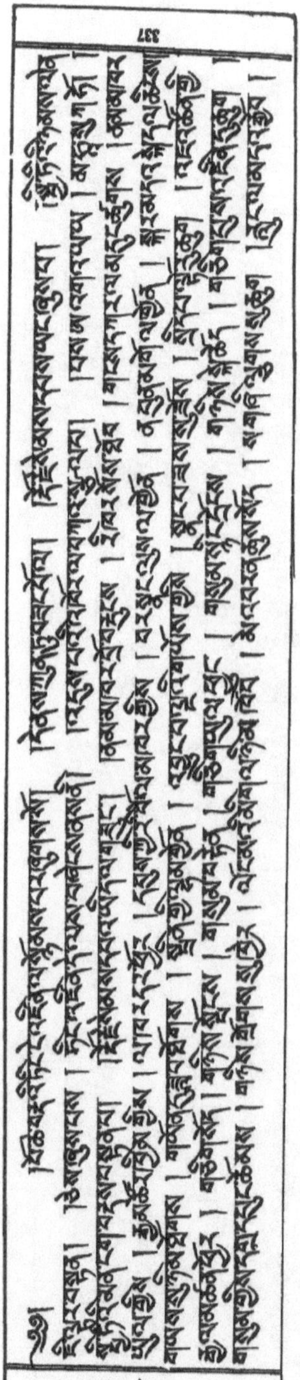

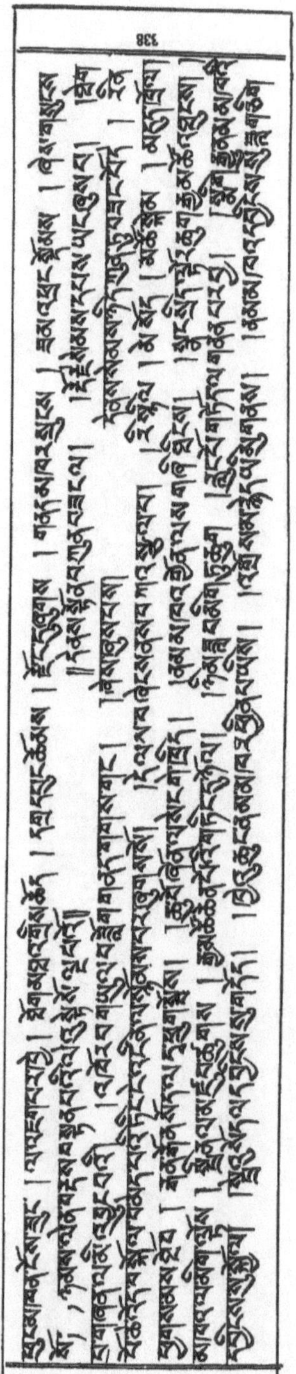

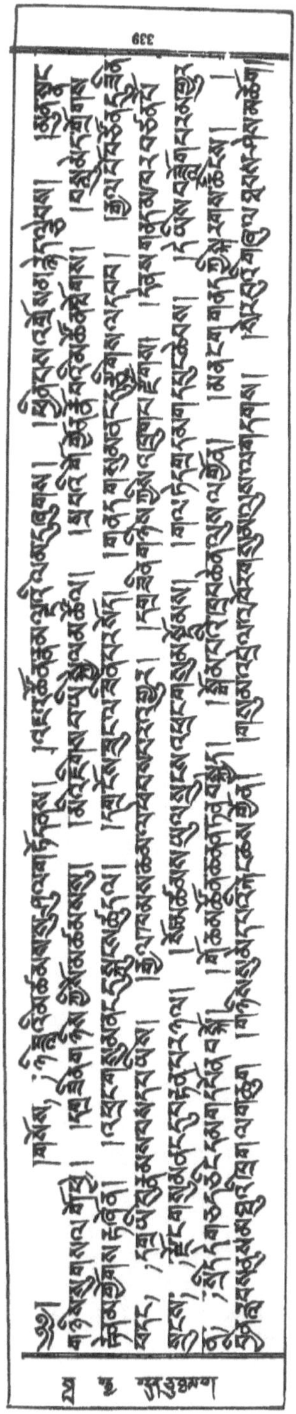
339

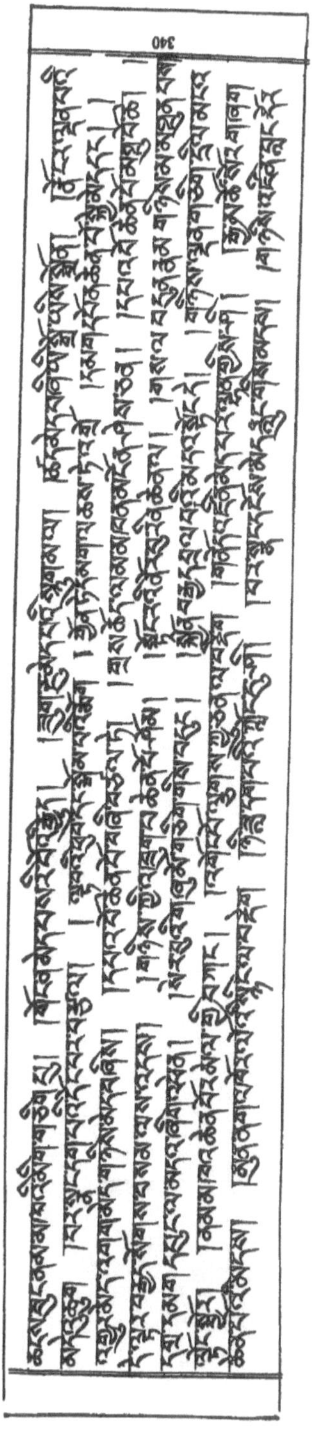
340

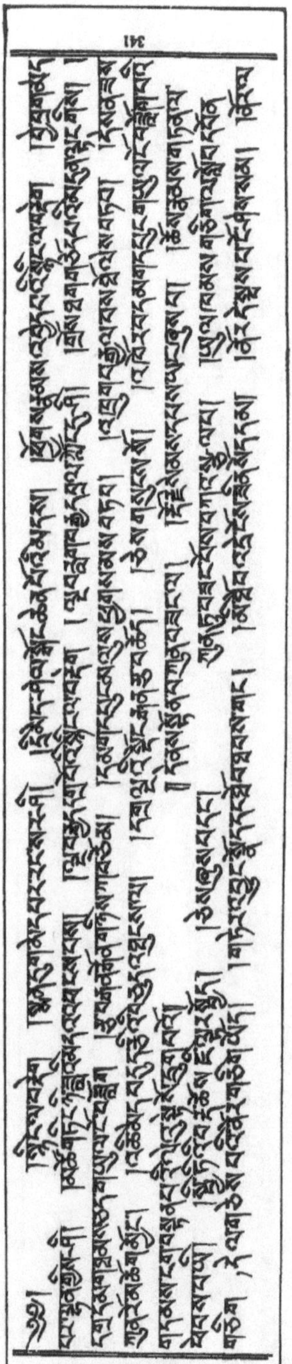

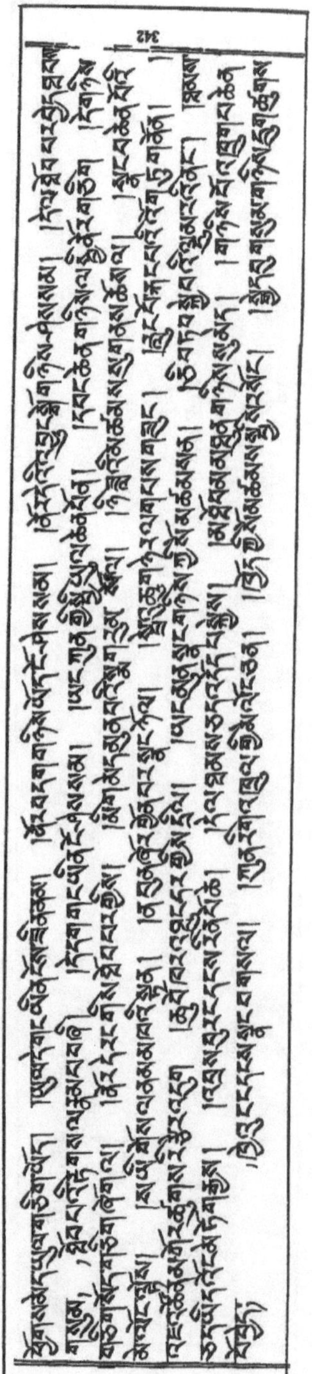

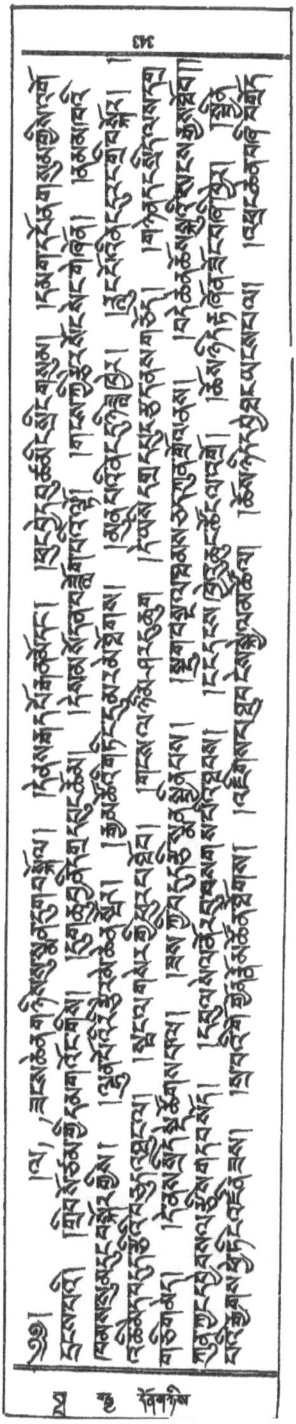

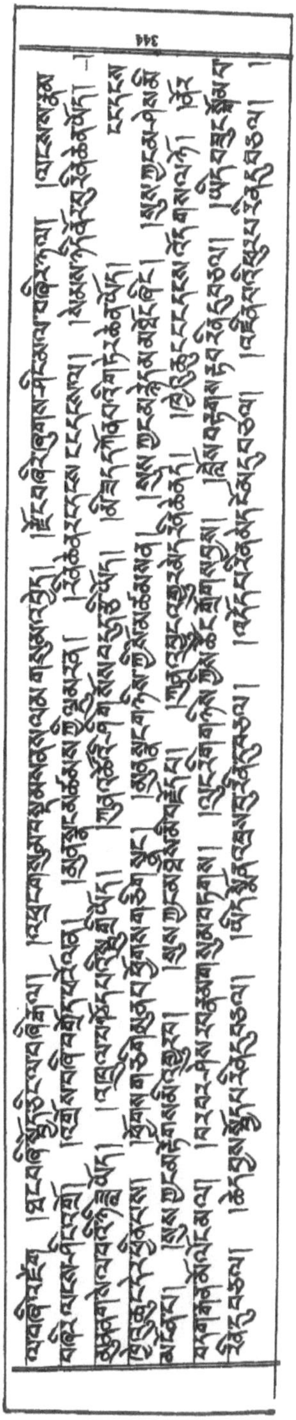

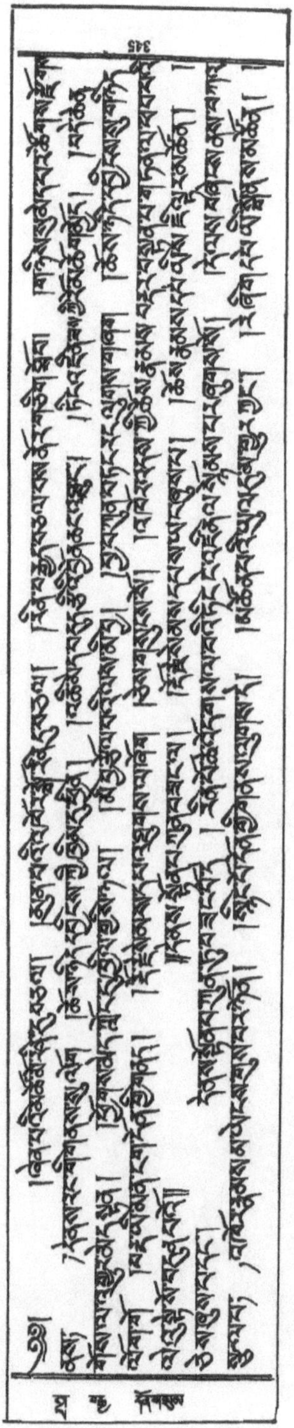

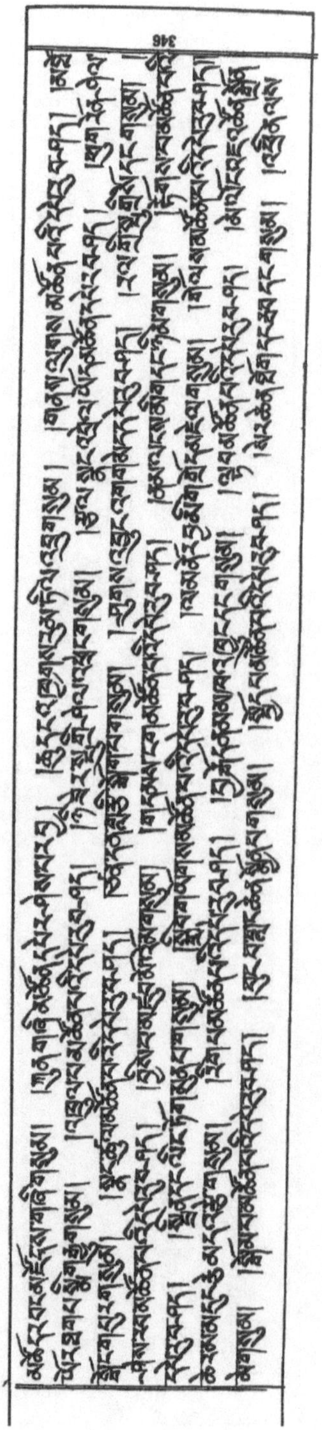

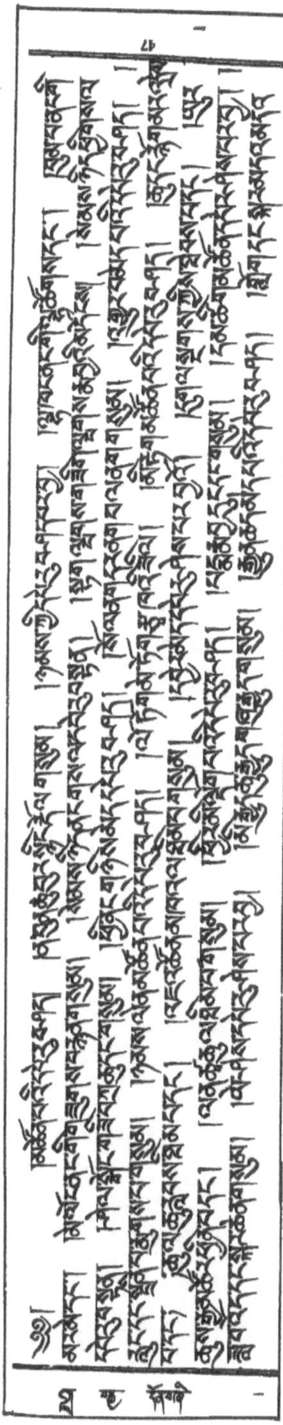

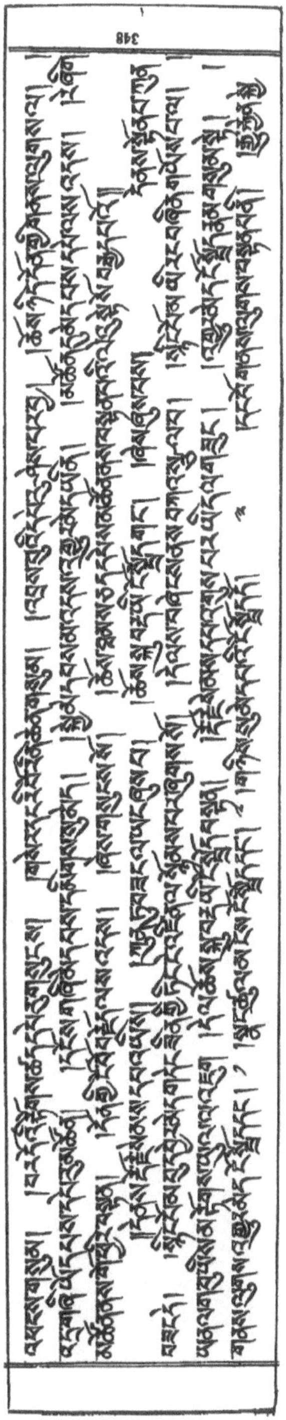

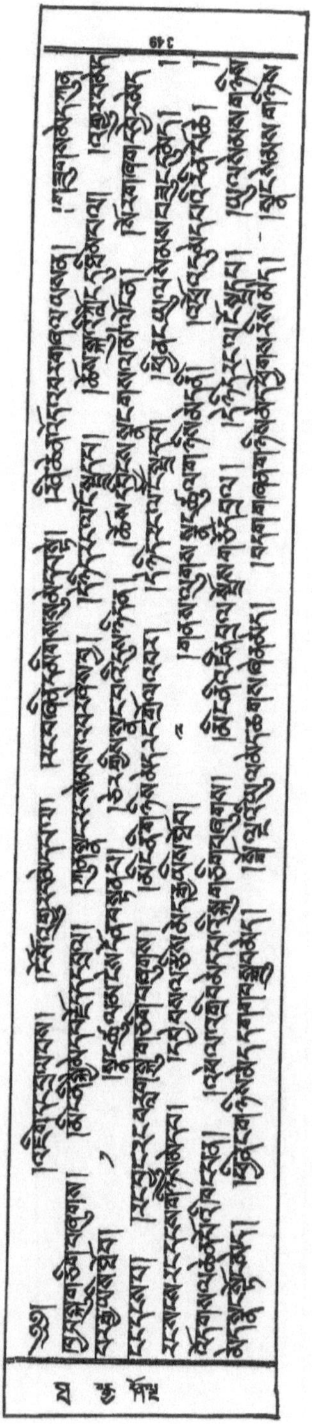
349

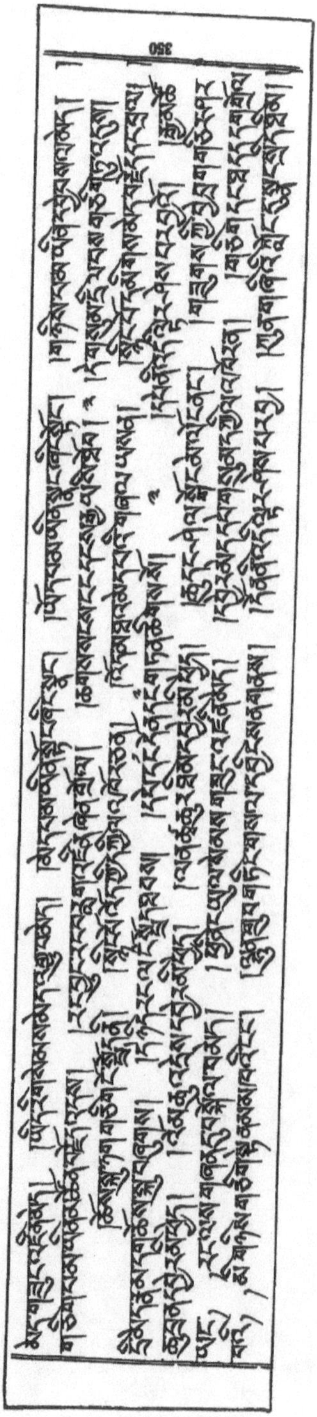
350

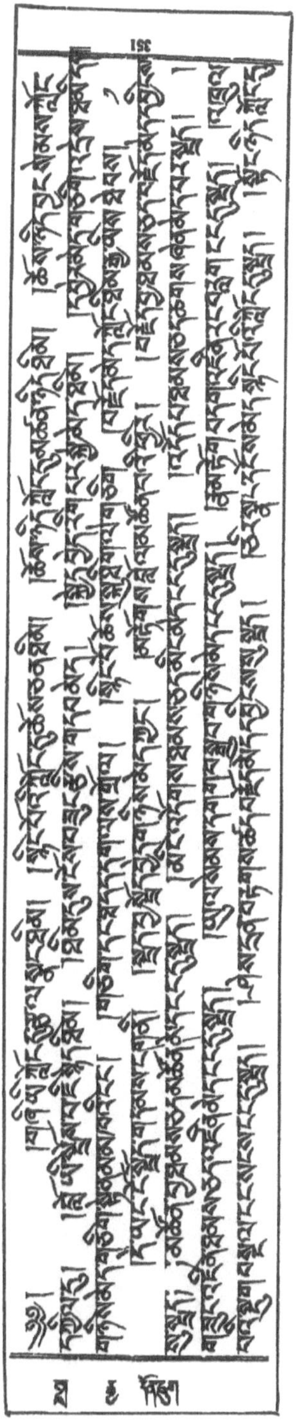

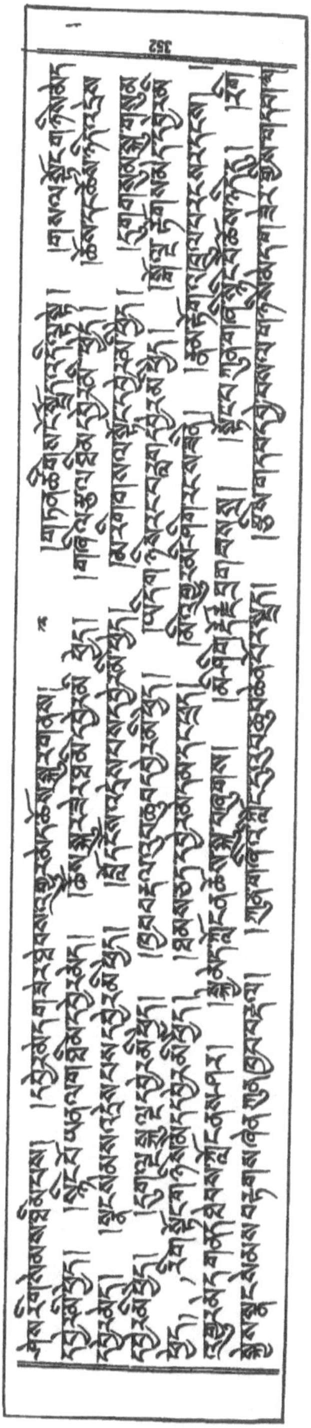

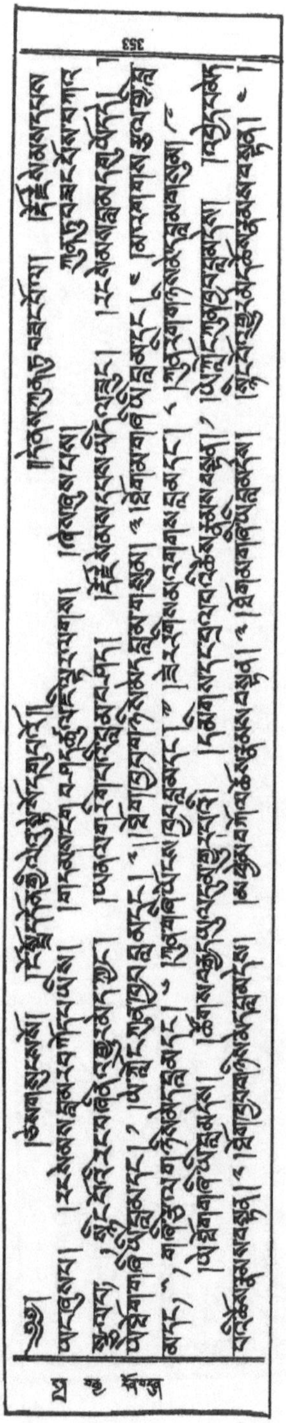

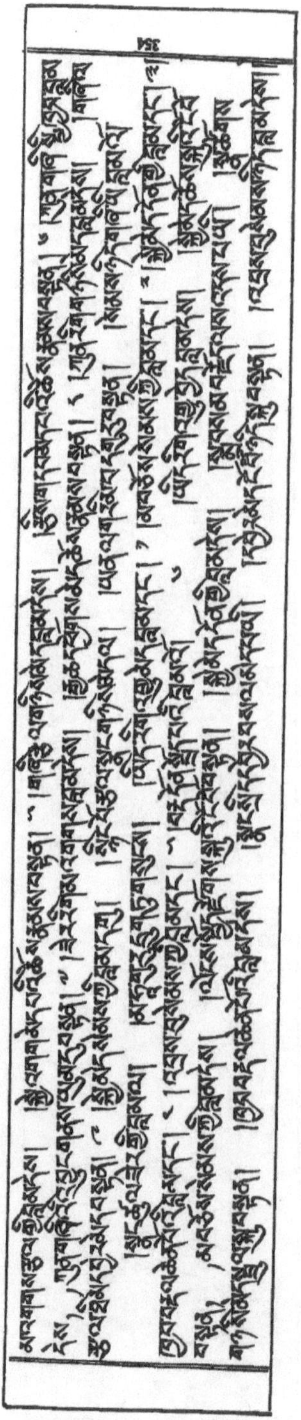

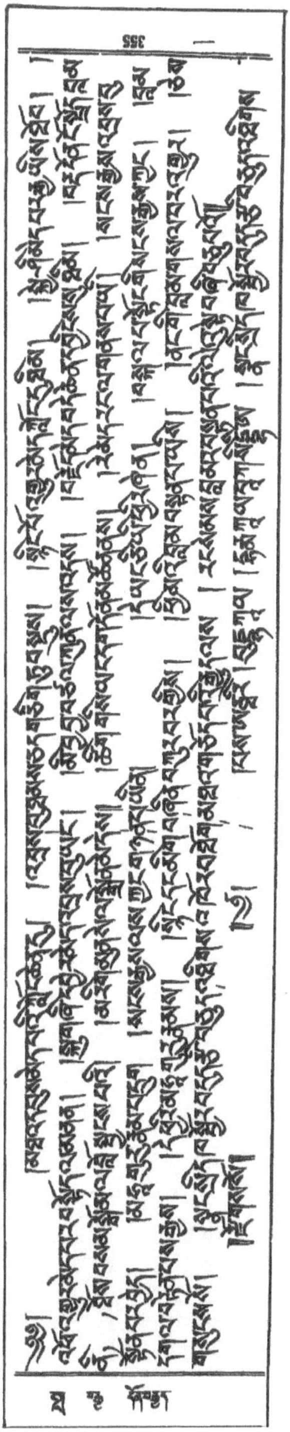

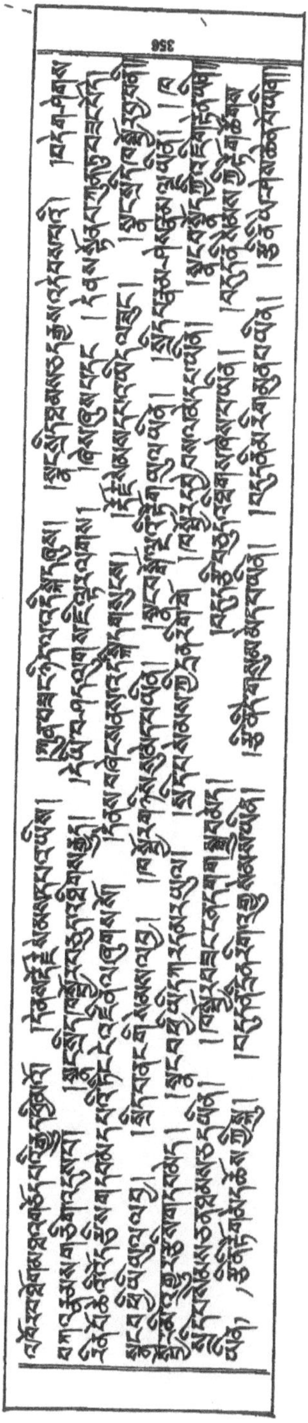

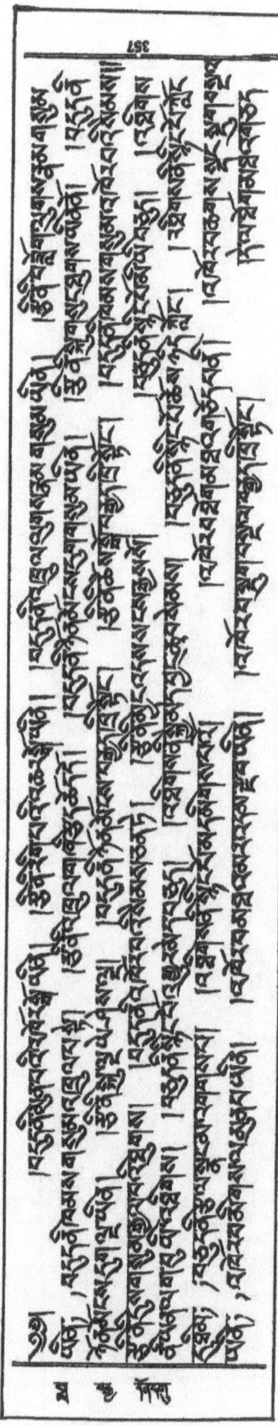

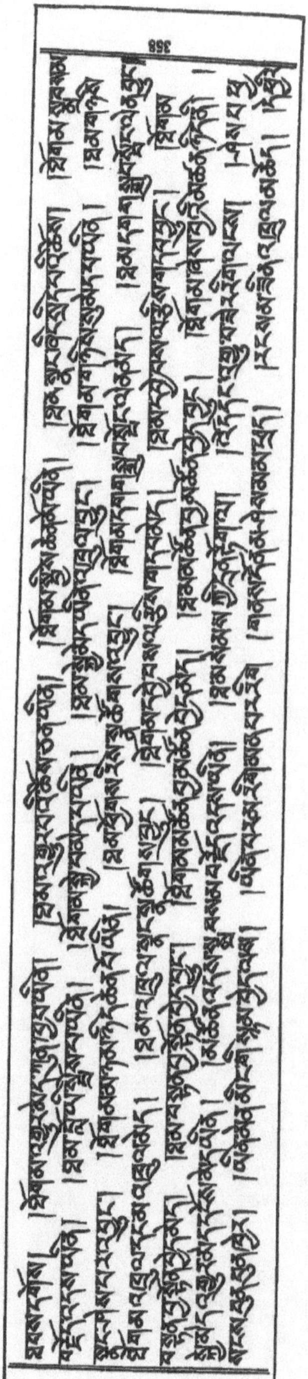

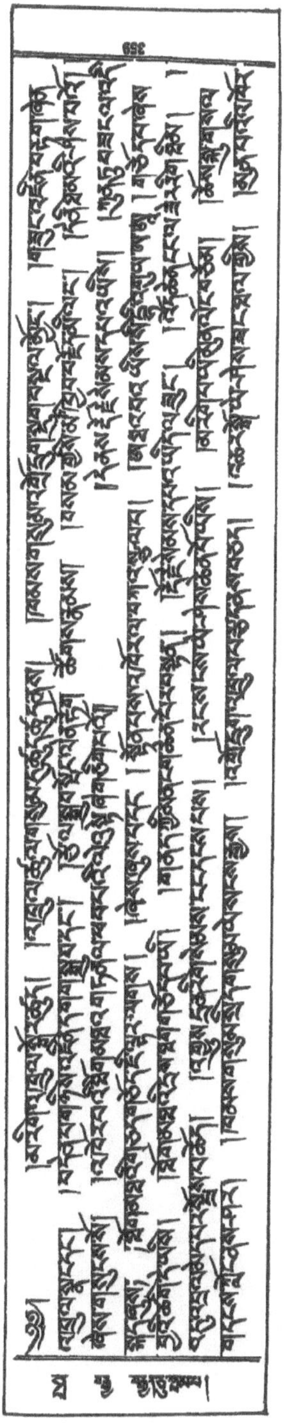

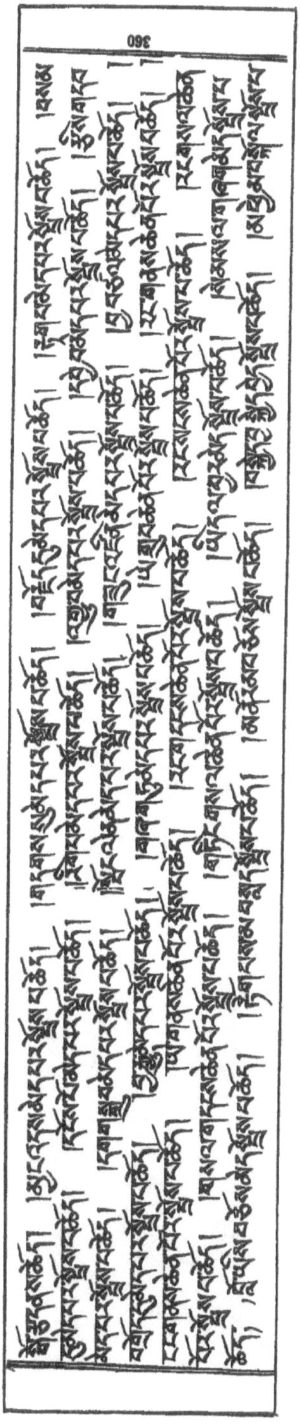

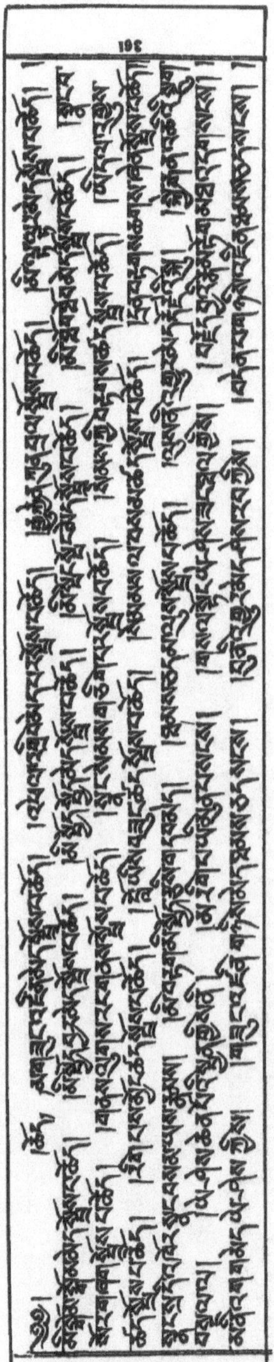

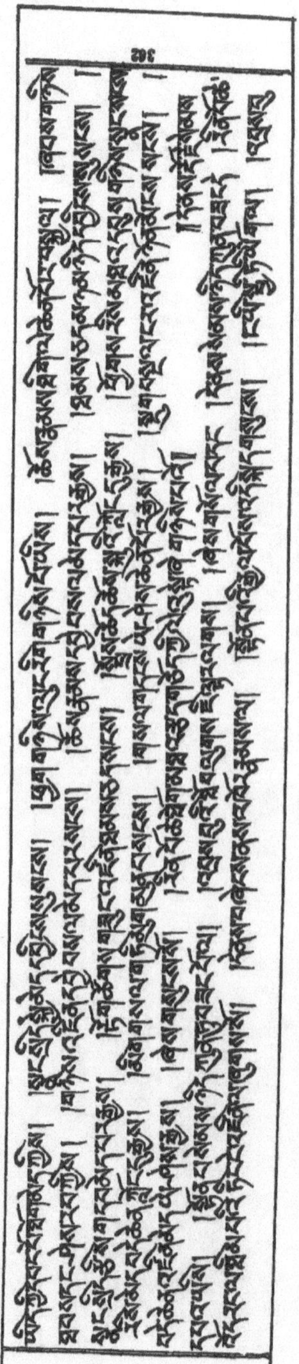

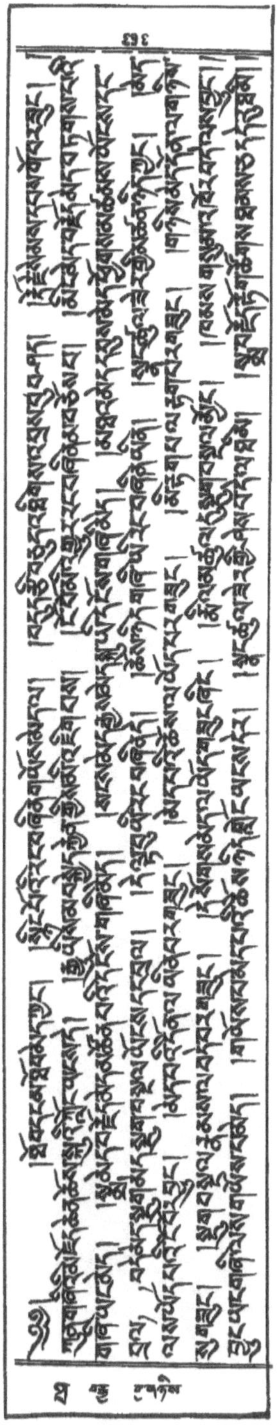

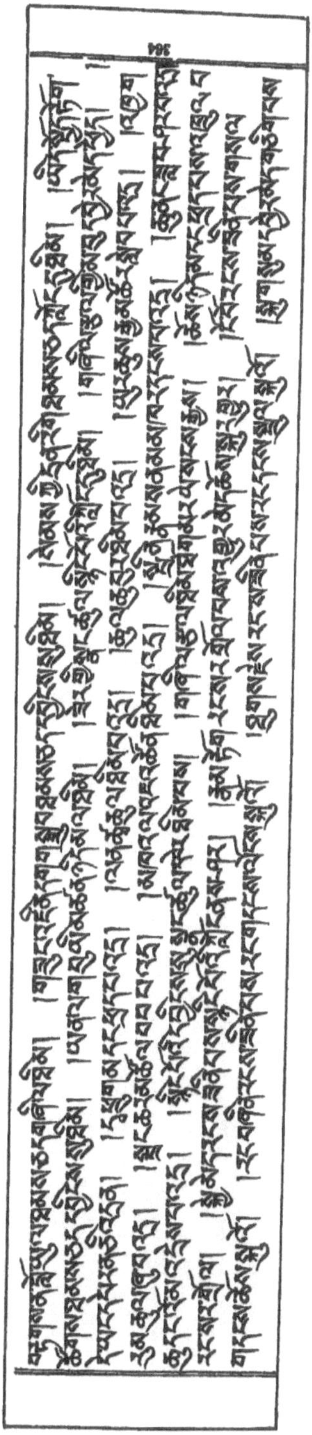

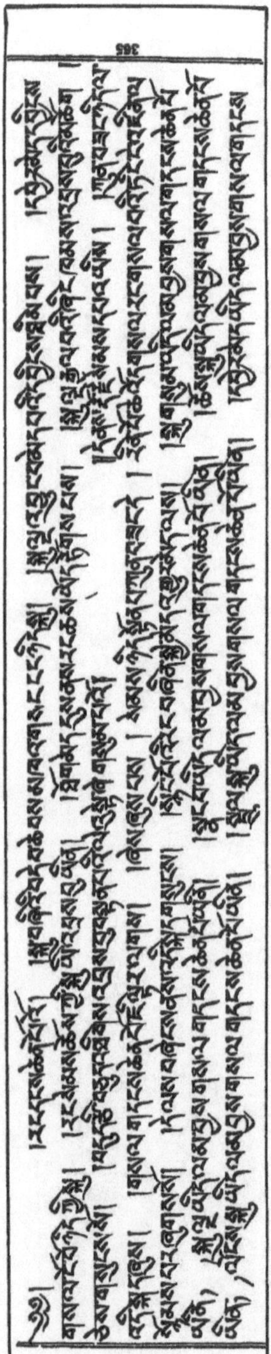

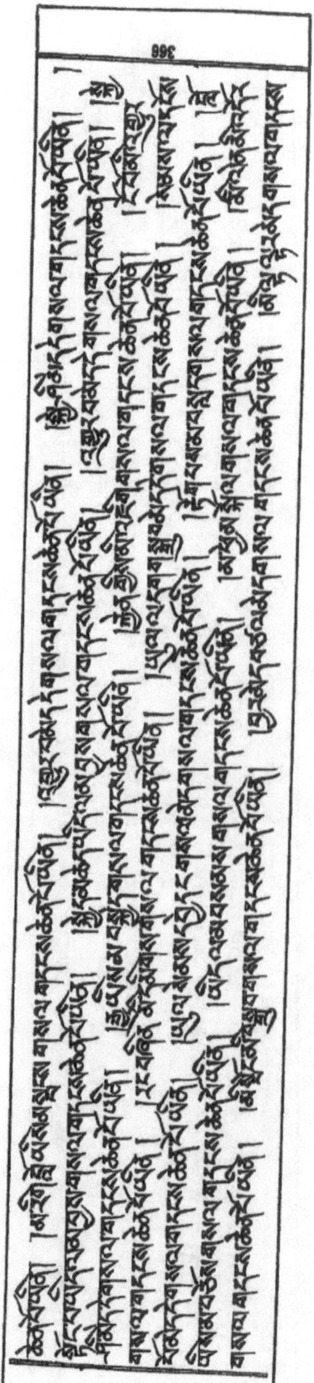

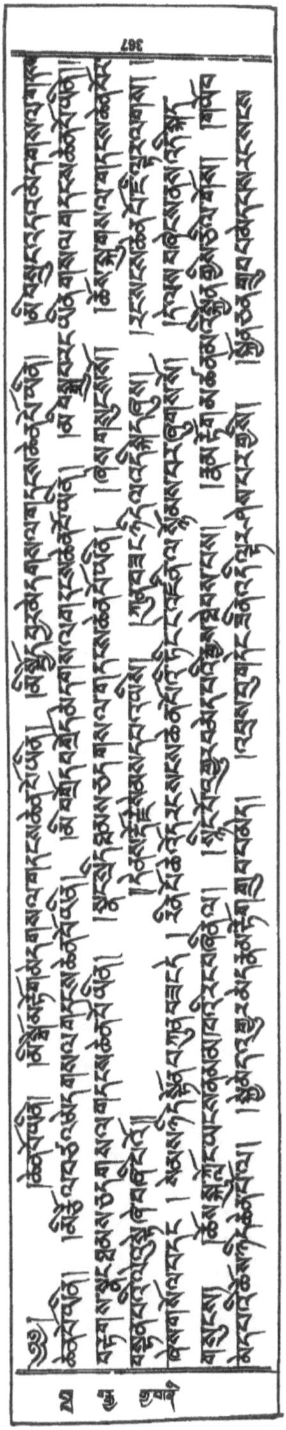

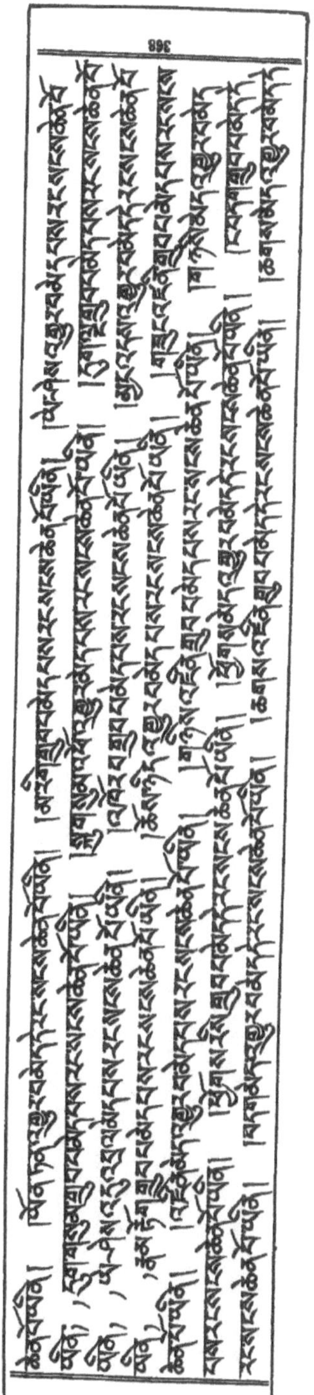

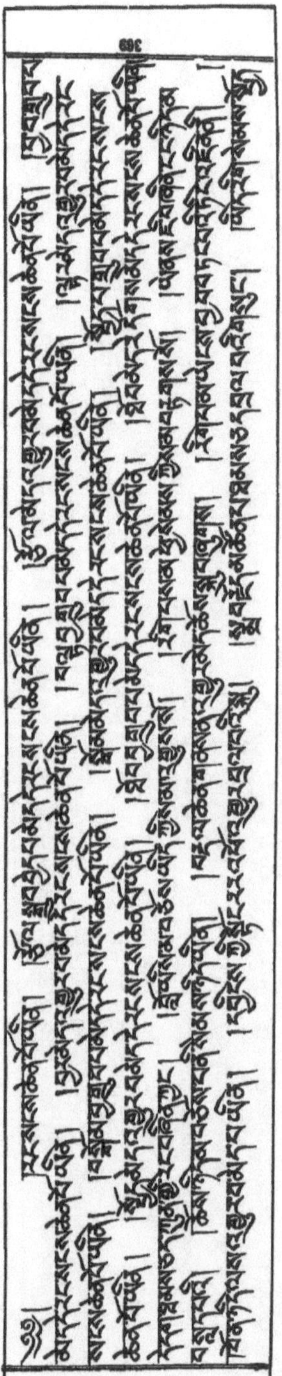

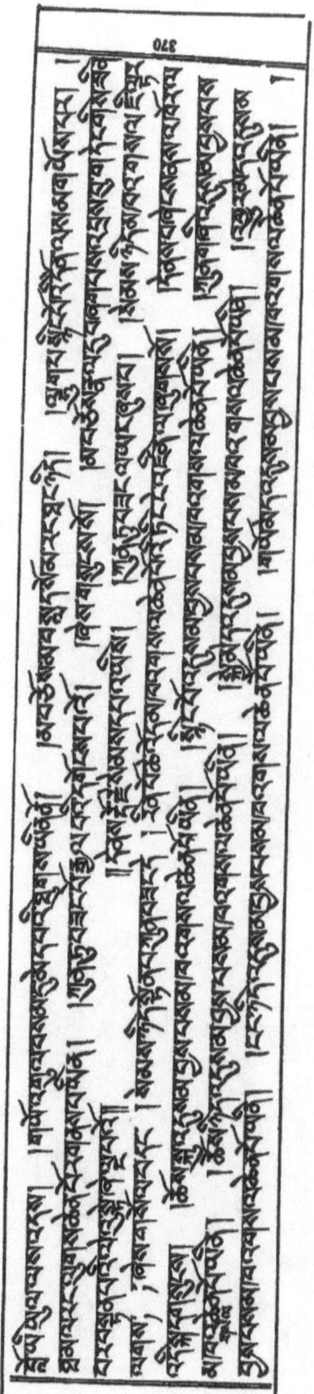

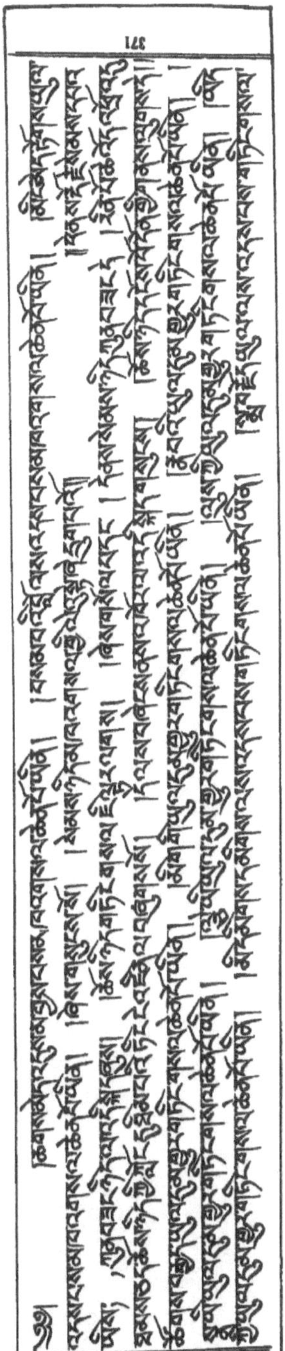

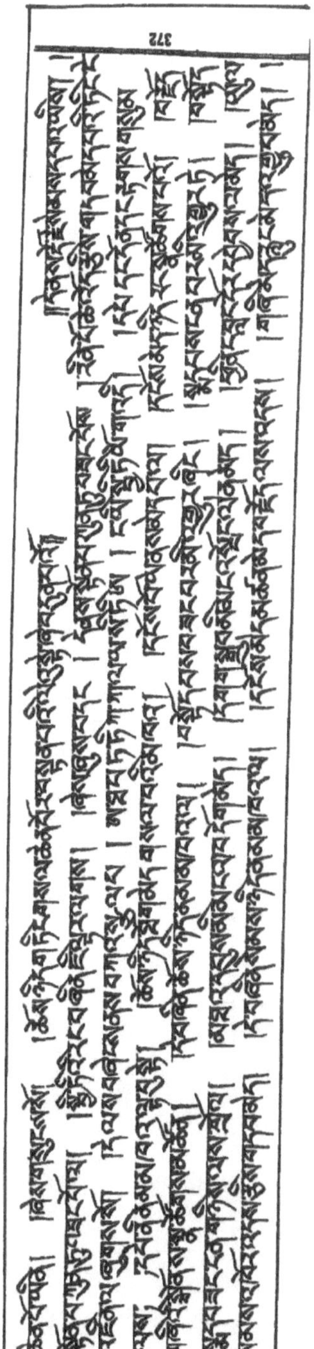

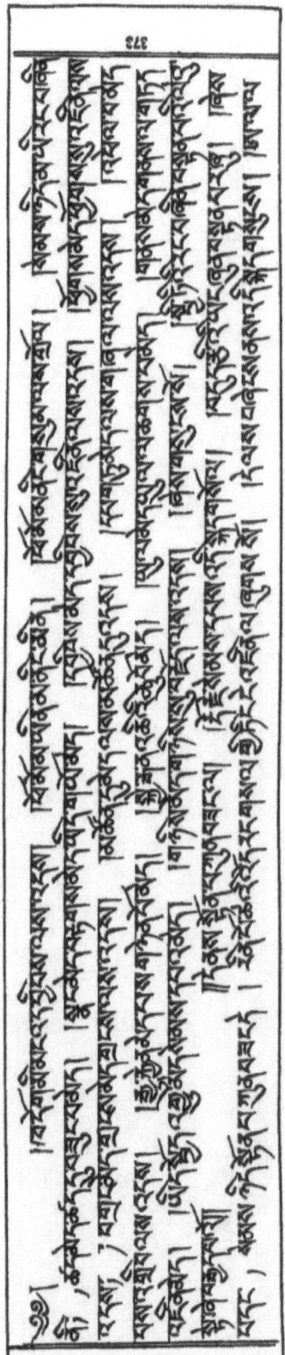
373

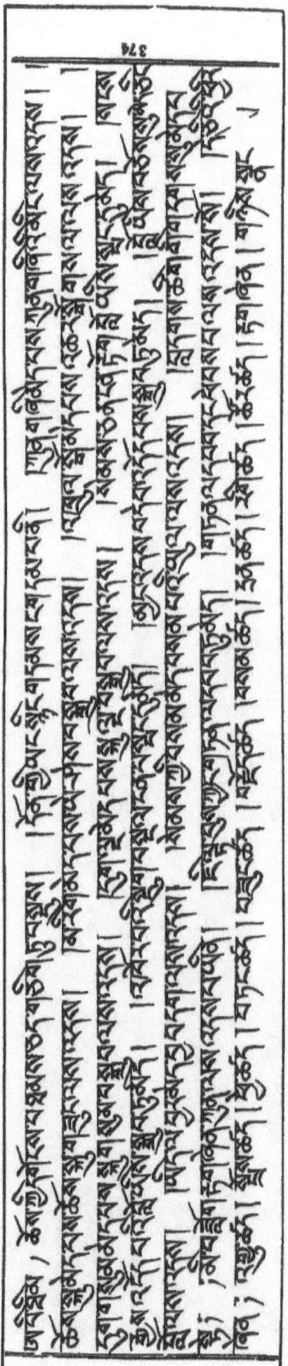
374

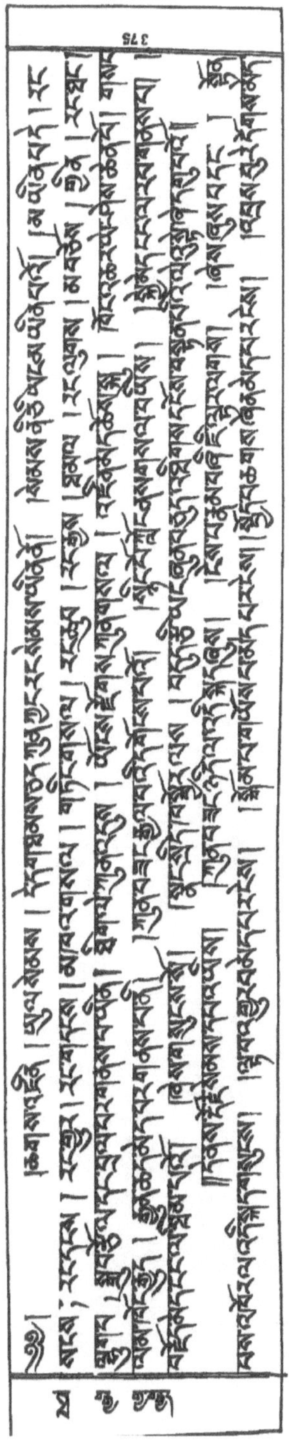

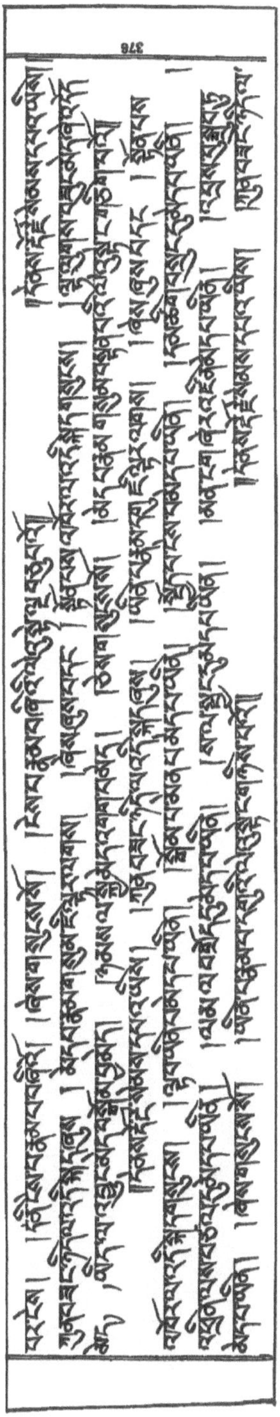

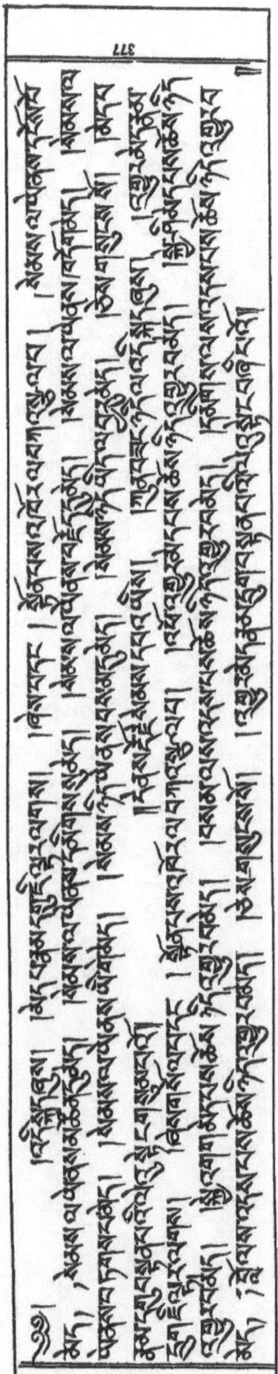

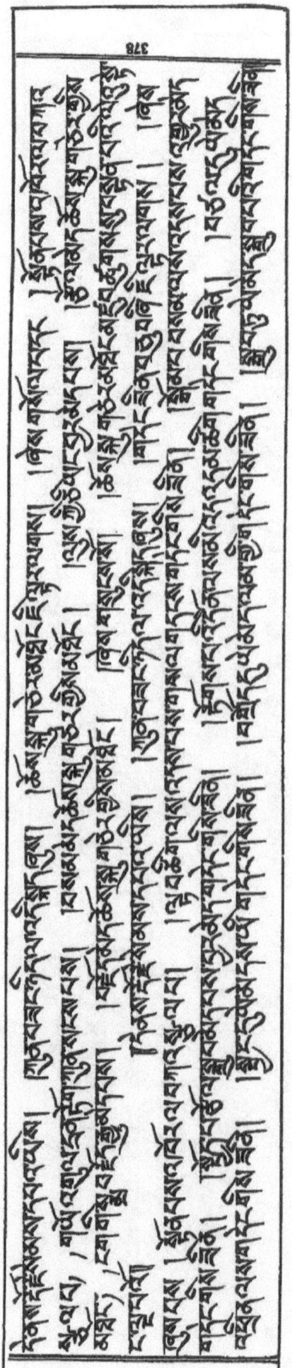

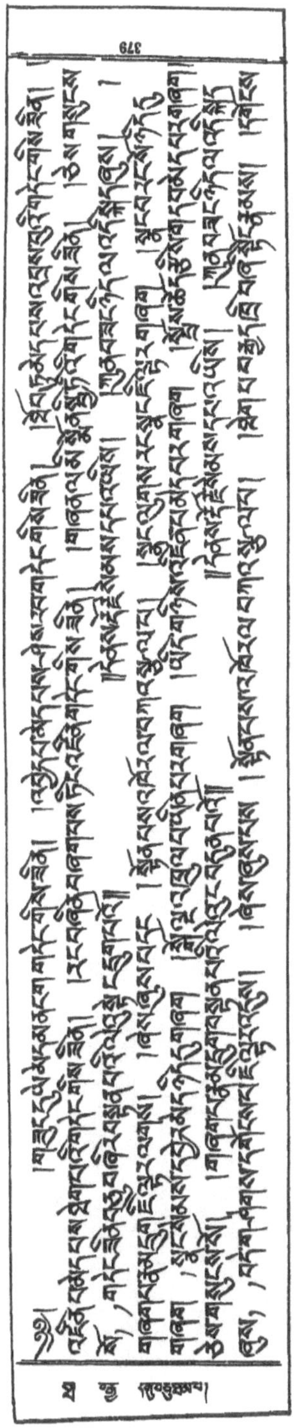

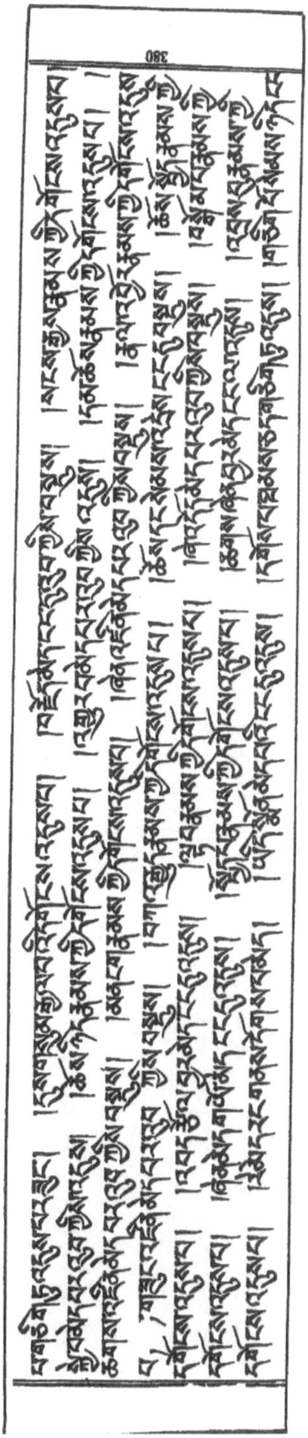

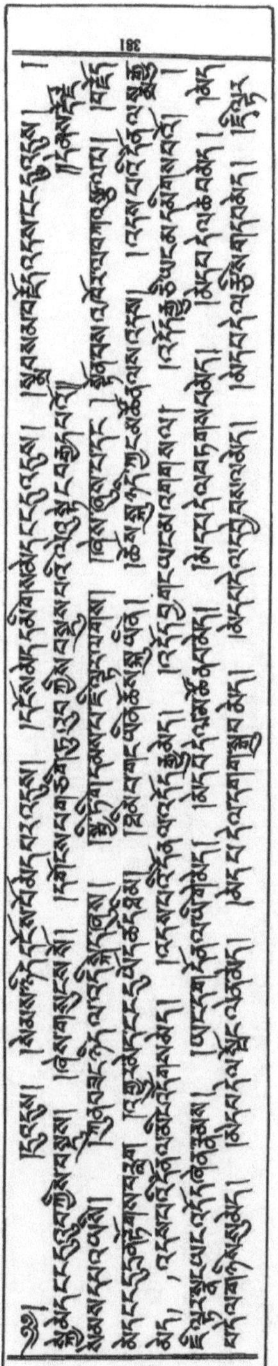
381

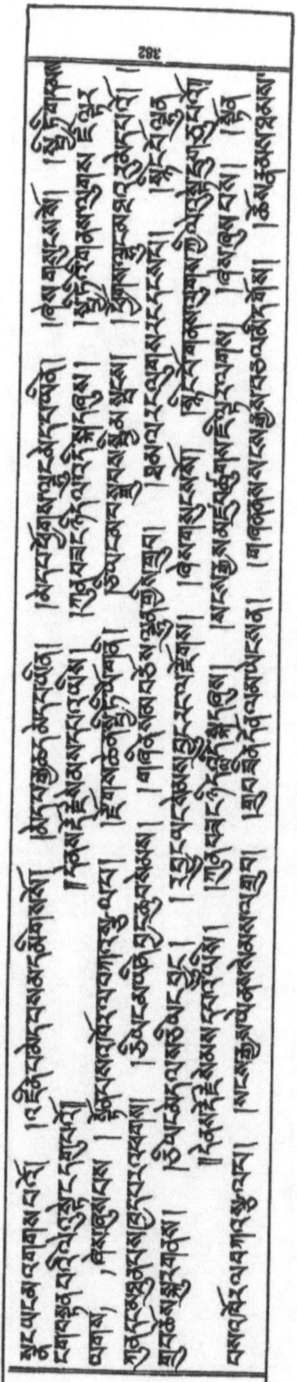
382

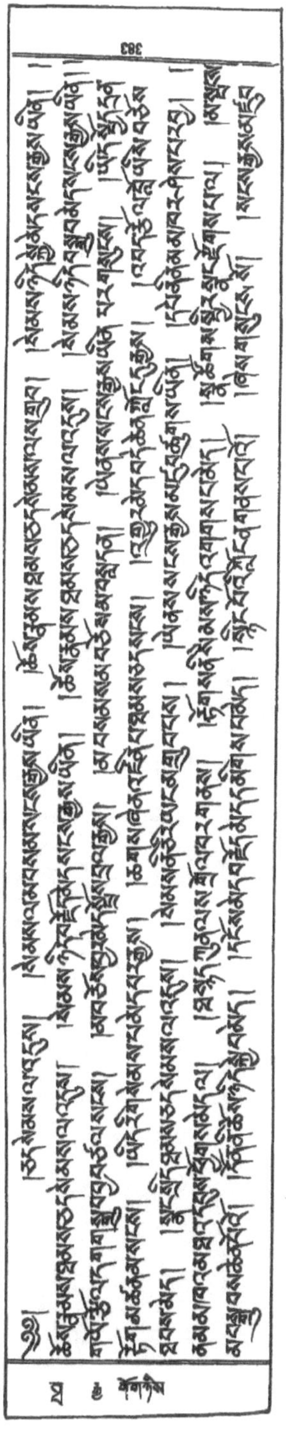

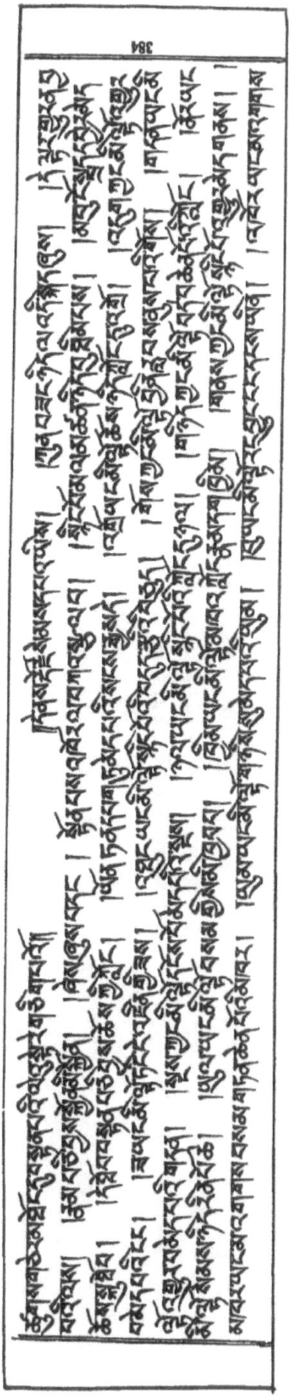

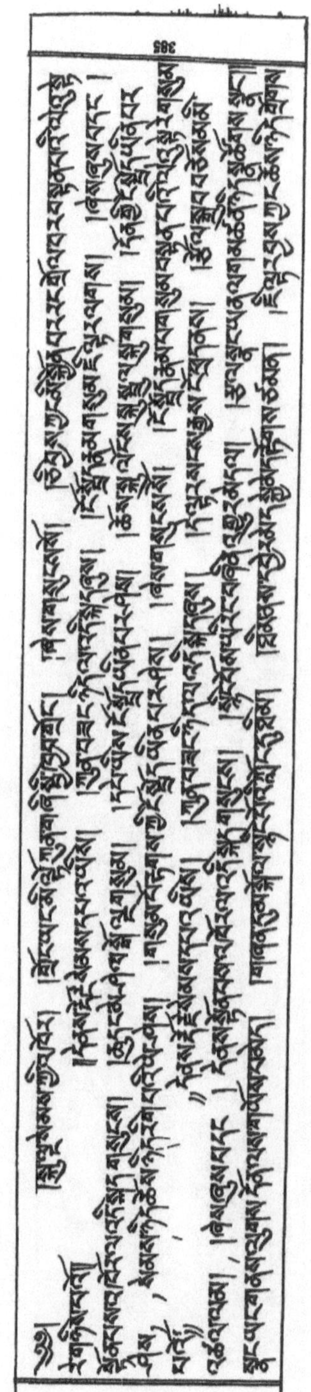

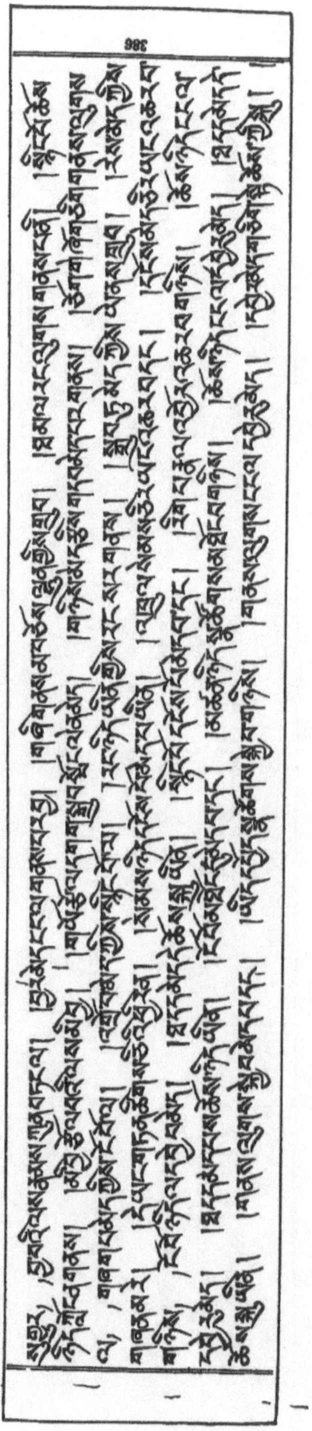

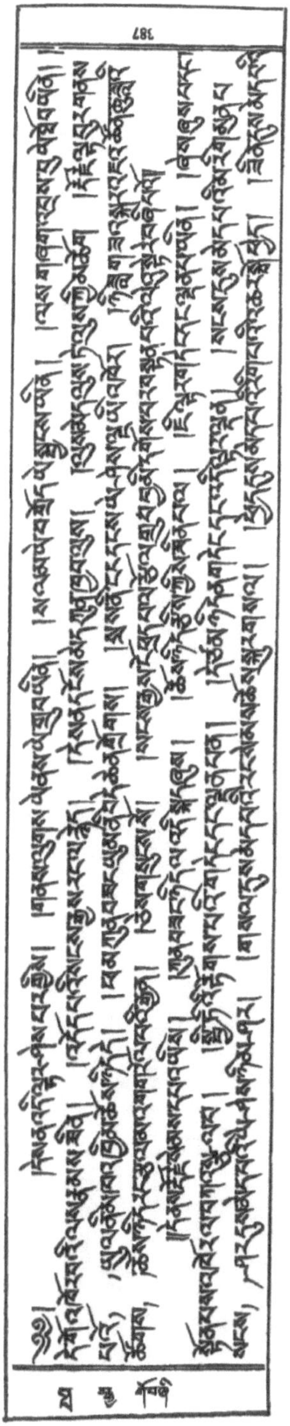

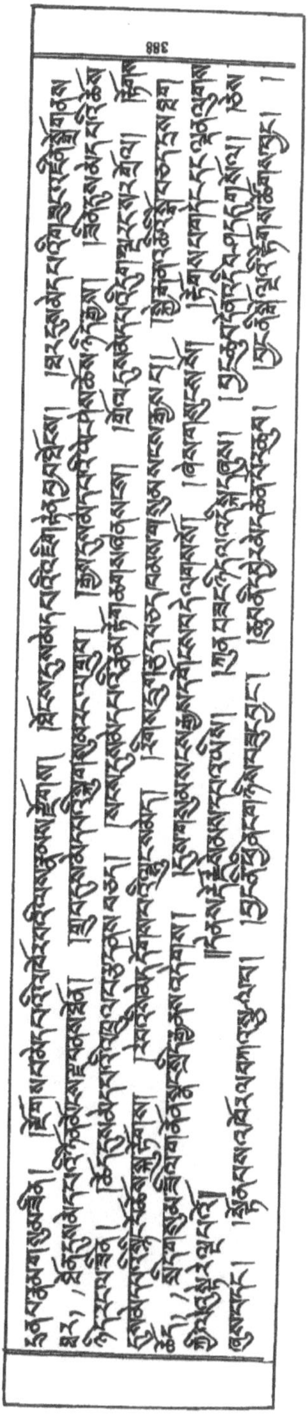

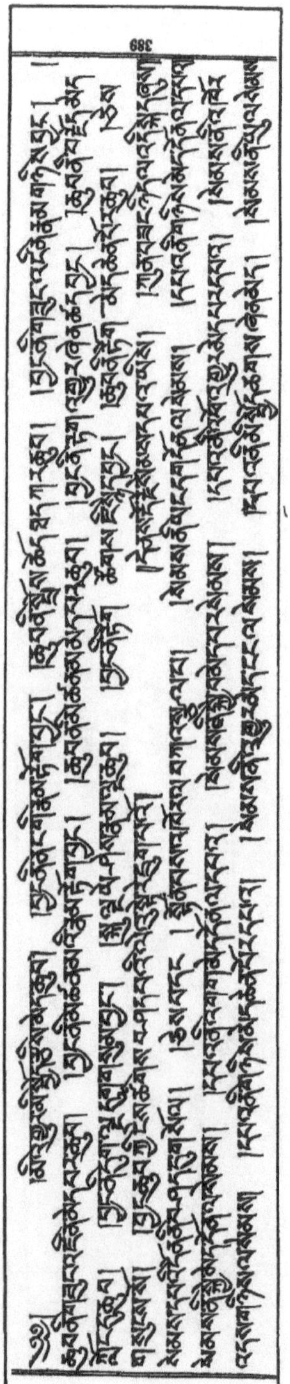

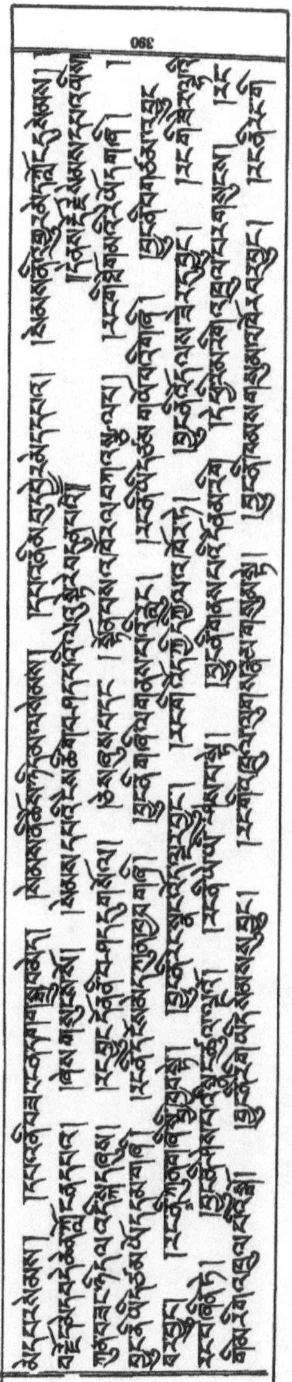

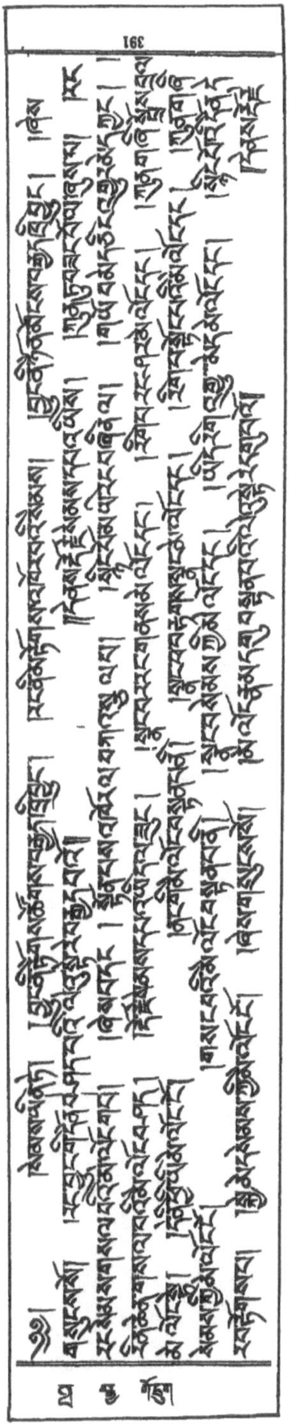

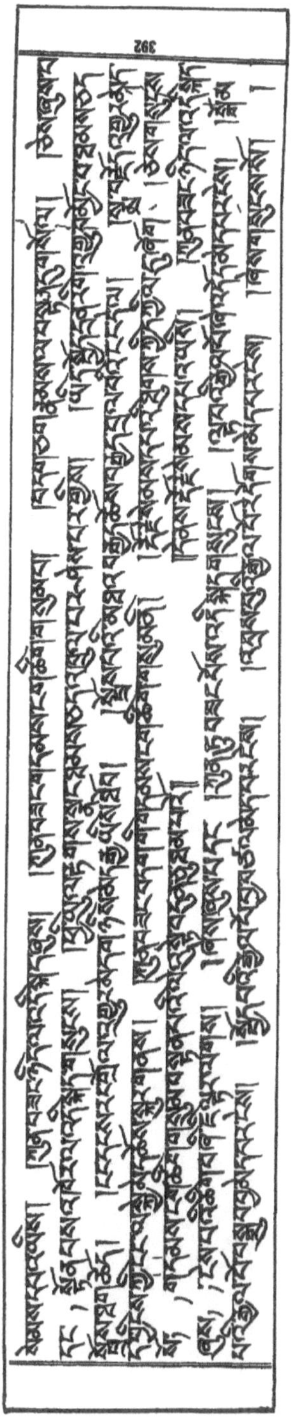

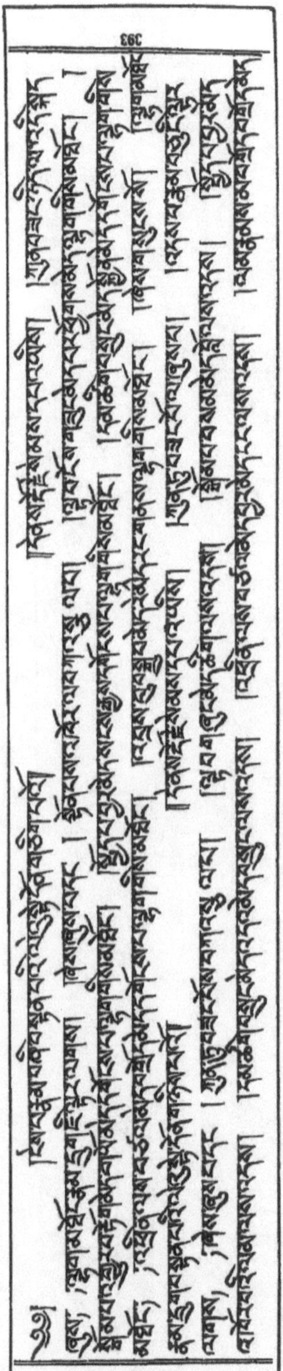

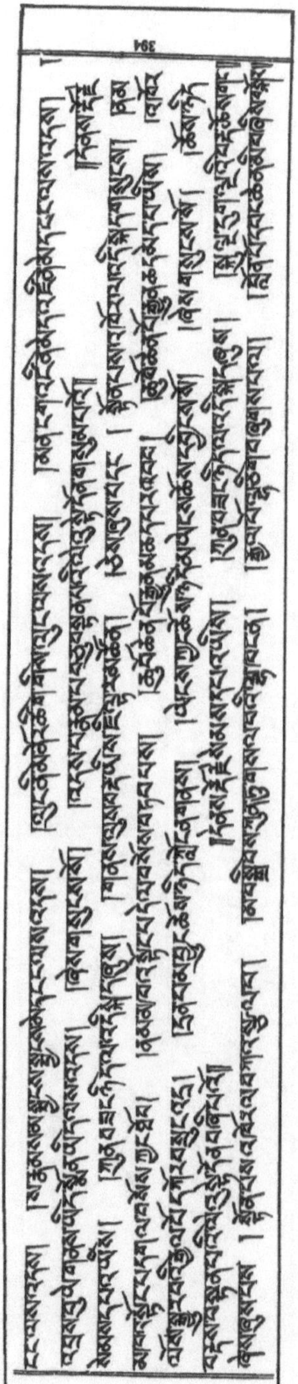

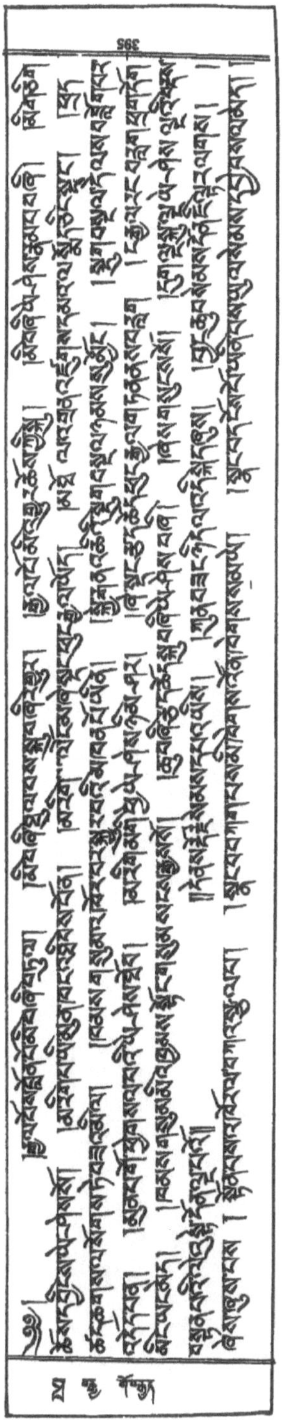

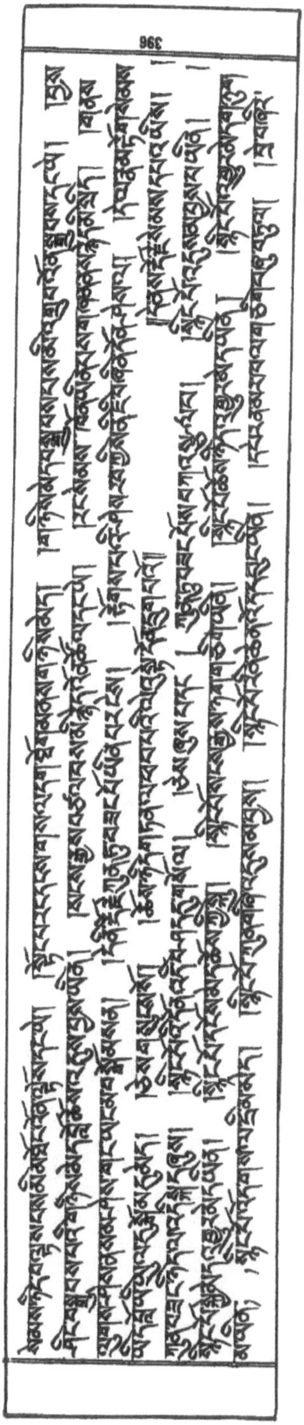

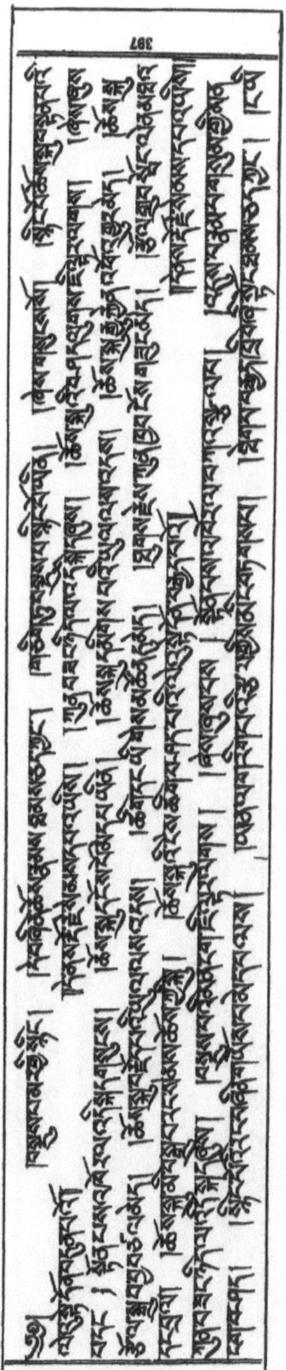

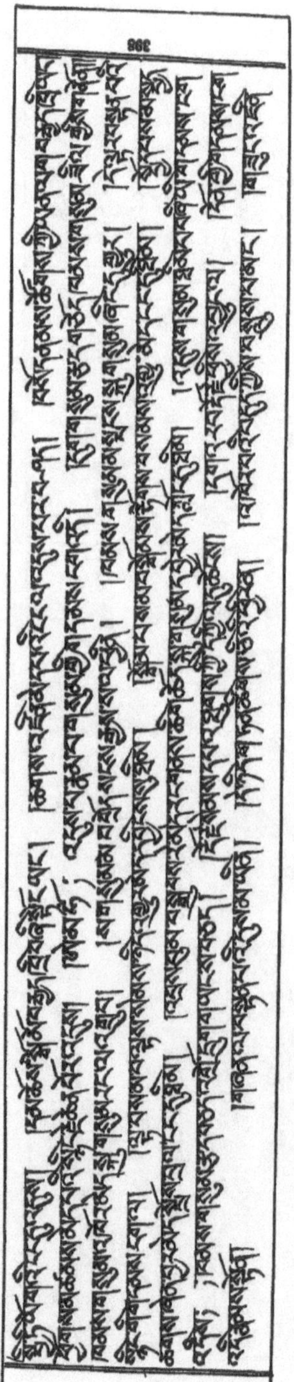

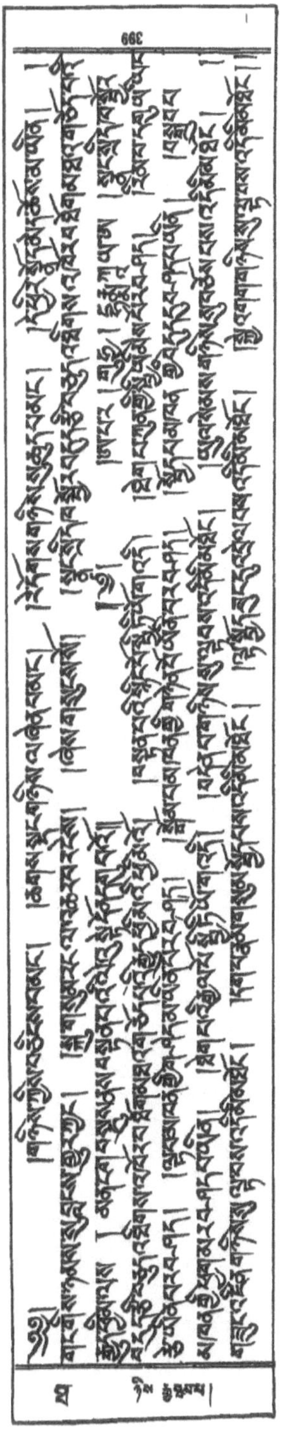

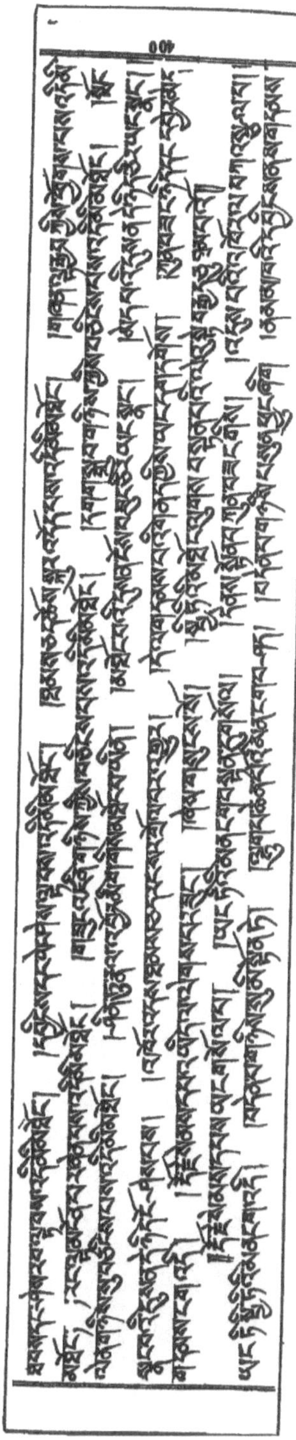

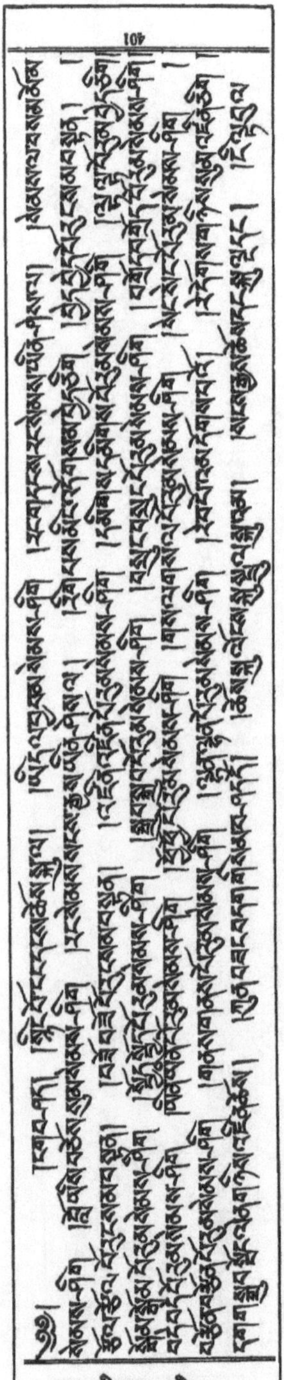

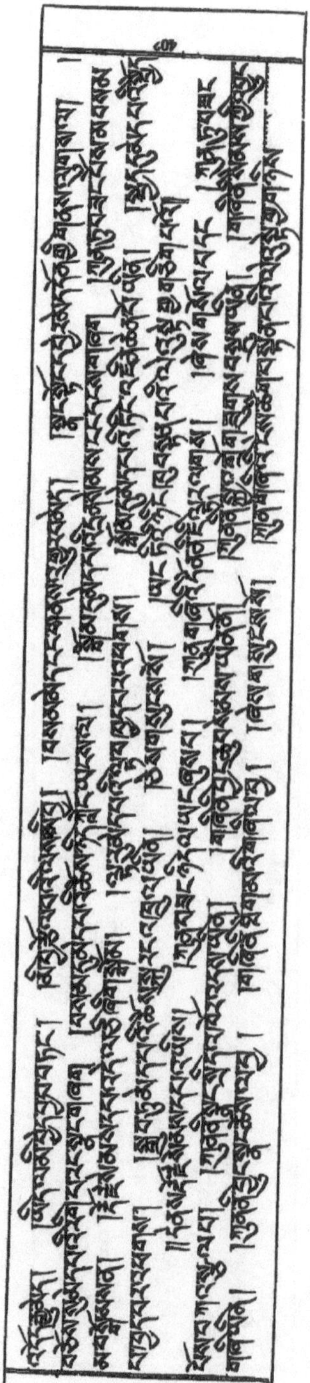

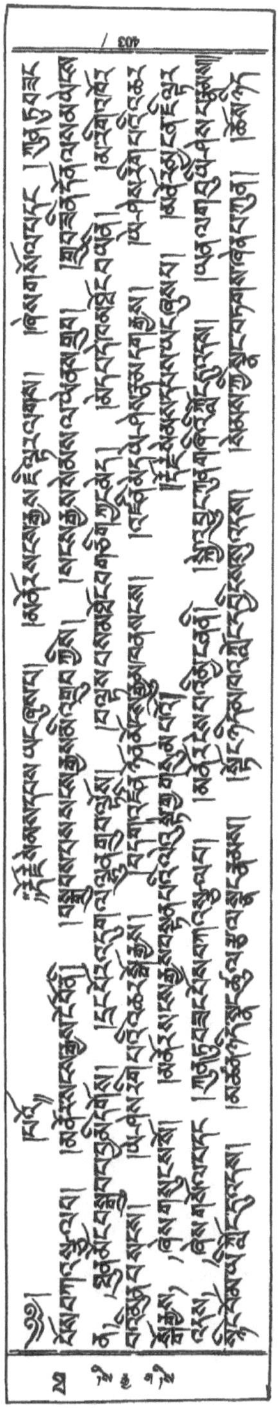

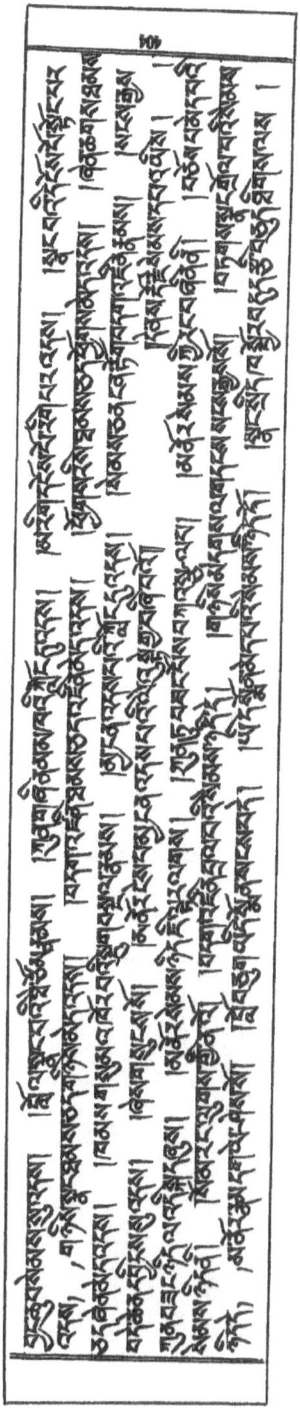

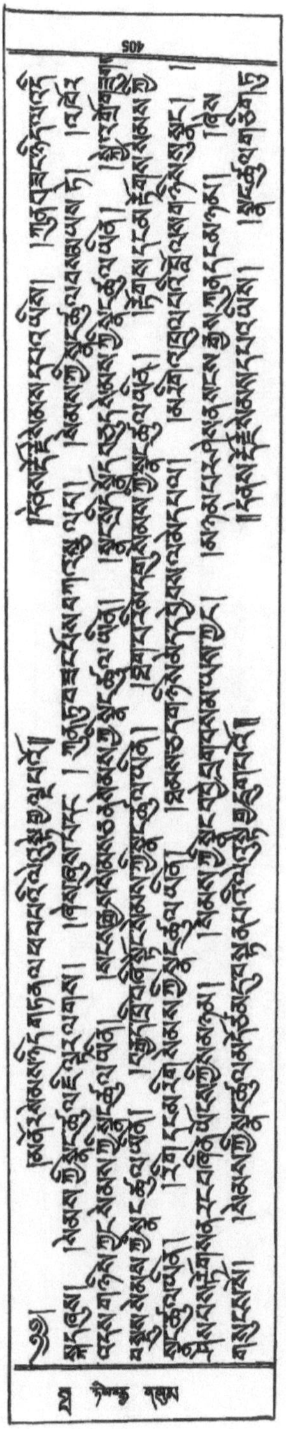

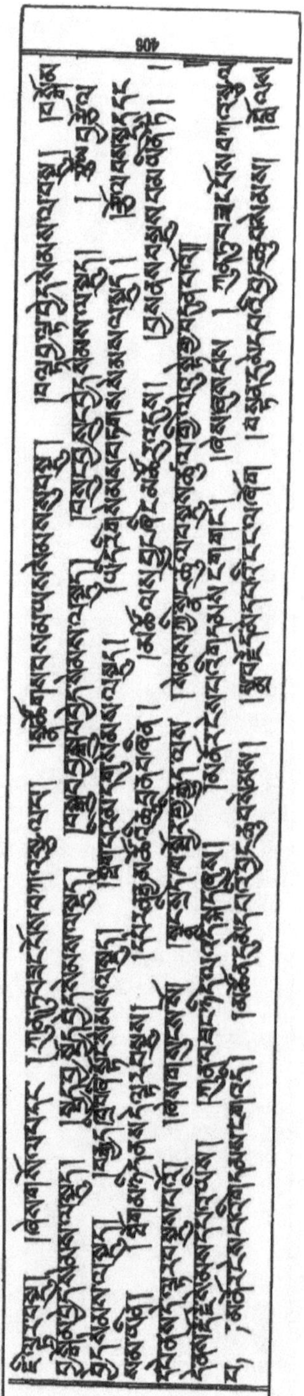

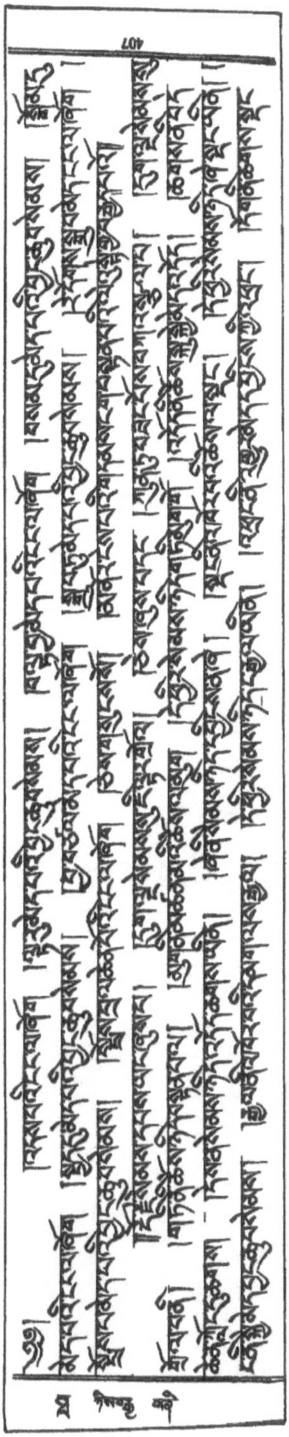
407

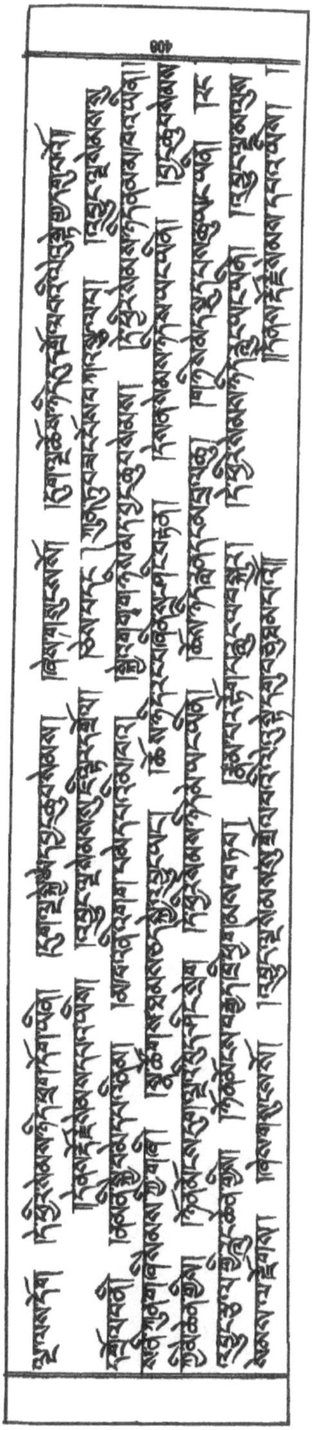
408

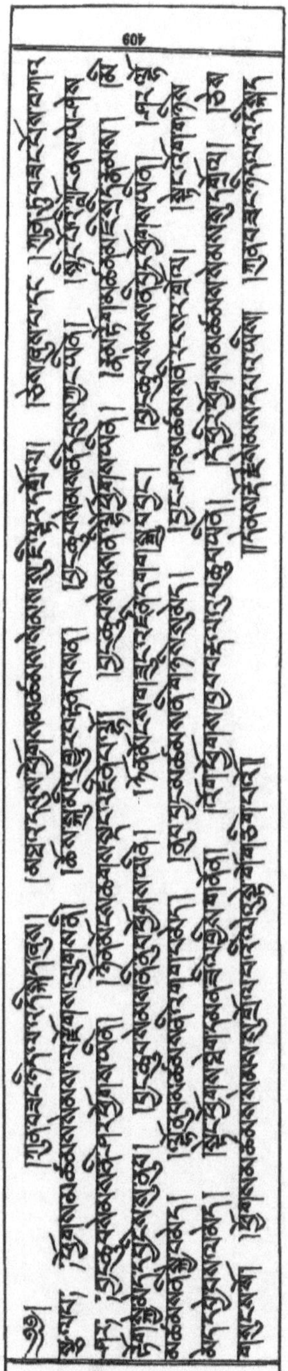

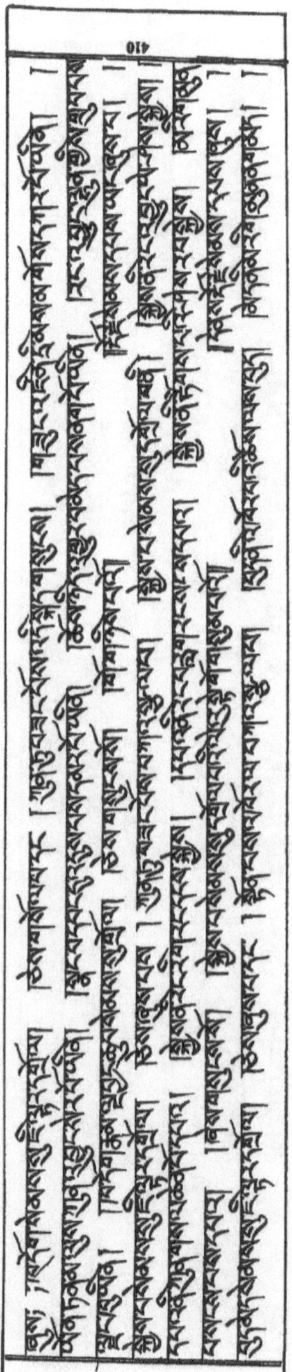

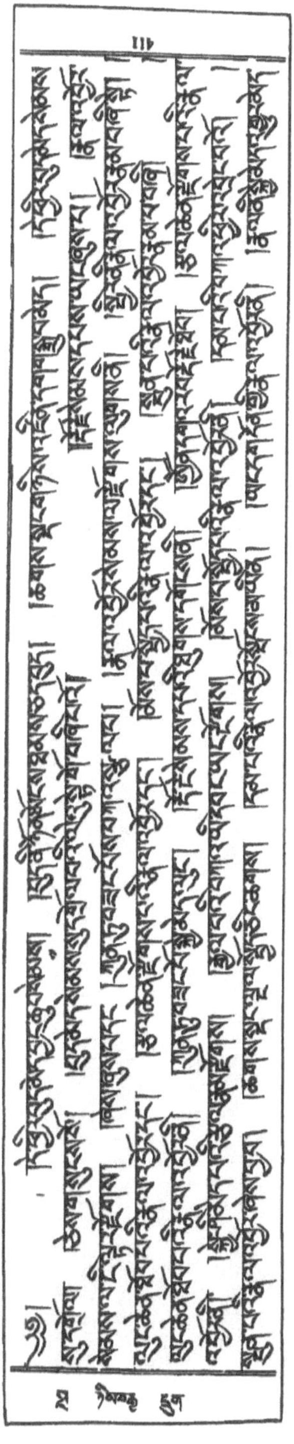

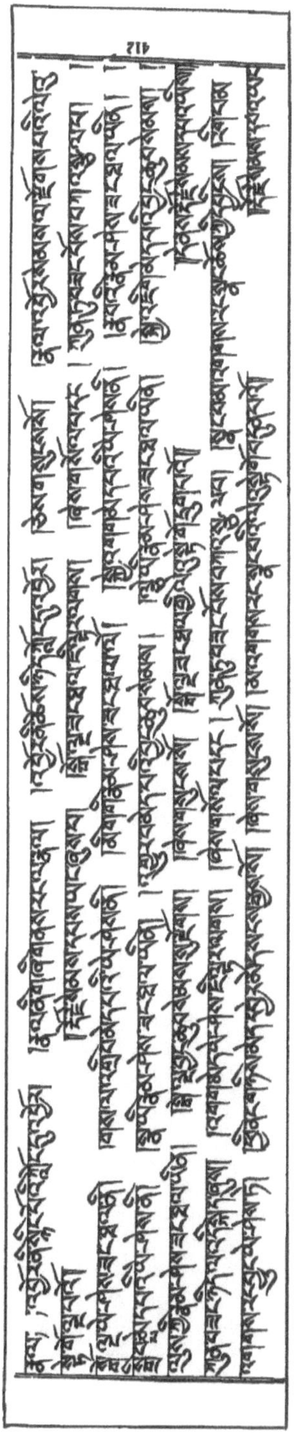

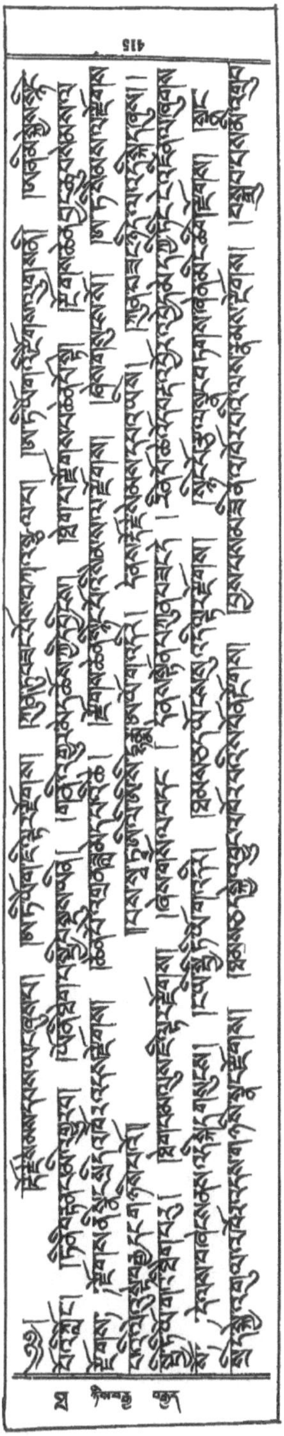

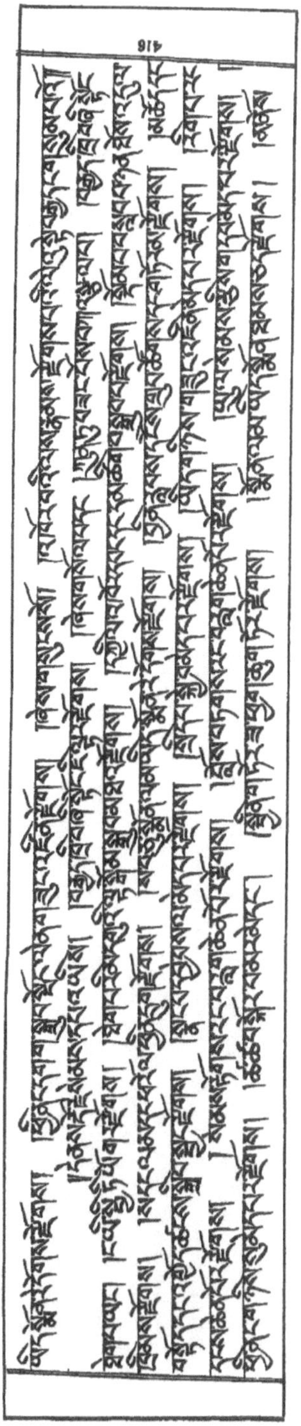

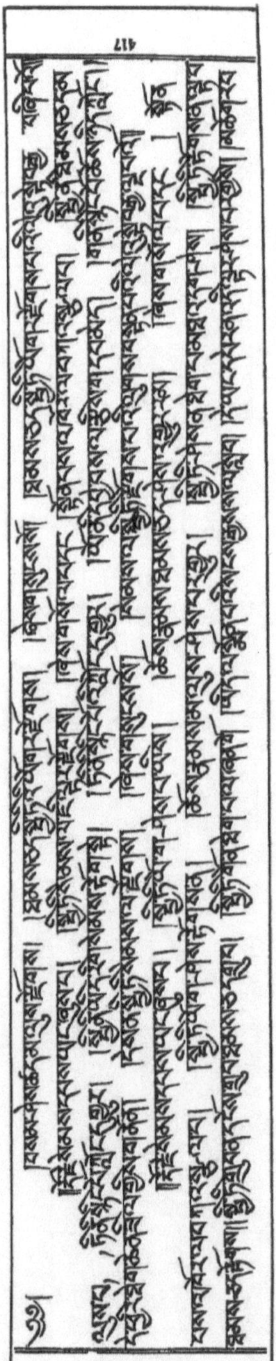

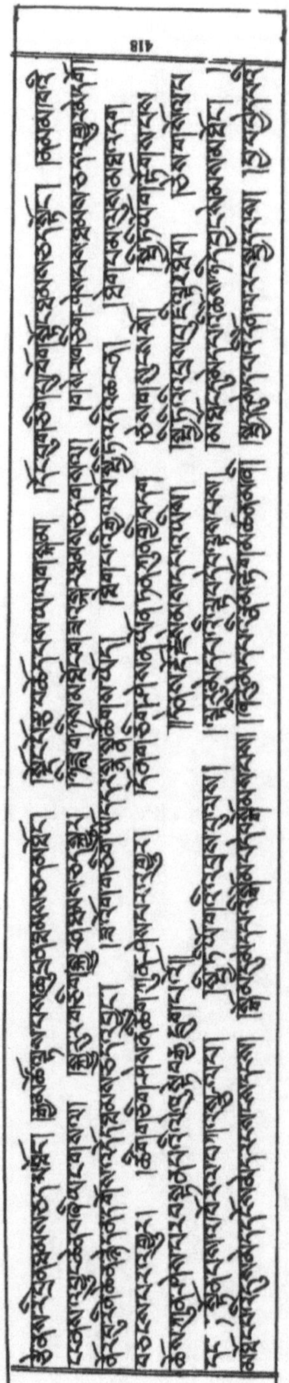

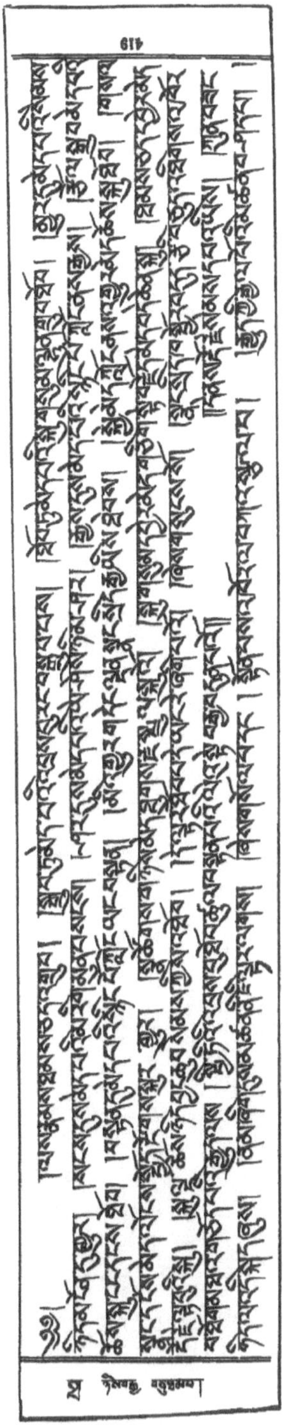
419

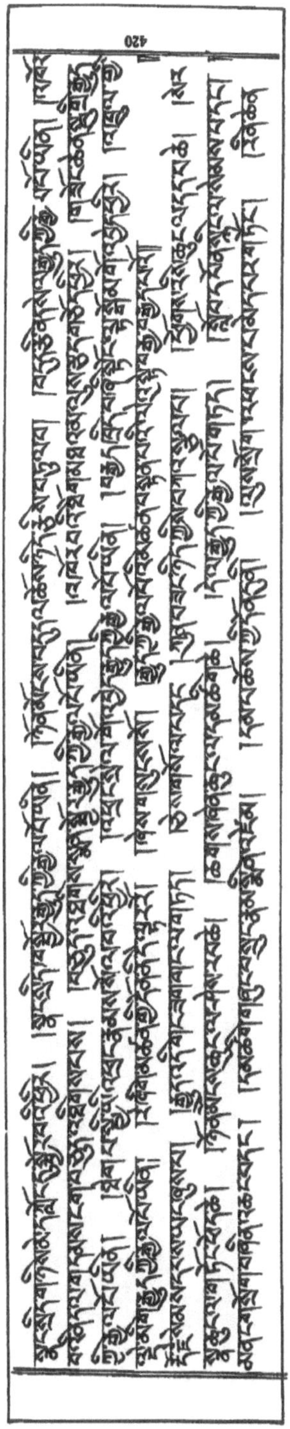
420

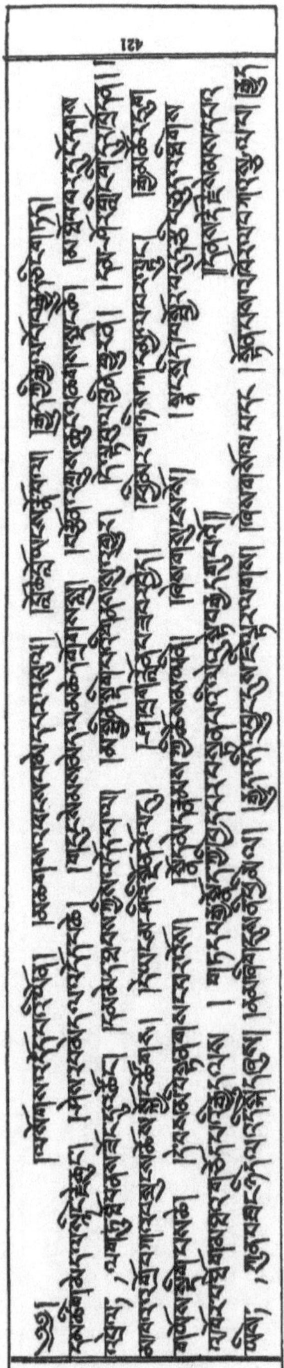

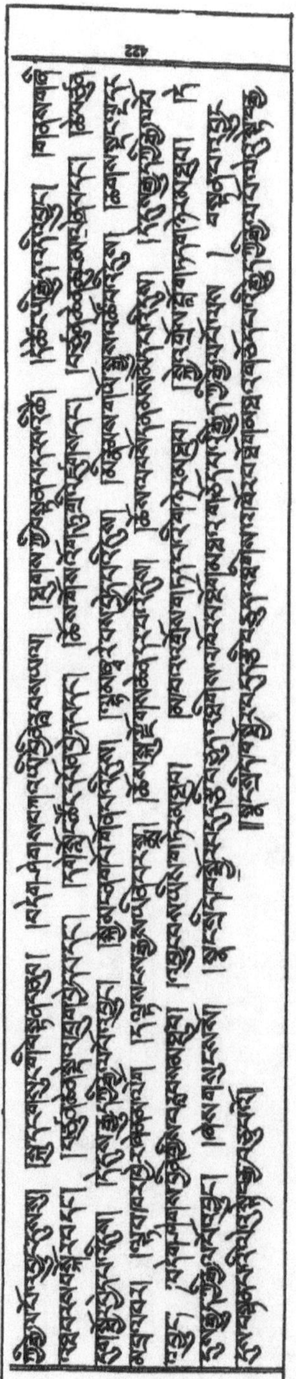

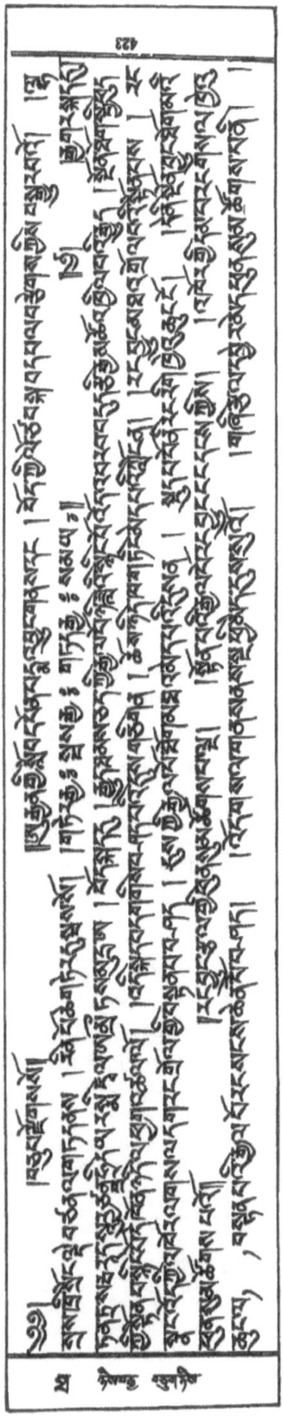

ABOUT THE TRANSLATOR

Christopher Wilkinson began his career in Buddhist literature at the age of fifteen, taking refuge vows from his guru Dezhung Rinpoche. In that same year he began formal study of Tibetan language at the University of Washington under Geshe Ngawang Nornang and Turrell Wylie. He became a Buddhist monk, for three years, at the age of eighteen, living in the home of Dezhung Rinpoche while he continued his studies at the University of Washington. He graduated in 1980 with a B.A. degree in Asian Languages and Literature and another B.A. degree in Comparative Religion (College Honors, Magna Cum Laude, Phi Beta Kappa). After a two-year tour of Buddhist pilgrimage sites throughout Asia he worked in refugee resettlement programs for five years in Seattle, Washington. He then proceeded to the University of Calgary for an M.A. in Buddhist Studies. He proceeded to work on a critical edition of the Sanskrit text of the 20,000 line Perfection of Wisdom in Berkeley, California, followed by an intensive study of Burmese language in Hawaii. In 1990 he began three years' service as a visiting professor in English Literature in Sulawesi, Indonesia, exploring the remnants of the ancient Sri Vijaya Empire there. He worked as a research fellow for the Shelly and Donald Rubin Foundation for several years, playing a part in the early development of the Rubin Museum of Art. He was a Research Fellow at the Centre de Recherches sur les Civilisations de l'Asie Orientale, Collège de France, for twelve years, and taught at the University of Calgary as an Adjunct Professor for five years. He has published forty-four volumes of translations of Tibetan literature, and is currently engaged in further translation of these great classics.